MW01121436

D ABUSE

TH DISABILITIES

DISABILITY STUDIES

JOAV MERRICK - SERIES EDITOR -

MEDICAL DIRECTOR, MINISTRY OF SOCIAL AFFAIRS,
JERUSALEM, ISRAEL

Child Abuse: Children with Disabilities
*Vincent J Palusci, Dena Nazer,
Donald E. Greydanus,
and Joav Merrick (Editors)*
2017. ISBN: 978-1-53612-035-6

Pediatric Pain: Current Aspects
*Hatim A. Omar, Dilip R. Patel,
Donald E. Greydanus,
and Joav Merrick (Editors)*
2016. ISBN: 978-1-63485-505-1

**Recent Advances on Using Virtual
Reality Technologies for Rehabilitation**
Paul M. Sharkey and Joav Merrick (Editors)
2016. ISBN: 978-1-63484-027-9

**Technology, Rehabilitation and
Empowerment of People with
Special Needs**
*Lena Pareto, Paul M Sharkey
and Joav Merrick (Editors)*
2015. ISBN: 978-1-63482-713-3

**Virtual Reality: Rehabilitation in Motor,
Cognitive and Sensorial Disorders**
Paul M. Sharkey and Joav Merrick (Editors)
2014. ISBN: 978-1-63321-773-7

**Virtual Reality:
People with Special Needs**
*Paul M. Sharkey
and Joav Merrick (Editors)*
2014. ISBN: 978-1-63321-729-4

**Quality of Life and Intellectual
Disability: Knowledge Application to
other Social and Educational Challenges**
*Roy I. Brown and Rhonda M. Faragher
(Editors)*
2014. ISBN: 978-1-62948-264-4

**Intellectual Disability:
Some Current Issues**
*Joav Merrick, Donald E Greydanus
and Dilip R. Patel (Editors)*
2014. ISBN: 978-1-63321-855-0

**From One Century to the Next:
A History of Wrentham State School
and the Institutional Model in
Massachusetts**
Ingrid Grenon
2014. ISBN: 978-1-63117-711-8 (Hardcover)
2014. ISBN: 978-1-63483-805-4 (Softcover)

Pain and the Elderly
Joav Merrick and Mimi M.Y. Tse
2013. ISBN: 978-1-62948-468-6

**Pain: International Research
in Pain Management**
*Joav Merrick, Patricia Schofield
and Mohammed Morad (Editors)*
2013. ISBN: 978-1-62948-423-5

CHILD ABUSE

CHILDREN WITH DISABILITIES

VINCENT J PALUSCI,
DENA NAZER,
DONALD E GREYDANUS
AND
JOAV MERRICK
EDITORS

nova
science publishers
New York

NOTICE TO THE READER

Library of Congress Cataloging-in-Publication Data

Names: Palusci, Vincent J., editor.
Title: Child abuse : children with disabilities / editors, Vincent J Palusci, M.D., Dena Nazer, M.D., Donald E Greydanus, M.D. and Joav Merrick, M.D. (Medical Director, Health Services, Division for Intellectual and Developmental Disabilities, Jerusalem, Israel, and others.
Description: Hauppauge, New York : Nova Science Publishers, Inc., [2017] | Series: Disability studies | Includes index.
Identifiers: LCCN 2017022235 (print) | LCCN 2017023962 (ebook) | ISBN 9781536120561 |
ISBN 9781536120356 (hardcover) | ISBN 9781536120561 (ebook)
Subjects: LCSH: Children with disabilities--Abuse of. | Children with disabilities--Abuse of--Prevention.
Classification: LCC HV888 (ebook) | LCC HV888 .C476 2017 (print) | DDC   362.4083--dc23
LC record available at https://lccn.loc.gov/2017022235

Published by Nova Science Publishers, Inc. † New York

CONTENTS

DEDICATION

Richard Alan Kaplan, MD (1950-2013)

Richard Alan Kaplan, MD, was professor of pediatrics and the director of the Center for Safe and Healthy Children at the University of Minnesota Amplatz Children's Hospital. He passed away on Monday, August 19, 2013, at his home in Northfield, MN, from complications of progressive muscular atrophy. After an early career in social work, Dr Kaplan (or "Rich as he repeatedly instructed us to call him) received his MD from the University of South Dakota and completed his residency in pediatrics at Phoenix Children's Hospital. He joined the faculty of the University of Minnesota in 2004 and rose to the rank of professor in 2012.

Kaplan grew up in Waterloo, Iowa, and often engaged in political activism, resulting in an often recounted youthful stint in jail. He was an exceptional man and dedicated his life to helping others. Before leading the University of Minnesota Children's Hospital child abuse program, he had worked in the Dakotas and Indian Country to provide sorely needed child abuse pediatric care. He made teaching a priority and served as head of the section for Safe and Healthy Children in the division of academic general pediatrics. Rich loved the outdoors and made frequent pilgrimages to the Boundary Waters in Minnesota, which he considered his sanctuary. Those of us who portaged canoes with him feel especially lucky to have shared that time with him. And always there were his wife, Avonne; and his children, Jennifer, Max, Lindsay, Alex and Sophie.

Kaplan was internationally recognized for his work in child abuse pediatrics, co-authoring a leading text in the field, lecturing internationally, and leading courses in child abuse and neglect at the MidWest Regional Child Advocacy Center, across the United States and internationally. He was expert in the US federal rules of evidence as well as rules in several states, often teaching colleagues (and lawyers) about the best ways to handle child abuse cases in the courts. He received numerous awards and honors including Outstanding Front Line Professional in 2009 from the American Professional Society on the Abuse of Children and the 2003 Commissioner's Award from the US Department of Health and Human Services for Outstanding Leadership and Service in the Prevention of Child Abuse and Neglect.

Many in the field have fond memories of Kaplan and his unique approach to children and families. He could put a child, a parent, a colleague (and even a lawyer) at ease as he explained what we do and how we do it while minimizing further trauma to the child and family. Sometimes this was with him wearing shorts, polo shirts and sandals. Sometimes he showed an earring or tattoo. Always it was with a gentleness and kindness that was unique among pediatricians and social workers as well. Many of us also remember his sharp mind and wit and how, when necessary, he could be blunt and swift when needed to protect a child, teach an important point, or properly instruct a judge and jury (or lawyer) on how things ought to be done.

We dedicate this book to Rich Kaplan, because of all this and his inspiring and contagious compassionate care of children. He continues to be missed by his colleagues in the United States and internationally.

INTRODUCTION

In: Child Abuse: Children with Disabilities
Editors: V. J Palusci, D. Nazer et al.

ISBN: 978-1-53612-035-6
© 2017 Nova Science Publishers, Inc.

Chapter 1

CHILDREN WITH DISABILITIES

Vincent J Palusci[1,], MD, MS, FAAP,*
Dena Nazer[2], MD, FAAP,
Donald E Greydanus[3], MD, DrHC(Athens), FAAP
and Joav Merrick[4-8], MD, MMedSc, DMSc

[1]New York University School of Medicine, New York, New York, US
[2]Wayne State University School of Medicine, Detroit, Michigan, US
[3]Western Michigan University Homer Stryker MD School of Medicine, Kalamazoo, Michigan, US
[4]National Institute of Child Health and Human Development, Jerusalem
[5]Office of the Medical Director, Health Services, Division for Intellectual and Developmental Disabilities, Ministry of Social Affairs and Social Services, Jerusalem
[6]Division of Pediatrics, Hadassah Hebrew University Medical Center, Mt Scopus Campus, Jerusalem, Israel
[7]Kentucky Children's Hospital, University of Kentucky School of Medicine, Lexington, Kentucky, US
[8]Center for Healthy Development, School of Public Health, Georgia State University, Atlanta, Georgia,US

---

* Corresponding author: Vincent J Palusci, Professor of Pediatrics, New York University School of Medicine, Bellevue Hospital Center, 462 First Avenue, New York, NY 10016, United States. E-mail: Vincent.palusci@nyumc.org.

This chapter reviews abuse and neglect among children with disabilities, serving as an introduction to the definitions, causes, epidemiology, international aspects, assessment, treatment and legal responses which will be addressed in this book. We highlight the importance of identifying abuse and neglect in this vulnerable population because of their increased risk and harmful effects which result from a complex interaction of disability and our professional responses and their special needs which can result in ongoing victimization. Disability and maltreatment are defined and addressed internationally. Patterns of presentation of victimization are discussed and suggestions are given to aid in recognition, assessment and treatment. Developmental considerations in the evaluation and treatment are reviewed as are special situations with siblings and neglect of special medical needs. We conclude with a discussion of prevention and recommendations to improve our understanding of how to best identify child maltreatment and to improve practice among children with disabilities so they may maximize their developmental and intellectual potentials.

INTRODUCTION

It is only relatively recently that we have come to understand the profound effects of abuse and neglect on persons with disability. At the time of the classic description of the battered child by C Henry Kempe (1922-1984) in 1962, physical abuse and neglect were not a stranger to children with disabilities (1). People with intellectual and developmental disabilities (IDD) faced almost complete exclusion from schools, communities, and sometimes even homes. Families were regularly counseled to place children with IDD in state-run facilities and were assured that their children would be cared for and protected. Unfortunately, the facilities were often riddled with systemic neglect and abuse. It was within this context that the Federal Government began providing funds to enhance institutions, and parents and others provided private special-education classes and sheltered workshops for children and adults who were living with their families. In 1989, the United Nations Convention on the Rights of the Child set out the rights that must be realized for children to develop their full potential, free from hunger and want, neglect and abuse (2). In the US, there are a number of agencies have been put in place at different levels (e.g., local, state, federal) to improve our response. More recently, the United Nations Convention on the Rights of Persons with Disabilities codified rules and regulations which provided special protections and accommodations for people with physical and other impairments (3).

While these changes have dramatically improved our responses to child maltreatment and disabilities, a variety of persisting societal attitudes that had resulted in these inhumane conditions in institutions for children and adults with IDDs highlight how far we still have far to go. Both then and now, children and adults present with any one of the variety of injuries associated with abuse, including fractures, bleeding, traumatic brain injuries, bruising, soft tissue and organ injuries, and death. Likewise, in addition to their higher rates of abuse and neglect, they have a disproportionately higher percentage with physical abuse as a cause of their disabilities. Children and adults with disabilities are also victims of sexual abuse, the evaluation for which is made all the more difficult because their developmental delays affect their behavior and communication. Child protective systems strive to protect all children but are especially challenged to help children with disabilities, those who are medically fragile, and parents coping with their own disabilities who also face their own increased risk for abuse and neglect as vulnerable adults (4). Legal systems designed to intervene and to reduce potential harm from maltreatment may be unable to integratively approach both maltreatment and disability to maximize children's growth and development. Unfortunately, these systems are also ill-equipped to support parents with disabilities and their families, resulting in disproportionately high rates of continued involvement with child welfare services and devastatingly high rates of parents with disabilities losing their parental rights.

DEFINITIONS

Abuse and neglect have sometimes distinct definitions in different professional fields, for children and adults, and are codified under different federal, state and national statutes. Maltreatment, a more encompassing term which includes abuse, neglect and exploitation, is often used, and several types are discussed, such as physical abuse, sexual abuse, neglect, medical care neglect and emotional/psychological abuse and neglect. Physical abuse can be further subdivided into abusive head trauma, abusive fractures and other injuries, while sexual abuse is often categorized as penetrating or non-penetrating, contact or non-contact or sexual exploitation. The broadest category, neglect, has been further classified as physical neglect (lack of appropriate food, clothing or shelter), medical care neglect (lack of appropriate medical attention, dental care or medications), and supervisional neglect (lack of developmentally appropriate surveillance and protection from environmental or other dangers).

While the US has codified child abuse and neglect under the federal Child Abuse Prevention and Treatment Act and state statutes, there are specific subtypes which have been used in medical and social research which are further reviewed later by chapters in this book. Overall, the most useful definitions for international comparisons have been provided by the World Health Organization (WHO), which has broadly defined these types of maltreatment for data collection and intervention (5):

- Physical abuse is the intentional use of force against a child that results in, or has a high likelihood of resulting in, harm to the child's health, survival, development or dignity. This includes hitting, beating, kicking, shaking, biting, strangling, scalding, burning, poisoning and suffocating.
- Sexual abuse is the involvement of a child in sexual activity that he or she does not fully comprehend, is unable to give informed consent to, or for which he or she is not developmentally prepared, and/or that violates the laws or social taboos of society. This can be by adults or other children who, by virtue of their age or development, are in a position of responsibility, trust or power over the child.
- Psychological maltreatment is a pattern of failure over time on the part of the parent or caretaker to provide bonding and a developmentally appropriate and emotionally supportive environment. This includes restriction of movement, belittling, blaming, threatening, frightening, discriminating against, ridiculing and other non-physical hostile treatment.
- Neglect is defined as isolated incidents and patterns of failure over time on the part of the parent or caretaker, when in a position to do so, to provide for the food, clothing, shelter, health, education, nutrition and safety of the child.

Children and adults with disability are a heterogeneous group of individuals who possess a variety of skills and experience a range of difficulties. Disability can affect, for example, a person's physical and cognitive abilities, language skills, memory, emotions, behavior, mobility and/or interpersonal interactions. Although there are commonalities among individuals diagnosed with specific disabilities such as autism, each person demonstrates unique qualities. Early in life, intellectual or developmental disability (IDD) can affect a child's cognitive and adaptive functioning, and studies have demonstrated that children with IDD are at greater risk for abuse and maltreatment and report more severe forms of abuse than the general child population (6). In addition, the more profound the disability, the more severe the abuse.

Disability is variably defined in medical and child welfare systems because of its political, policy, societal and economic implications. Various models of disability have been described, the predominant ones being a medical model and a social model. Various agencies and institutions define disability differently serving their explicit narrow purpose, and there are international variations which have occurred through culture and context across the world. A widely used construct of disability comes from the World Health Organization, and is called the International Classification of Functioning, Disability, and Health–Children and Youth Version (7). Physical disability and intellectual disability also differ in terms of their conceptualization and implications. The definition of intellectual disability has evolved significantly over the past decade, with IDD characterized by deficits in cognitive and adaptive abilities that initially manifest before 18 years of age. In this book, Professors Patel and Brown provide a framework describing how to approach disability to best understand abuse and neglect among this vulnerable population.

BIOLOGY, EPIDEMIOLOGY AND RISK FACTORS

Studies in the US have linked adverse childhood experiences (ACEs) to leading causes of adult morbidity and mortality. Abuse and neglect have specific long term effects genetically, behaviorally and physically, and it appears that disabilities associated with interpersonal and behavioral difficulties are most strongly associated with further victimization risks. Children with disabilities have greater risk for maltreatment, however, despite this reported vulnerability, reports of child maltreatment among youth with IDD are less likely to occur and less likely to be believed (8). Stigma, discrimination and ignorance about disability are factors which place people with disabilities across the world at higher risk of violence, and prevention and early detection of maltreatment are therefore important goals of global public health. In his discussion in this book, Professor Merrick reviews international disability prevalence and explores the connection between disability and maltreatment across the world.

Advances in biology are providing deeper insights into genetic changes associated with disability and how early experiences are built into the body with lasting effects on learning, behavior, and health. Numerous evaluations of interventions for young children facing adversity have demonstrated multiple effects but they have been highly variable and difficult to sustain or scale. The growing knowledge base shows that we need to shift our thinking about policy and practice. We need to recognize that early experiences affect lifelong health, not just learning, and that healthy brain development requires protection from toxic stress, not just enrichment. More effective interventions will be needed in the prenatal period and first 3 years after birth for the most disadvantaged children and families. Achieving breakthrough outcomes for young children facing adversity will require more than just addressing child-level risk factors by also supporting the adults who care for them to transform their own lives. Shonkoff (9) has concluded that the time has come to leverage 21st-century science to catalyze the design, testing, and scaling of more powerful approaches for reducing lifelong disease by mitigating the effects of early adversity.

In this book, Professor Gupta reviews genetics and new research on plasticity and critical periods in development, increasing understanding of how gene-environment interaction affects variation in stress susceptibility and resilience, and the emerging availability of measures of toxic stress effects that are sensitive to intervention. These provide much-needed fuel for science-informed innovation in the early childhood arena. It has become apparent that elements of our environment, including maltreatment, can physically affect our DNA and the flow of genetic information. These events can lead to immediate and accumulating physiological effects that can be transmitted to progeny in a non-Mendelian fashion. The goal of his discussion is to introduce the underlying mechanisms of these "marks" on our genomes as it relates to the outcomes of child abuse and maltreatment, and he discusses our understanding of genetics in a modern perspective with a special emphasis on the emerging concepts of epigenetics and their underlying molecular bases.

In the child welfare system, children who were reported to child protective services with any of the following risk factors were considered as having a disability in the US National Child Abuse and Neglect Data System (NCANDS): intellectual disability, emotional disturbance, visual or hearing impairment, learning disability, physical disability, behavioral problems or other medical problems (10). During 2005-2011, a progressively increasing proportion of children being reported have had an identified disability. Behavior problems and other medical problems had the greatest frequency, followed by emotional disability, and then intellectual disability, sensory disability, and physical disability. There were almost 800,000 substantiated cases of child abuse or neglect in 2011 in NCANDS, and 3% of the children confirmed for abuse or neglect in NCANDS had one or more of these disabilities, although this is thought to be an undercount (10).

Initial reports of child maltreatment in the special needs pediatric population were anecdotal rather than addressing the true population-based incidence. In the 1986 National Incidence Study for child abuse in the United States, 35.5 per 1,000 children with disabilities were maltreated, compared to 21.3 per 1,000 children without disabilities, suggesting an epidemiologic connection (11). Physical abuse alone has been reported to be 3 times more likely among children with disabilities than among the general pediatric population (9% versus 31%). Spencer et al. (12) found similar increases in the UK. Another study found increasing proportions of children with physical and emotional disabilities associated with recurrence of abuse and neglect. However, a systematic review concluded that the evidence base for an association of disability with increased abuse and neglect was weak, and another found that physical disability did not increase the risk for any type of victimization once confounding factors and co-occurring disabilities were controlled (13).

When demographic risk factors are assessed, it is apparent that not all types of disability are equally related to child, family and community factors. In 2011, sexual abuse was statistically significantly higher among children with confirmed maltreatment when mental retardation/intellectual disability, sensory disability or physical disability was present. Similar relationships were not found for physical abuse and neglect. Some demographic factors were seen more frequently in some forms of disability, as were child and family problems with drugs, alcohol and other disabilities. Interestingly, children with disabilities were actually less likely to have other family violence present but were more likely to have services provided after child protective services investigation than were non-disabled children (4).

Children with IDD are often isolated in environments that place them at an increased risk for abuse. Some environments provide potential perpetrators easy access to this vulnerable population. In addition, staff turnover in institutions can decrease the likelihood of employed caregivers getting to know their child clients well, with less monitoring and less recognizing changes indicative of abuse. Society's lack of experience with youth and adults who have IDD can increase their isolation and promote misperceptions such as people with IDD are different, weak and vulnerable and/or lack the experiences of the community at large. It has been proposed that decreased isolation of individuals with IDDs may decrease their vulnerability to abuse (14). Premature infants may be at increased risk due to the lack of bonding created by their prolonged neonatal stay in hospital and the prolonged stress associated with this and with separation from their parents. Infants who may be seen for assessment and referral for early intervention services have histories which include being low birth weight or small for gestational age, being one of multiple births, having other structural anomalies such as spina bifida, chronic problems such as chronic lung or heart disease, chromosomal anomalies, including trisomy 21, and visual and hearing impairments. Subtle maltreatment can also occur in hospitalized children who are physically-challenged, as such children with cognitive limitations may not have procedures explained to them in a developmentally appropriate manner by staff and/or may not have their privacy as well respected as do more vocal children who are able to complain.

Children with IDD are also sexually abused at higher rates than typically developing children (14). Several risk factors for sexual abuse in this population have been identified. These include characteristics of the child, the perpetrator of abuse and the child's environment and culture. For example, children with IDD may not feel they have the control or power to address or change a situation. Many undergo intrusive medical, educational and/or behavioral interventions that leave others in charge of their functioning and blur their sense of personal space and boundaries. Children with hearing and visual problems have increased risk for sexual abuse because of their inability to adequately report victimization. In addition, delays in cognitive, social and emotional skills can contribute to the difficulties of disclosing sexual abuse. Children receiving bowel and bladder routines due to neurologic incontinence may be accustomed to having these performed by a variety of health care professionals and their index of suspicion may be lowered. They may also have reduced access to developmentally-appropriate sex education services. They may not question or understand the inappropriate sexual behavior of others and may not know how to seek help. Young children have particularly increased risk (15). The reported incidence and prevalence of maltreatment of children with disability in the US highlights the impact of disability on child abuse and neglect in the United States and internationally. In this book, Professor Palusci expands upon our knowledge about the epidemiology and risk factors for maltreatment. Patterns of victimization are defined and discussed in categories of different types of maltreatment, including physical and sexual abuse, psychologic maltreatment, and neglect. The effects of disabilities of various types on this epidemiology are discussed, serving as an introduction to the problem of child abuse and neglect as well as describing potentially intervenable risk factors among the population of disabled children.

ABUSE AS A CAUSE OF DISABILITY

Frasier (16) reviewed the unquestionably negative effect of child abuse on the growth, emotional, social, and cognitive development of children. Psychological and emotional trauma, violence, abandonment, neglect, and failure to nurture can impact brain development at neuronal, functional, and neurodevelopmental levels. Abusive head trauma as a form of direct physical trauma can result in brain damage with global, pervasive developmental disabilities that affect a child and family for life. Conversely, patients with spinal cord injury, accidental drowning, suffocation, and burns who are disabled may also have been abused. Spinal cord injuries in young children are rare and are usually associated with high impact injuries such as motor vehicle accidents; however, in younger children, spinal cord injury is often caused by abusive head trauma. These injuries may present clinically with neurological findings without radiographic abnormalities on spinal films, although MRI studies can be confirmatory of the lesions. Clinical lesions may be initially overlooked due to the severity of the head injuries even when upper cervical spine level injuries are sustained.

In patients admitted to a pediatric rehabilitation unit, an overall incidence of 27% for abuse and neglect of patients was reported over a 3-year period (17). About 20% of the patients had been directly abused de novo, and the remainder of patients suffered from secondary neglect in association with their pre-existing disabling condition. In facilities where a greater number of patients with traumatic brain injuries were served, the percentage of admitted children who are directly abused approached 33%. Males were more likely to be affected. In Hagbergs' study of the changing panorama of cerebral palsy (18), child abuse is not mentioned as an etiology, but victims of inflicted traumatic brain injury have been noted to have motor deficits (60%), visual deficits (48%), epilepsy (20%), speech and language abnormalities (64%), and behavioral problems (52%).

One population-based study found the incidence of shaken baby syndrome to be 29.7 per 100,000 among infants and 3.8 per 100,000 in the second year of life (19). The average age for occurrence of shaken baby syndrome was 4-6 months, and these patients exhibited variable patterns of intracranial, retinal and preretinal hemorrhages, hematomas, edema, axonal injury and fractures. Younger children were more prone to tears of the tentorium and venous structures due to the weakness of their neck musculature that allows for their heads to be "snapped" back and forth. The prognosis was not always be apparent at presentation and could take up to several months to evolve as interruption of brain growth may take this long to manifest. The full extent of the neuropsychological and behavioral sequelae may not evolve for 3-6 years and may make the retrospective diagnosis difficult. Even in the absence of structural abnormalities, verbal and performance IQ scores are often suppressed and mandated intervention for special education services, cognitive remediation, and speech therapy are required (20).

In this book, Drs. Feifer and Descartes-Walker present the evidence for physical abuse and child neglect as contributors to disability statistics in the United States and worldwide. They explore the epidemiology, mechanism, and overall costs of abuse-related sequelae using abusive head trauma as the injury best studied in the context of pervasive disability, but they also explore the limited research around other forms of physical abuse and child neglect in the form of failure to thrive as etiologies for impairment of intellectual development and social functioning.

ASSESSMENT, LEGAL RESPONSE AND TREATMENT

Children with disability often have contact with healthcare and other service providers whose role it is to support their safety and well-being (4). However, the presentation of certain disabilities may disguise potential indicators of child abuse. Beliefs and attitudes can also affect how professionals view, assess and attend to children with intellectual and developmental disabilities. For example, beliefs such as that children with IDD cannot provide accurate information regarding their personal experiences; children with IDD are not affected by abuse and/or cannot benefit from interventions after a traumatic experience; and children with IDD are stressful or undesirable to work with, can negatively impact service providers' and investigators' interactions with this population and lead to unsupportive and less effective interventions.

These tragedies are made more apparent by Professors Greydanus, Hawver and Merrick in their discussion in this book about sibling abuse of children with disabilities. The world's literature and research by scientists have attested to the high frequency and the severe consequences of sibling abuse seen in families around the world. Often hidden or ignored by society, such exploitation is the most common form of abuse found in humans and appears increased among children with IDD. Underpinnings to this phenomenon of desecration of our children are many, but tend to focus on family dysfunction, lack of education in parenting provided to most parents, and the underlying biology and violent nature of humankind. This discussion presents concepts of sibling abuse found in all societies for thousands of years that has been hinted at in children's fables and finally studied by research in the 20th and 21st centuries.

Sexual development begins in infancy and continues throughout the human lifecycle. Children develop across many domains: emotional, social and physical, and at different rates and developmental stages. The topic of sexual development is often overlooked as an expected area of development. This could be due to societal beliefs and/or parental, cultural or religious differences. The normative progression of sexual development may not apply within a clear framework if a child has a developmental disability or delay. This topic has not been frequently studied historically, but more clinicians and researchers are now looking at how young people with disabilities experience sexual feelings or behaviors—whether at a normative rate, as a result of trauma or abuse, or the possibility of another explanation—using a developmental psychopathology framework. Unfortunately, children with IDD experience sexual abuse at a higher rate than peers who are not developmentally delayed (21). These children are especially at risk due to cognitive, social and emotional deficits. As with typically developing peers, problematic sexual behavior can occur in children with IDD as a result of sexual abuse, but there may also be other factors at play. In this book, Mandel and Datner will discuss sexualized behaviors in youth diagnosed with IDD and their assessment and treatment. They present a brief overview of normative and problematic sexual behaviors in youth and then explore some of the reasons why they are prevalent in developmentally-delayed populations, focusing on children and adolescents diagnosed with higher functioning autism spectrum disorder formerly known as Asperger's syndrome. They then discuss various methods to assess sexual behaviors and treatment options for this population.

The presence of a disability may not in and of itself change some of the basic findings of maltreatment on physical examination. Key concepts in assessing the potentially abusive nature of injuries in all age groups include the mobility and developmental abilities of the victim, the severity of the injury, the contribution of underlying medical conditions, and the ability of the victim to disclose what, if anything happened. As infants, patients are relatively immobile and passive in ways similar to frail adults. It is only with successful rehabilitation and mobilization that a child or adult may later become more vocal and more demanding of care, prompting an alleged event of abuse or neglect. When there is an unclear or inconsistent mechanism of injury reported, the caretaker-patient dyad should be observed closely and a full psychosocial assessment by a multidisciplinary team should be obtained (22).

Children and adults who have pathological bruising or fractures may be suspected of having inflicted injuries. Bruise patterns shaped like objects and located on specific target zones (face, ears, neck, torso) are particularly concerning. Unusually shaped lesions, such as cigarette burns, belt marks, or other objects, are grounds for report to protective services. Bruising may be confused with congenital hemangiomas alone, in association with a more generalized syndrome, or with Mongolian spots. Unexplained generalized bruising requires evaluation with a complete blood count and coagulation studies regardless of the associated diagnoses to exclude the possibility of a hematologic abnormality and/or medication effect. Glutaryl-Co-A-dehydrogenase deficiencies, particularly glutaric aciduria type 1, are inherited metabolic disorders with encephalopathic findings in association with neurological degeneration. When there is potential for malabsorption or inadequate vitamin D supplementation as a cause for fractures, screening tests for serum calcium, phosphate and alkaline phosphatase should be obtained with mono- and dihydroxy-vitamin D levels since serum chemistries alone may not reveal any abnormalities. Pathologic femur fractures may occur even in younger patients with spina bifida, as they may in patients with cerebral palsy, osteogenesis imperfecta, non-ossifying fibromas, osteoporosis, aneurysmal bone cyst, and fibrous dysplasia. In patients where the mechanism for abusive fracture is clear, the clinician needs to advocate for the accurate diagnosis despite the presence of additional chronic conditions (23).

Skin breakdown is clearly a risk in patients who have loss of sensation even in the absence of inflicted injury. Children and adults with chronic skin ulcers below their sensory levels which are permitted to fester and get infected, with unreported and fetid drainage under casts and poor hygiene with secondary infection, also pose a group of victims who should be admitted for skin care in addition to restorative services and should be reported. In such instances, if it is determined that the parent or guardian does not pose a direct threat to the patient, they should be directly supervised and involved with medical specialists and nursing to learn how to best provide care. If there are concerns that caregivers are directly harming the child, steps should be taken to restrict access pending investigation. Another example of potential medical neglect includes failure to keep appointments such as to have a medication pump refilled when there is prior knowledge that medication withdrawal is not only associated with rebound spasticity, but also with seizures, altered mental status, fever, and other serious morbidities.

The assessment of medical neglect is often made much more complex when children have physical disabilities and special medical needs. The failure to comply with treatments and diagnostic testing is a marker of parental/caretaker noncompliance and potential neglect (24). Children in need of diagnostic testing, therapy for progressive limb contractures, or provision of orthotics and varied treatments will not perform as well when not provided with these services. These lapses may extend to the lack of provision of general medical care and failure to properly immunize children which would not only place them at jeopardy but also, in the absence of medical contraindications, limit their participation in center-based and rehabilitative programs. Intentionally not permitting a physically-challenged adult or child to access their augmentative communication and other technological devices or intentional breakage of such devices upon which they are dependent is also a form of maltreatment. Children with medical care neglect have been underidentified and underreported (25).

Once concern has arisen, the medical evaluation for potential physical and sexual abuse and neglect in children with IDD requires special training, assistance, and resources to best identify their needs while reducing further trauma from the evaluation. In this book, Professor Nazer frames this evaluation in the context of their vulnerability because of their age and disability because the presence of disability makes the evaluation complex while conferring greater risk for abuse as compared to children with no disabilities. Her chapters differentiate the medical evaluations for physical abuse and neglect from sexual abuse given the different objectives during assessment, classes of findings expected, and potential for additional traumatic stress from the process. In this book, Dr Okun addresses recognizing and responding to suspected medical neglect among children with medical complexity/disability, how medical complexity is defined, what distinguishes it from related conceptualizations (e.g., children who are medically fragile), and some of the issues that arise for mandated reporters in the domains of ethics and professionalism.

The perception that all children with IDD are unreliable witnesses and lack the ability to provide accurate information can lead investigators to discount their disclosures and/or behaviors and fail to conduct forensic interviews that consider children's individual capabilities and needs (26,27). As with any child, children with IDD should receive individualized treatment when being interviewed about child abuse. Investigators and courts should avoid making assumptions about their functioning, should take into account the individual abilities of each child, and should obtain information about a particular child before conducting an interview. Many children with IDD have the capacity to provide accurate accounts of their personal experiences, but more research is needed on these abilities in order to inform investigators and improve the effectiveness of child abuse evaluations.

If a child discloses information or behaves in such a way that leads to a suspicion of abuse or neglect, a variety of professionals and agency staff members can be legally mandated (each state/country according to their laws) to make a report to the governmental entity designed to receive such reports. This entity determines if there is enough evidence to prompt an investigation and/or begins an investigation which includes assessing the safety of the home, interviewing family members and others known to the patient, and obtaining medical and other records. This investigation can involve law enforcement and child or adult protective services. Some jurisdictions have Child Advocacy Centers where child protective services and police are co-located and conduct forensic interviews and investigations. If abuse occurs in an institution or in foster care, the agencies involved may also conduct their own investigation. Given the variety of agencies that can become involved when a child or adult discloses abuse, collaboration and awareness of the needs of the patient and his/her family are essential. Efforts should be made to decrease the number of interviews conducted by different agencies. Multiple interviews have the potential to create stress, confusion, and frustration for patients and families and lead victims to think they are not believed or are in trouble, to avoid disclosing information, accurate or not, to cope with the repetitive process. For victims with IDD, these potential negative effects can be exacerbated by their difficulties coping with and understanding the investigation process. Difficulties conducting a sound and informed interview can ultimately fail to protect a victim, halt an abuse investigation, and negatively impact subsequent civil and/or criminal legal proceedings (4).

Despite the multiple potential risks for child abuse in populations with IDD and the higher rates of reported abuse, few reported cases end up in the court system or result in disciplinary action against the perpetrator of abuse. In addition, criminal cases have been dismissed because of uninformed interviewers who do not ask sound questions (28). Investigators of child abuse should take into account the individual abilities of each child before and during a forensic interview (29). Parental disability also needs to be taken into account given the high rates of termination of parental rights in this population (30). In this book, Professors Vandervort and Kay examine the legal framework in the US which is applicable when child maltreatment and disability intersect. They begin with a brief description of the constitutional foundation for parent-child-state relations and then review relevant federal child welfare laws which today shape each state's child protection system. They then consider the application of various federal laws governing work with children and families when a child has a disability. In doing so, they consider the Americans with Disabilities Act, the Individuals with Disabilities Education Act, Section

504 of the Rehabilitation Act, and Social Security benefits for children. This chapter does not examine child well-being legislation that establishes and funds programs such as Temporary Assistance to Needy Families (TANF), Supplemental Nutrition Assistance Program (SNAP), or publicly funded health care for children such as the State Children's Health Insurance Program.

PREVENTION

Those caring for children with disabilities have many reasons for wanting to prevent child abuse and neglect, not the least of which are to reduce pain and suffering and future health problems. These goals are particularly relevant for the weak and vulnerable in our population. In order to identify and prevent abuse and neglect, a high index of suspicion needs to be maintained. Clinicians and advocates need to be able to identify and report patterns of maltreatment while excluding mimics and other confounders. Children and adults with disabilities are seen by many subspecialists, and it is important that there is one individual or group of professionals who follow them on a consistent basis, preferably in a defined "medical home" integrated with community services. This can reduce the risk of abuse or neglect and permit proactive, preventative services to be put into place. With mandated early intervention referrals, children are now more readily identified, and several studies have shown the potential positive effects when supportive social services, parent education, respite services, and counseling are provided earlier in life (31-33). It is clinically believed that such interventions reduce emotional trauma and recidivism because of the additional emotional support that enhances child development.

However, the details of why, how, when, and where health care professionals can promote prevention may seem murky or ill-defined, especially as maltreatment of children with disability remains undercounted and underaddressed by many segments of society and by many of the systems designed to improve child welfare. Scott et al. (34) note that contemporary approaches to child protection are dominated by individualized forensically-focused interventions that provide limited scope for more holistic preventative responses to children at risk and the provision of support to struggling families and communities. Investigatory and removal approaches are failing in critically important ways, particularly regarding reducing the inequities that underpin neglect and abuse. There have been increasing calls for a health systems-based model for the protection of children, and it is precisely the population of children with disabilities who would most benefit from this approach. In this book, Professor Palusci provides both the rationale and strategies for prevention as well as some concrete ideas about how professionals in the health system can integrate it into the day-to-day care of children with disabilities. He also assesses the cost effectiveness of a number of current programs and argues that they are justified based on their financial savings as well as their human benefits.

CONCLUSION

The National Survey on Abuse of People with Disabilities found that "[T]oo many people are abused too much, with very little on the response side to help in the aftermath" (35). The need for a coordinated response is urgent. Such response, however, is not complete until it also addresses the needs of persons with developmental and intellectual disabilities and their unique struggles. Their plight has been so invisible that waiting for the attention they deserve is no longer an option.

While mandatory training for health care professionals in the identification of child abuse and neglect is required in many states, little or no training is available addressing the needs of adults with disabilities. School personnel and other professionals, especially those dealing with special education populations, need additional training beyond baseline mandatory courses. In addition, there are several other services that need to be in place to prevent abuse and neglect among people with disabilities. Programs for identification, education and prevention need to be extended to professionals, parents and guardians for all young children and those in early intervention and preschool programs.

Daro (36) has noted that today's society is at odds with planning a public health response to child maltreatment prevention. A critical component of this problem is the absence of a public policy framework and related infrastructure, particularly for disabled children, which can create common ownership of the problem while recognizing the vast differences in individual willingness and capacity to alter their parenting behaviors. To address this challenge, it seems prudent to begin building a universal system of assessment and support that will touch all children and all families at multiple points in the developmental process. She notes that such a system would not simply identify those at highest risk but would be built on the premise that all parents have issues and concerns and differ only in the extent to which they have the capacity to address these issues. Her commentary outlines the key elements of such a system and its benefits in strengthening both the impacts of interventions and the collective will to support children.

The chapters in this book highlight the importance of identifying abuse and neglect in this vulnerable population because of their increased risk and the harmful effects which can result from a complex interaction of disability, special needs, and our professional responses which can result in ongoing victimization. Developmental considerations must be included in any professional response to maltreatment in children with disability, and additional research is needed to improve our understanding of how to best identify maltreatment and to improve practice in this vulnerable population so they may maximize their developmental and intellectual potentials.

REFERENCES

[1] Kempe CH, Silverman FN, Steele BF, Droegemueller W, Silver HK. The battered-child syndrome. JAMA 1962;181:17-24.

[2] United Nations General Assembly. Convention on the Rights of the Child A/RES/44/25. Adopted 20 November 1989.

[3] United Nations General Assembly. Convention on the Rights of Persons with Disabilities A/RES/61/106. Adopted 24 January 2007.

[4] Palusci VJ, Datner E, Wilkins C. Abuse and neglect. In: Rubin IL, Merrick J, Greydanus DE, Patel DR, eds. Rubin and Crocker, 3rd edition: Health care for people with intellectual and developmental disabilities across the lifespan. Cham, Switzerland: Springer International Publishing 2016;2011-32.

[5] World Health Organization. Report of the consultation on child abuse prevention. Geneva: WHO Press. Document WHO/HSC/PVI/99.1, 1999. URL: http://whqlibdoc.who.int/hq/1999 /WHO_HSC_PVI_99.1.pdf.

[6] Hershokowitz D, Lamb ME, Horowitz D. Victimization of children with disabilities. Am J Orthopsychiatr 2013;77(4):629-35.

[7] World Health Organization. The international classification of functioning, disability and health, Children and youth version. Geneva: WHO, 2007. URL: http://www.who.int/classifications/icf/en/.

[8] Poole DA, Lamb ME. Investigative Interviews of Children: A guide for helping professionals. Washington, DC: American Psychological Association, 1998.

[9] Shonkoff JP. Capitalizing on advances in science to reduce the health consequences of early childhood adversity. JAMA Pediatrics 2016. doi:10.1001/ jamapediatrics.2016.1559. Published online August 22, 2016.

[10] US Department of Health and Human Services, Administration on Children Youth and Families. Child maltreatment 2005-2011. Washington, DC: US Government Printing Office, 2007-2012.

[11] Sedlak AJ, Mettenburg J, Basena M, Petta I, McPherson K, Greene A, Li S. Fourth National Incidence Study of Child Abuse and Neglect (NIS–4): Report to Congress, Executive Summary. Washington, DC: US Department of Health and Human Services, Administration for Children and Families, 2010.

[12] Spencer N, Devereux E, Wallace A, Sundrum R, Shenoy M, Bacchus C, Logan S. Disabling conditions and registration for child abuse and neglect: A population-based study. Pediatrics 2005;116:609-13.

[13] Turner HA, Vanderminden J, Finkelhor D, Hamby S, Shattuck A. Disability and victimization in a national sample of children and youth. Child Maltreat 2001;16:275-86.

[14] Ballard MB, Austin S. Forensic interviewing: Special considerations for children and adolescents with mental retardation and developmental disabilities. Educ Train Ment Retard Dev Disabil 1999;34(4):521-5.

[15] Palusci VJ. Risk factors and services for child maltreatment among infants and young children. Child Youth Serv Rev 2011;33:1374-82.

[16]   Frasier LD. Abusive head trauma in infants and young children: A unique contributor to developmental disabilities. Pediatr Clin North Am 2008; 55: 1269-85.

[17]   Wolfe AE, Hwang ME, Palusci VJ. Child maltreatment in developmentally-delayed children. GRAMEC Research Day, Grand Rapids, MI: April 20, 1999.

[18]   Hagberg B, Hagberg G. The changing panorama of cerebral palsy in Sweden: 5. The birth year period 1979-82. Acta Paediatr Scand 1989; 78: 283-90.

[19]   Keenan HT, Runyan DK, Marshall SW, Nocera MA, Merten DF, Sinal SH. A Population-based study of inflicted traumatic brain injury in young children. JAMA 2003; 290: 621-6.

[20]   Hennes H, Kini N, Palusci VJ. The epidemiology, clinical characteristics and public health implications of shaken baby syndrome. In: Lazoritz S, Palusci VJ, eds. The shaken baby syndrome: A multidisciplinary approach. Binghamton, NY: Haworth Maltreatment Trauma Press 2001: 19-40.

[21]   Palusci VJ, Cox EO, Cyrus TA, Heartwell SW, Vandervort FE, Pott ES. Medical assessment and legal outcome in child sexual abuse. Arch Pediatr Adol Med 1999; 153(4): 388-92.

[22]   Adams JA, Kellogg ND, Farst KJ, Harper NS, Palusci VJ, Frasier LD, et al. Updated guidelines for the medical assessment and care of children who may have been sexually abused. J Pediatr Adolesc Gyn 2016; 29(2): 81-7.

[23]   Servaes S, Brown SD, Choudhary AK, Christian CW, Done SL, et al. The etiology and significance of fractures in infants and young children: A critical multidisciplinary review. Pediatr Radiol 2016; 46(5): 591-600.

[24]   Jenny C, American Academy of Pediatrics. Recognizing and responding to medical neglect. Pediatrics 2007; 120: 1385-9.

[25]   Palusci VJ. Some thoughts on counting medical neglect. Maltreat Sci 2015 Jan 16. URL: http://www.maltreat.info/index.php/contribution-articles? download= 9:some-thoughts-on-counting-medical-neglect-reports.

[26]   Anderson J, Heath R. Forensic interviews of children who have developmental disabilities, Part 1 of 2. Natl Center Prosecution Child Abuse Update 2006; 19(1).

[27]   Anderson J, Heath R. Forensic interviews of children who have developmental disabilities, Part 2 of 2. Natl Center Prosecution Child Abuse Update 2006; 19(2).

[28]   Ericson K, Perlman N, Isaacs B. Witness competency, communication issues and people with developmental disabilities. Dev Disabil Bull 1994; 22(2): 101-9.

[29]   Cederborg A, Lamb ME. How does the legal system respond when children with learning difficulties are victimized? Child Abuse Negl 2006; 30(5): 537-47.

[30]   Lightfoot E, Hill K, LaLiberte T. The inclusion of disability as a condition for termination of parental rights. Child Abuse Negl 2010; 34: 927-34.

[31]   Palusci VJ, Zeemering W, Bliss RC, Combs A, Stoiko MA. Preventing abusive head trauma using a directed parent education program. Pediatric Academic Societies Meeting. Atlanta, GA: April 29, 2006

[32]   Palusci VJ, Ondersma SJ. Services and recurrence after psychological maltreatment confirmed by child protective services. Child Maltreat 2012; 17(2): 153-63.

[33]   Palusci VJ, Bliss R, Crum P. Outcomes after groups for children exposed to violence with behavior problems. Trauma Loss 2007; 7(1): 27-38.

[34]   Scott D, Lonne B, Higgins D. Public health models for preventing child maltreatment: Applications from the field of injury prevention. Trauma Violence Abuse 2016;17(4):408-19.

[35]   Balderian NJ, Coleman TF, Stream J. Abuse of people with disabilities: Victims and their families speak out. A report on the 2012 National Survey on Abuse of People with Disabilities. Disability Abuse Project, Los Angeles, CA: Spectrum Institute, 2013.

[36]   Daro D. A public health approach to prevention: What will it take? Trauma Violence Abuse 2016;17(4):420-1.

SECTION ONE: ASPECTS OF MALTREATMENT AND DISABILITY

In: Child Abuse: Children with Disabilities
Editors: V. J Palusci, D. Nazer et al.

ISBN: 978-1-53612-035-6
© 2017 Nova Science Publishers, Inc.

Chapter 2

GENETICS, EPIGENETICS AND THE MOLECULAR MARKS OF STRESS: A PRIMER

Kushol Gupta*, PhD
Department of Biochemistry and Biophysics,
Perelman School of Medicine, University of Pennsylvania, Philadelphia,
Pennsylvania, United States of America

In recent years it has become apparent that elements of our environment, including abuse, can physically affect our DNA and the flow of genetic information. These events can lead to immediate and accumulating physiological effects that can be transmitted to progeny in a non-Mendelian fashion. The goal of this discussion is to introduce the underlying mechanisms of these "marks" on our genomes, as it relates to the outcomes of child abuse and maltreatment. This review will discuss our understanding of genetics in a modern perspective, with a special emphasis on the emerging concepts of epigenetics and their underlying molecular bases.

INTRODUCTION

In the 21st century, it remains the case that the maltreatment of children represents a major public health concern worldwide (1), with some 700,000 reports in the US alone

* Correspondence: Kushol Gupta, Department of Biochemistry and Biophysics, Perelman School of Medicine, University of Pennsylvania, 242 Anatomy-Chemistry Building, Philadelphia, Pennsylvania, United States. E-mail: kgupta@upenn.edu.

each year (2). A steadily growing number of studies have linked this maltreatment with poor health outcomes, including hypertension, diabetes, asthma, heart disease, inflammation, and obesity (3-6). Early life stress is associated with an increased susceptibility to major psychiatric disorders including major depression, bipolar disorder, post-traumatic stress disorder (PTSD), alcohol and drug abuse, and schizophrenia (7). By cataloging the biological markers that accumulate as a result of these traumas, specific understanding in the underlying bases for these health problems can be gathered and treatments devised.

How can traumatic events early in childhood, including physical and mental abuse and malnutrition, underlie increased incidence of disease later in life? How does our environment affect our genome, sometimes in a heritable way? Why can twins with identical DNA sequences display different features? Why does Mendelian genetics alone fall short of describing a number of afflictions, including cancer and mental retardation? To appreciate some of the answers to these questions, we must not only understand the most basic aspects of genetics, but also a rapidly emerging field of study called epigenetics. There is now a convincing body of evidence that connects epigenetics to the underlying bases for changes in DNA expression changes in response to early life experiences (8).

OUR GENOME IN A MODERN PERSPECTIVE

For much of the 20th century, our understanding of biology and its most fundamental tenets were guided by the seminal contributions of figures such as Gregor Mendel and Charles Darwin, which include the concepts of traits, heredity, and evolution. Preceding the Nobel-prize winning work of the team of Francis Crick, James Watson, Maurice Wilkins, and Rosalind Franklin in the 1950s (9,10) was a growing body of evidence supplied by geneticists that it was deoxyribonucleic acid (DNA) and not the protein in chromosomes that was responsible for heredity among species. The work of this quartet of scientists ultimately illuminated the molecular basis of these heritable units in 1953 with their discovery of the double-helix structure of DNA using X-ray crystallography. At its most basic level, DNA is seemingly simple: a polymer comprised of four chemical bases (adenine (A), thymine (T), guanine (G), and cytosine (C)) (see Figure 1). Between the strands of the DNA double-helix, adenine only pairs with thymine and guanine only pairs with cytosine, creating a base pair between two strands. However, the potential information content across the entire DNA content of a cell is expansive. A genome is the complete set of DNA found within the cell of an organism. In the nuclei of each of the $\sim10^{13}$ cells in the human body, the approximately three billion pairs of DNA of the human genome reside across 23 pairs of chromosomes. In typewritten form, the sequence of the human genome would occupy some one million pages. Contained within the genome are units of sequences called genes which encode for biopolymers called proteins. The basic building blocks of proteins are called amino acids, of which twenty naturally occurring units are known. Proteins in turn serve a variety of chemical and structural roles that underlie basic cellular functions. The term "proteome" refers to the entire collection of proteins that can exist within a cell during its lifetime.

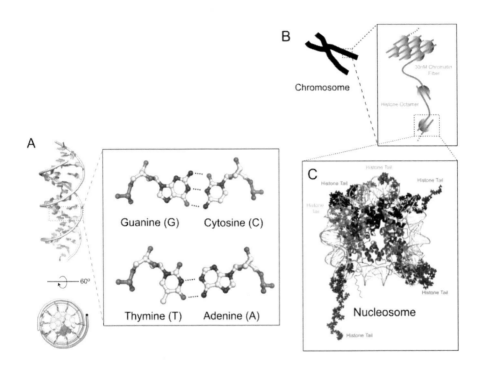

Figure 1. The structure of DNA and chromatin. A. Shown are orthogonal views of standard "B-form" DNA. Shown in the inset are the canonical base pairings that occur between components of the genetic code within double-stranded DNA. B. Chromatin structure. Chromosomes are comprised of chromatin fibers, which are highly compacted chains of nucleosome particles. The nucleosome is the basic unit of chromatin, comprised of ~147 base pairs of DNA (grey) wrapped around eight small proteins called histones (colored). Shown extending from each histone protein are tails that are the targets of enzymes that chemically modify them.

In its fully-extended form, the DNA of one cell is approximately a meter in length, yet tightly packaged into a cellular compartment (the nucleus) of a cell with a diameter of ~10 microns. How is this feat accomplished? Within the cell, DNA is tight wound around an octet of small proteins known as histones, creating what appears to be a node on a string. Each of these nodes is what is called a nucleosome, which wraps around ~165 base pairs (bps) of DNA. This string of pearls in turn can be wound to form higher order compact species called chromatin fibers, in the way one can continually wind a rubber band from its extended form to a more condensed form. Chromatin generally exists in one of two states: a less compacted form called *euchromatin* and a more compacted form called *heterochromatin* (see Figure 2). Generally, less compacted chromatin allows for access by cellular factors to read the genetic information, whereas more compacted forms are less accessible and hence not read. Using an analogy of a university library, the difference between euchromatin and heterochromatin is akin to the difference in one's ability to access books sequestered away in high-density shelving versus a book that is comfortably within reach on a shelf or table. The state of DNA in its packaged form dictates the flow of information and resulting products.

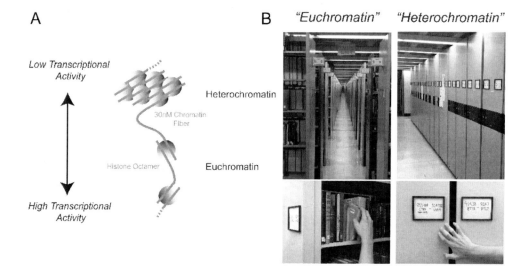

Figure 2. Chromatin remodeling and transcriptional activity. A. The condensation of chromatin structure by various factors controls the flow of genetic information in the form of transcription. B. By analogy, this is much like the book stacks of a library. Stacks that are not condensed facilitate the access of information, while condensed stacks disfavor access to information.

First articulated by Francis Crick in 1956 and again in 1970 (11), the Central Dogma of Biology is the core principle that underlies our understanding of all of biology (see Figure 3). This elegant and canonical model provides a conceptual framework for the transfer of information between different kinds of biopolymers common to all forms of life. DNA is routinely copied and transferred to progeny in a process are called DNA replication. In a process called transcription, ribonucleic acid (RNA) is an intermediary molecule synthesized from DNA templates; these RNA molecules are subsequently read by molecular machines called ribosomes to yield proteins in a process called translation.

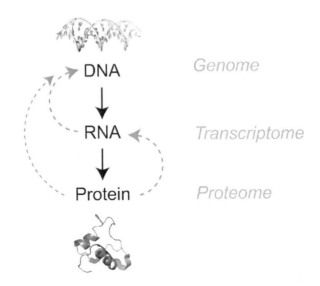

Figure 3. The central dogma of biology in a modern perspective. In the original presentation of this canonical concept, the flow of genetic information proceeds in one direction, from DNA to RNA to protein. However, since its original presentation, we now know that both RNA and protein can act to regulate the flow of this information at different levels. In the modern perspective, these elements are viewed on a global level: the genome, the transcriptome, and the proteome.

The advent of the Genomics Age and subsequent discoveries has revealed that the relationship between DNA, RNA, and protein is far more complex and nuanced than what was initially conceived by Mendel, Darwin, and Crick. As mentioned, in each cell are some three billion base pairs, providing the potential for considerable information content. The Human Genome Project was a thirteen year-long multi-national collaborative research project that set out to determine the sequence of base pairs within the human genome. The biggest surprise learned upon the completion of the project in 2003 was that there were far fewer protein-encoding genes in the human genome that initially believed: ~19,000, which is only a fraction what was originally predicted (~100,000). In comparison, the genome of *C. elegans* – a model-system roundworm – contains a similar number of genes (20,040). Humans only differ from one another by ~0.1%-0.4% of base pairs and from apes by about 1.2%. In the context of the Central Dogma, an ongoing fundamental question has been how such complexity between and within species of life can be achieved.

WHAT IS EPIGENETICS?

Over the past two decades, a relatively new area of intense investigation called "*epigenetics*" has arisen to provide at least some explanations to this driving question and other aspects that fall outside of the scope of traditional genetic concepts. This field of study is still in its relative infancy, insofar as even the definition of the term is still debated. Epigenetics can be defined as the study of natural changes in the expression of a gene without concomitant changes in its primary DNA sequence. Phenotypes can be altered without affecting the underlying genotype and hence do not obey Mendelian genetics; further, the alterations may or may not be heritable. This latter point has created ongoing disagreement on the scope of the definition of this field of study. The term has also been defined to describe anything other than DNA sequence that influences the temporal and spatial control of gene activity in the development of an organism (12, 13). This concept has been further extended to the coinage of the term *"epigenome,"* which is a reference to the overall epigenetic state of a cell. Efforts to map out the *"epigenomic code"* refer to the initiatives which look to measure the various forms of epigenetic "marks" that alter phenotypes, on a global level. A steadily increasing number of studies have revealed that misregulation of the epigenome on its different levels can result in disease, placing this field of study at the forefront of biomedical research and human health.

LAYERS OF COMPLEXITY

In the modern perspective, the Central Dogma has a very different and layered appearance. While it's original proposal implied directionality in the flow of information (e.g., DNA → RNA → protein), in reality RNA and protein play pivotal roles in the management of the instructions encoded in DNA. In addition to mRNAs corresponding to protein-encoding genes, the transcriptome – the collective of all of the messenger RNA molecules in the cell - there exists a population of non-coding RNAS (ncRNAs) which act to regulate the expression and function of gene products on different levels. Additionally, protein-encoding RNA transcripts can also be alternatively spliced to form variants of native proteins with modified activities.

A vast number of proteins encoded for within the genome act to regulate DNA and RNA, either by recognition and binding to specific sequences (like transcription factors) or by chemically decorating the nucleosome to modulate its compactness and signal the recruitment of other cellular factors, or by chemically modifying DNA and RNA sequences directly to alter their behavior and packaging in the context of chromatin.

A

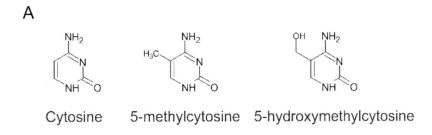

B

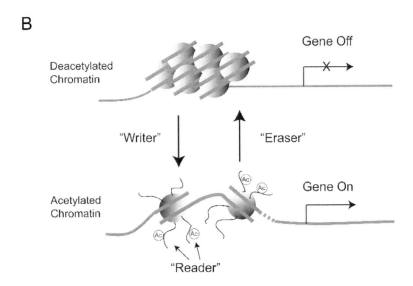

Figure 4. Epigenetic mechanisms. A. Chemical structure of the DNA base cytosine and its modified forms. Methyltransferases such as DNMT1 transfer a methyl moiety to the fifth carbon of the cytosine ring. The hydroxylase TET1 further hydroxylates the methyl moiety. B. Effects of acetylation on chromatin remodeling. Enzymes that acetylate the histone tails of chromatin ("Writers") catalyze the opening of chromatin structure, allowing proteins that recognize these marks ("Readers") to promote transcriptional activity. Enzymes that remove this mark ("Erasers") promote the condensation of chromatin structure, lowering transcriptional activity.

Epigenetic regulation of transcription and the flow of genetic information is a dynamic process mediated by an array of cellular protein factor that include an assorted variety of DNA and chromatin-modifying enzymes and non-coding RNAs (14-18). These enzymes generally fall into three general categories: 1) "writers," which are enzymes that decorate DNA or protein with a chemical modification, 2) "readers," which are proteins that recognize these modified DNA and protein molecules, precipitating subsequent molecular events, and 3) "erasers," which are enzymes that remove these marks from protein or DNA(19) (see Figure 4).

TRANSCRIPTION FACTORS

Cellular processes are highly coordinated both temporally and spatially by signaling pathways. The typical destinations of these pathways are the transcription factors which promote the flow of genetic information. The primary consequence of epigenetic misregulation is the inability of transcription factors to carry out their role by either occluding direct interaction with the DNA of interest (e.g., promoters), or preventing the transition of chromatin to a less compact and more accessible form via chromatin remodeling enzymes. Mutations in transcription factors and epigenetic enzymes are most frequently observed in cancer (20-22), including histone modifiers, methyltransferases, and non-coding RNA processing enzymes.

GENOMIC IMPRINTING AND DNA METHYLATION

The best-studied of the mechanisms for epigenetic regulation of the genetic code is genomic imprinting. In classic Mendelian genetics, one copy of a gene (an allele) is received from each parent and expressed. However, for some genes, only one copy is expressed, depending on the parent from whom the allele was received. This phenomenon is reversible, as the "marks" which underlie this are erased, re-rendered, and maintained during cell cycle. The methylation of DNA underlies the molecular bases of these marks on DNA and the phenomenon of genomic imprinting. The methylation of DNA is associated with the inactivation of a gene. The maintenance of DNA methylation during cell division is catalyzed by enzymes called DNA (cytosine-5) methyltransferases (DNMTs). These enzymes decorate the fifth carbon cytosine bases in dense regions of the genome enriched in CpG dinucleotides called CpG islands across the genome, accounting for some 1% of the total DNA bases in the human genome (23), with mature sperm and egg cells showing even higher levels of methylation.

In mammals, improper imprinting has been related to defects in embryonic and neonatal growth and can results in neurological disorders such as Prader-Willi syndrome and Angelman syndrome (24). Other imprinting disorders with disease phenotypes include Beckwith-Wiedemann syndrome, psuedohypoparathyroidism, and Silver-Russell syndrome.

Methylated cytosine has been found to be converted to another form called 5-hydroxymethylcytosine (5hmC) by enzymes which decorate the methyl group with an additional hydroxyl (the ten-eleven translocation (TET) family of enzymes) (25). The highest levels of these marks have been mapped to the nervous system (0.03-0.7% of the genome) (26) and have been implicated in neurodegeneration and aging (26). The role of 5hmC remains poorly understood, but has been implicated in development and tumor development and progression (28-30). Experimentally, it is difficult to distinguish 5mC from 5hmC from standard methods used to identify methylated DNA (such as methylation-specific polymerase chain reaction (PCR) and bisulfite pyrosequencing), slowing progress in fully discerning the biological roles of these chemical marks.

A growing number of human and animal studies provide evidence that the environment affects the epigenetic and hence the transcriptional state of the cell. It is most likely that a combination of many environmental factors such as diet and early life stress (e.g., abuse) and stochastic events collectively contribute to epigenomic variation. The understanding of epigenetic mechanisms alongside the availability of cutting edge technology such as high resolution tandem mass spectrometry and RNA sequencing methods has allowed investigators to more rigorously examine the scope of molecular changes on a global level and in a quantitative fashion.

For example, studies of monozygotic twins has shown that epigenotypes can change from very similar early in life to more divergent later in life with regards to DNA methylation amount and distribution and histone acetylation (31). In another study of maltreated children, methylation patterns at CpG sites correlated strong with depression (32). In 2014 Suderman and colleagues (33) analyzed the promoters of over 20,000 genes to identify 997 differentially methylated promoters associated with verbal, emotional, or sexual abuse. Clear examples of how early experiences and parental behavior impact the epigenome on the molecular level are emerging, with the best examples determined using mouse model systems (34, 35). It has been shown that frequent licking and grooming by mother rats modulate DNA methylation in the gene promoter for glutocorticoid receptor in the hippocampus region of their pups (35-39). The glucocorticoid receptor is involved in stress hormone levels and stress response. Nurtured pips have lower DNA methylation and increased histone acetylation at the promoter, which is associated with higher gene activity.

TELOMERES

The region at the end of a chromosome is enriched in repetitive DNA sequences (in vertebrates, a TTAGGG sequence), serving the primary function of protecting the chromosome from a phenomenon referred to as "the end replication problem": the enzymes that duplicate the chromosomes during cell division cannot continue all the way to the end of the chromosome, resulting in the progressive loss of genetic content. Telomeres serve as buffer regions that are lost during cellular division and subsequently replenished by an enzyme call telomerase. By analogy, they are like the aglets (tips) on the ends of shoelace which serve to prevent the fiber from unraveling. They have been proposed to serve as a "molecular clock," with their length being related to age (40, 41). Telomeres exist in chromatin, and a number of posttranslational modifications at the nucleosome have been additionally related to their regulation, which might work to regulate access of telomerase to the telomere.

A number of age-related diseases have been associated to premature shortening of the telomeres, including cancer, Werner syndrome, Bloom syndrome, Fanconi anaemia, and several others (42). A number of studies in recent years have related telomere shortening to childhood abuse and early life stress, including studies of adults (43) and environmental-risk longitudinal studies in twins (44). In one study, depression related to adverse childhood experiences were related to increased telomerase activity without any change in telomere length relative to the healthy group control (45). To test the hypothesis that telomere length could be a biological indictor of exposure to early adversity and serve as an early indicator to negative health outcomes later in life, in 2014 Drury *et. al.* examined children exposed to family stress and violence in the home and confirmed that children exposed to interpersonal violence and disruption in the home had significantly shorter telomere (46). Similar results were found with children exposed to maltreatment, domestic violence, and frequent bullying (44). Such studies may pave the way for future interventions which offset the resulting effects on telomeres by stimulating restoration of the chromosome ends.

CHROMATIN AND THE HISTONE CODE

The remodeling of chromatin from a heterochromatin ("silent") to euchromatin ("active") state to facilitate the access of transcriptional machinery to genes is regulated by an array of enzymes that affect the positioning, chemical compositions, and structure of the nucleosome units. One means by which this is accomplished is via "remodeling complexes." These large amalgams of proteins called ATP-dependent chromatin remodeling complexes regulate gene expression on a higher level by physically restructuring, removing, and rebuilding nucleosomes. These processes are essential to basic biological processes including DNA replication and repair, chromosome segregation, normal cell-cycle, and development. Dysfunction of this machinery has been implicated in cancer.

The other way by which this regulation is accomplished is on local level via chemical modification. As mentioned, nucleosomes are comprised in part by small proteins call histones. A distinctive feature of the nucleosome is its protein "tails:" extended floppy regions that comprise over a quarter of the protein mass of the nucleosome and are enriched in amino acids such as lysine, arginine, and serine, all of which are susceptible to chemical modification by an array of enzymes ("writers"). These modifications affect the arrangement of chromatin in such a ways as to loosen or tighten chromatin between silent and active states. These chemical marks come in different varieties, including methylation, acetylation, phosphorylation, and ubiquitination. Over twenty types of histone chemical modifications have been identified to date (47). Collectively these chemical modifications are referred to as the alphabet of the "histone code," which together with DNA methylation underlies the molecular bases for epigenetic regulation. Complexity in this code is achieved by preferential modifications of different variants of histones. These marks are read by "readers," resulting in different cellular processes. The two best-characterized modifications to date are acetylation and methylation. Acetylation is a mark commonly associated with active genes (euchromatin) while methylation is a mark commonly associated with silenced genes (heterochromatin). Histone marks are generally viewed as the most important and most well-studied group of epigenetic marks. They are highly stable modifications that are inheritable during cellular division and correlate strongly with global gene expression patterns (47-53). Chemical compounds which block the writers and erasers are promising targets for pharmaceuticals that are just entering the clinic.

NON-CODING RNAS

Of the different mechanisms discussed herein, non-coding RNAs (ncRNAs) are perhaps the least explored of the epigenetic mechanisms. There are different varieties that include microRNAs (miRNA), silencing RNA (siRNA), piwi-interacting RNA (piRNA), and large noncoding RNA (lncRNA). Generally, these ribonucleic acid chains, which can vary in size from <30 nucleotides to >200, function at the transcriptional and post-transcriptional levels to regulate the flow of genetic information. In many of the cases known, they augment existing epigenetic mechanisms that include histone modification and DNA methylation. For example, miRNAs act by targeting messenger RNA, blocking translation of gene products. Two miRNAs have been identified to regulate the imprinted gene Rtl1, which is involved in placenta formation in mice (54). While there have been little work relating non-coding RNAs to child abuse and trauma, recent work has related lncRNAs to drug abuses and changes in the brain (55).

FUTURE DIRECTIONS

A number of measureable changes in regions of the brain such as the hippocampus and the amygdala have been correlated with early life stress and traumatic events including poverty (8, 56), but it remains to be determined if these physiological changes correlate with epigenetic marks, and if these changes are preventable and reversible. Future studies that correlate the molecular marks now known to occur in response to stress and abuse early in life with resulting phenotypes and outcomes using state-of-the-art technologies will continue to illuminate our fundamental understanding in this area.

ACKNOWLEDGMENTS

Special thanks to Thomas Hensle and the Van Pelt Library system at the University of Pennsylvania.

REFERENCES

[1]   Gilbert R, Widom CS, Browne K, Fergusson D, Webb E, Janson S. Burden and consequences of child maltreatment in high-income countries. Lancet 2009;373(9657):68-81.

[2]   US DHHS. Child maltreatment 2009. Washington, DC: Administration of Children and Families, Children's Bureau, 2011.

[3]   Danese A, Pariante CM, Caspi A, Taylor A, Poulton R. Childhood maltreatment predicts adult inflammation in a life-course study. PNAS 2007;104(4):1319-24.

[4]   Flaherty EG, Thompson R, Litrownik AJ, Theodore A, English DJ, Black MM, et al. Effect of early childhood adversity on child health. Arch Pediatr Adolesc Med 2006;160(12):1232-8.

[5]   Wegman HL, Stetler C. A meta-analytic review of the effects of childhood abuse on medical outcomes in adulthood. Psychosom Med 2009;71(8):805-12.

[6]   Widom CS, Czaja SJ, Bentley T, Johnson MS. A prospective investigation of physical health outcomes in abused and neglected children: New findings from a 30-year follow-up. AJPH 2012;102(6):1135-44.

[7]   Nemeroff CB. Paradise lost: The neurobiological and clinical consequences of child abuse and neglect. Neuron 2016;89(5):892-909.

[8]   Kundakovic M, Champagne FA. Early-life experience, epigenetics, and the developing brain. Neuropsychopharmacol 2015;40(1):141-53.

[9]   Watson JD, Crick FHC. Molecular structure of nucleic acids - A structure for deoxyribose nucleic acid. Nature 1953;171(4356):737-8.

[10] Watson JD, Crick FHC. Genetical Implications of the Structure of Deoxyribonucleic Acid. Nature 1953;171(4361):964-7.

[11] Crick F. Central dogma of molecular biology. Nature 1970;227(5258):561.

[12]   Holliday R. DNA methylation and epigenetic inheritance. Phil Trans Royal Soc London Ser B, Biol Sci 1990;326(1235):329-38.

[13]   Holliday R. Genomic imprinting and allelic exclusion. Dev Suppl 1990:125-9.

[14]   Dawson MA, Bannister AJ, Gottgens B, Foster SD, Bartke T, Green AR, et al. JAK2 phosphorylates histone H3Y41 and excludes HP1 alpha from chromatin. Nature 2009;461(7265):819-29.

[15]   Bannister AJ, Kouzarides T. Regulation of chromatin by histone modifications. Cell Res 2011;21(3):381-95.

[16]   Piatti P, Zeilner A, Lusser A. ATP-Dependent Chromatin Remodeling Factors and Their Roles in Affecting Nucleosome Fiber Composition. Int J Mol Sci 2011;12(10):6544-65.

[17]   Sutcliffe EL, Bunting KL, He YQ, Li J, Phetsouphanh C, Seddiki N, et al. Chromatin-associated protein kinase c-theta regulates an inducible gene expression program and micrornas in human T lymphocytes. Mol Cell 2011;41(6):704-19.

[18]   Jin BL, Ernst J, Tiedemann RL, Xu HY, Sureshchandra S, Kellis M, et al. Linking DNA methyltransferases to epigenetic marks and nucleosome structure genome-wide in human tumor cells. Cell Rep 2012;2(5):1411-24.

[19]   Gardner KE, Allis CD, Strahl BD. OPERating ON chromatin, a colorful language where context matters. J Mol Biol 2011;409(1):36-46.

[20]   Ley TJ, Ding L, Walter MJ, McLellan MD, Lamprecht T, Larson DE, et al. DNMT3A mutations in acute myeloid leukemia. New Engl J Med 2010;363(25):2424-33.

[21]   Kadoch C, Hargreaves DC, Hodges C, Elias L, Ho L, Ranish J, et al. Proteomic and bioinformatic analysis of mammalian SWI/SNF complexes identifies extensive roles in human malignancy. Nat Genet 2013;45(6):592.

[22]   Shain AH, Pollack JR. The spectrum of SWI/SNF mutations: Ubiquitous in human cancers. Plos One 2013;8(1).

[23]   Ehrlich M, Gama-Sosa MA, Huang LH, Midgett RM, Kuo KC, McCune RA, et al. Amount and distribution of 5-methylcytosine in human DNA from different types of tissues of cells. Nucleic Acids Res 1982;10(8):2709-21.

[24]   Barlow D, Bartolomei M. Genomic imprinting in mammals. In: Allis C, Jenuwein T, Reinberg D, Caparros M, eds. Epigenetics. Cold Spring Harbor, NY: Cold Spring Harbor Laboratory Press, 2007:357-75.

[25]   Tahiliani M, Koh KP, Shen Y, Pastor WA, Bandukwala H, Brudno Y, et al. Conversion of 5-methylcytosine to 5-hydroxymethylcytosine in mammalian DNA by MLL partner TET1. Science 2009;324(5929):930-5.

[26]   Globisch D, Munzel M, Muller M, Michalakis S, Wagner M, Koch S, et al. Tissue distribution of 5-hydroxymethylcytosine and search for active demethylation intermediates. Plos One 2010;5(12):e15367.

[27]   Sherwani SI, Khan HA. Role of 5-hydroxymethylcytosine in neurodegeneration. Gene 2015;570(1):17-24.

[28]   Madzo J, Liu H, Rodriguez A, Vasanthakumar A, Sundaravel S, Caces DB, et al. Hydroxymethylation at gene regulatory regions directs stem/early progenitor cell commitment during erythropoiesis. Cell Rep 2014;6(1):231-44.

[29]   Rampal R, Alkalin A, Madzo J, Vasanthakumar A, Pronier E, Patel J, et al. DNA hydroxymethylation profiling reveals that WT1 mutations result in loss of TET2 function in acute myeloid leukemia. Cell Rep 2014;9(5):1841-55.

[30] Moen EL, Mariani CJ, Zullow H, Jeff-Eke M, Litwin E, Nikitas JN, et al. New themes in the biological functions of 5-methylcytosine and 5-hydroxymethylcytosine. Immunol Rev 2015;263(1):36-49.

[31] Fraga MF, Ballestar E, Paz MF, Ropero S, Setien F, Ballestar ML, et al. Epigenetic differences arise during the lifetime of monozygotic twins. PNAS 2005;102(30):10604-9.

[32] Yang BZ, Zhang H, Ge W, Weder N, Douglas-Palumberi H, Perepletchikova F, et al. Child abuse and epigenetic mechanisms of disease risk. Am J Prev Med 2013;44(2):101-7.

[33] Suderman M, Borghol N, Pappas JJ, Pinto Pereira SM, Pembrey M, Hertzman C, et al. Childhood abuse is associated with methylation of multiple loci in adult DNA. BMC Med Gen 2014;7:13.

[34] Weaver IC, Cervoni N, Champagne FA, D'Alessio AC, Sharma S, Seckl JR, et al. Epigenetic programming by maternal behavior. Nature Neuroscience 2004;7(8): 847-54.

[35] Liu D, Diorio J, Tannenbaum B, Caldji C, Francis D, Freedman A, et al. Maternal care, hippocampal glucocorticoid receptors, and hypothalamic-pituitary-adrenal responses to stress. Science 1997;277(5332):1659-62.

[36] Johnson SB, Riley AW, Granger DA, Riis J. The science of early life toxic stress for pediatric practice and advocacy. Pediatrics 2013;131(2):319-27.

[37] Champagne FA, Francis DD, Mar A, Meaney MJ. Variations in maternal care in the rat as a mediating influence for the effects of environment on development. Physiol Behav 2003;79(3):359-71.

[38] Francis D, Diorio J, Liu D, Meaney MJ. Nongenomic transmission across generations of maternal behavior and stress responses in the rat. Science 1999;286(5442):1155-8.

[39] Szyf M, Weaver IC, Champagne FA, Diorio J, Meaney MJ. Maternal programming of steroid receptor expression and phenotype through DNA methylation in the rat. Front Neuroendocrinol 2005;26(3-4):139-62.

[40] Blackburn EH. Switching and signaling at the telomere. Cell 2001;106(6):661-73.

[41] Collins K, Mitchell JR. Telomerase in the human organism. Oncogene 2002;21(4):564-79.

[42] Blasco MA. Telomeres and human disease: ageing, cancer and beyond. Nat Rev Gen 2005;6(8):611-22.

[43] Tyrka AR, Price LH, Kao HT, Porton B, Marsella SA, Carpenter LL. Childhood maltreatment and telomere shortening: preliminary support for an effect of early stress on cellular aging. Biol Psychiatr 2010;67(6):531-4.

[44] Shalev I, Moffitt TE, Sugden K, Williams B, Houts RM, Danese A, et al. Exposure to violence during childhood is associated with telomere erosion from 5 to 10 years of age: a longitudinal study. Mol Psychiatr 2013;18(5):576-81.

[45] Chen SH, Epel ES, Mellon SH, Lin J, Reus VI, Rosser R, et al. Adverse childhood experiences and leukocyte telomere maintenance in depressed and healthy adults. J Affect Disord 2014;169:86-90.

[46] Drury SS, Mabile E, Brett ZH, Esteves K, Jones E, Shirtcliff EA, et al. The association of telomere length with family violence and disruption. Pediatrics 2014;134(1):e128-37.

[47] Huang H, Lin S, Garcia BA, Zhao Y. Quantitative proteomic analysis of histone modifications. Chem Rev 2015;115(6):2376-418.

[48] Egger G, Liang G, Aparicio A, Jones PA. Epigenetics in human disease and prospects for epigenetic therapy. Nature 2004;429(6990):457-63.

[49] Johnson L, Cao X, Jacobsen S. Interplay between two epigenetic marks. DNA methylation and histone H3 lysine 9 methylation. Curr Biol 2002;12(16):1360-7.

[50] Tamaru H, Selker EU. A histone H3 methyltransferase controls DNA methylation in Neurospora crassa. Nature 2001;414(6861):277-83.

[51] Jackson JP, Lindroth AM, Cao X, Jacobsen SE. Control of CpNpG DNA methylation by the KRYPTONITE histone H3 methyltransferase. Nature 2002;416(6880):556-60.

[52] Trojer P, Reinberg D. Histone lysine demethylases and their impact on epigenetics. Cell 2006;125(2):213-7.

[53] Kouzarides T. Chromatin modifications and their function. Cell 2007;128(4):693-705.

[54] Cui XS, Zhang DX, Ko YG, Kim NH. Aberrant epigenetic reprogramming of imprinted microRNA-127 and Rtl1 in cloned mouse embryos. Biochem Biophys Res Comm 2009;379(2):390-4.

[55] Bannon MJ, Savonen CL, Jia H, Dachet F, Halter SD, Schmidt CJ, et al. Identification of long noncoding RNAs dysregulated in the midbrain of human cocaine abusers. J Neurochem 2015;135(1):50-9.

[56] Luby J, Belden A, Botteron K, Marrus N, Harms MP, Babb C, et al. The effects of poverty on childhood brain development: The mediating effect of caregiving and stressful life events. JAMA Pediatr 2013;167(12):1135-42.

In: Child Abuse: Children with Disabilities
Editors: V. J Palusci, D. Nazer et al.

ISBN: 978-1-53612-035-6
© 2017 Nova Science Publishers, Inc.

Chapter 3

DISABILITY AND THE EPIDEMIOLOGY OF CHILD ABUSE AND NEGLECT

*Vincent J Palusci**, *MD, MS, FAAP*

New York University School of Medicine, New York, Frances L Loeb Child
Protection and Development Center, Bellevue Hospital,
New York, US

This chapter reviews abuse and neglect among children with disabilities and highlights the impact of disability on child abuse and neglect in the United States and internationally. Children with various disabilities have variable increases in their risk for maltreatment because of their increased vulnerability, difficulties in communication, and potential for ongoing victimization. Patterns of victimization are defined and discussed in categories of different types of maltreatment, including physical and sexual abuse, psychologic maltreatment, and neglect. The effects of disabilities of various types on this epidemiology are discussed, serving as an introduction to the problem of child abuse and neglect as well as describing potentially intervenable risk factors among the population of disabled children. Recommendations are given to improve our understanding of how to best identify child maltreatment among children with disabilities so they may maximize their developmental and intellectual potentials.

---

*Correspondence:Vincent J Palusci, MD, MS, Professor of Pediatrics, New York University School of Medicine, Bellevue Hospital Center, 462 First Avenue, New York, NY 10016, United States. E-mail: Vincent.palusci@nyumc.org.

INTRODUCTION

Child maltreatment (CM) continues to affect large numbers of children every year. In 2014, 700,000 children younger than 18 years were found to be victims after investigation by United States (US) child protective services (CPS) agencies (1). Despite being extant since the beginning of human civilization, it is only relatively recently that we have come to understand the profound effects of abuse and neglect on persons with disability. At the time of the classic description of the battered child by C Henry Kempe in 1962, physical abuse and neglect were not a stranger to children with disabilities, and people with intellectual and developmental disabilities (IDD) faced almost complete exclusion from schools, communities, and sometimes even homes. Families were regularly counseled to place children with IDD in state-run facilities and were assured that their children would be cared for and protected, but the facilities were often riddled with systemic neglect and abuse.

It was within this context that the Federal Government began providing funds to enhance institutions, and parents and others provided private special-education classes and sheltered workshops for children and adults who were living with their families (2). The United States Child Abuse Prevention and Treatment Act was passed in 1974 and reauthorized in 2010 to further develop state-based child abuse reporting and response systems, including foster care and home-based services (3). As a result, a number of agencies have been put in place at different levels (e.g., local, state, federal) to improve our response to abuse and neglect, and information has been collected about developmental and intellectual disabilities in the child welfare system. If a child discloses information or behaves in such a way that leads to a suspicion of abuse or neglect, a variety of professionals and agency staff members can be legally mandated (each state/country according to their laws) to make a report to the governmental entity designed to receive such reports. This entity determines if there is enough evidence to prompt an investigation and/or begins an investigation which includes assessing the safety of the home, interviewing family members and others known to the patient, and obtaining medical and other records. This investigation can involve law enforcement and child or adult protective services. If abuse occurs in an institution or in foster care, the agencies involved may also conduct their own investigation. This has been further codified and expanded throughout the world with the adoption of the United Nations Convention on the Rights of the Child (4) and Convention on the Rights of Persons with Disabilities in 2006 (5). The known and suspected causes of child maltreatment among children with disabilities are multifactorial, ranging from genetics, epigenetics, environment, and ecology to family demography, behavior, and social and societal norms.

Despite the existence of reporting, it is difficult to precisely determine the incidence and prevalence of child maltreatment in the US and across the world due to variations in the application of definitions in law and practice, different numbers of cases generated with voluntary versus mandated reports, large numbers of cases that are never known to CPS agencies, parenting and cultural practices, acceptability of corporal punishment and other family violence, and resources available for systematic epidemiologic case ascertainment. Some jurisdictions have little or no information about child maltreatment, while data systems have been in place in many countries such as the US for more than 20 years (1). Several models have been developed in various countries to capture the number of children coming to the attention of social services or legal authorities or the prevalence of behaviors that place children at risk for child maltreatment (6). In addition, population-based surveys using variations of the parent-child Conflict Tactics Scale, the Adverse Childhood Experiences (ACEs) questionnaire, the Lifetime Victimization Screening Questionnaire, and the International Society for the Prevention of Child Abuse and Neglect (ISPCAN) screening tools have all been variably used to assess child maltreatment worldwide (7).

The United States, Canada, England, and Australia often administratively report all types of child maltreatment as affecting 3% to 5% of all children, with fewer than half receiving investigation and fewer than a quarter being legally substantiated (8). Two large administrative sources provide information about the US annual incidence of child maltreatment: the National Child Abuse and Neglect Data System (NCANDS) and the National Incidence Studies of child abuse and neglect (NIS). NCANDS contains aggregate and case-level data on child abuse reports received by state Child Protective Service (CPS) agencies, and almost all US states and territories provide information annually about the outcomes of child abuse reports, types of maltreatment, child and family factors and services being provided (1). In contrast, NIS samples sentinel counties to identify under two standards: the harm standard (relatively stringent in that it generally requires that an act or omission result in demonstrable harm in order to be classified as abuse or neglect) and the endangerment standard (which allows children who were not yet harmed by maltreatment to be counted if the CM was confirmed by CPS or identified as endangerment by professionals outside CPS, either by their parents or other adults) (9).

Increasingly, non–English-speaking countries, such as the Netherlands, Greece, and Croatia, have reported population-based rates that are not substantially different (7). When individual countries such as the United States possess the resources to accurately count child maltreatment cases, additional obstacles often prevent an accurate comparison. Organizations such as WHO have decried poor public health surveillance of child maltreatment across the world, and there is active discussion on the world stage about measuring and reporting strategies (6). Each country (and sometimes provinces or states) has its own policy and practice around child maltreatment definitions and reporting and whether a report is substantiated. Such difficulties occur within countries over time as well.

Disabled children are often a hidden and difficult-to-determine part of these statistics. Child maltreatment occurs primarily in the family but also in schools, alternative care institutions and detention facilities, places where children work, and communities. After a variety of societal attitudes resulted in the inhumane conditions in institutions across the world for children with developmental and intellectual disabilities, their increasing placement back into the community has shown daylight on their numbers and needs, highlighting how far we have come while we still have far to go. In New York City, for example, among over 60,000 reports made annually for suspected abuse of maltreatment, our program for medical consultation identified 20% of the children as having special medical needs (10). These children included those with intellectual and developmental disabilities and also chronic medical conditions with the potential to disable a child. Likewise, in addition to their higher rates of abuse and neglect, there is a disproportionately large percentage of children with IDD with maltreatment as a cause of their disabilities. Children with disabilities are also victims of sexual abuse, the evaluation for which is made all the more difficult because of their disabilities, potential developmental delays, and difficulty with communication. Parenting practices and misunderstanding may lead to psychologic harm by a variety of mechanisms, and parents who have disabilities face heightened surveillance by a child welfare system seeking to reduce potential harm from the neglect to their children. For disabled parents, the limitations placed on them by their disabilities can contribute to all types of child maltreatment (11).

This discussion highlights our current definitions and knowledge about the incidence and prevalence of child maltreatment and its types as well as the potential risk and protective factors and concludes with recommendations to improve our understanding of how to best identify child maltreatment among children with disabilities.

DEFINITIONS AND RISK AND PROTECTIVE FACTORS

The World Health Organization and United Nations (6,12) broadly define these types of maltreatment for data collection and intervention:

1. Physical abuse (PA) is the intentional use of force against a child that results in, or has a high likelihood of resulting in, harm to the child's health, survival,

development or dignity. This includes hitting, beating, kicking, shaking, biting, strangling, scalding, burning, poisoning and suffocating.

2. Sexual abuse (SA) is the involvement of a child in sexual activity that he or she does not fully comprehend, is unable to give informed consent to, or for which he or she is not developmentally prepared, and/or that violates the laws or social taboos of society. This can be by adults or other children who, by virtue of their age or development, are in a position of responsibility, trust or power over the child.

3. Psychological maltreatment (PM) is a pattern of failure over time on the part of the parent or caretaker to provide bonding and a developmentally appropriate and emotionally supportive environment. This includes restriction of movement, belittling, blaming, threatening, frightening, discriminating against, ridiculing and other non-physical hostile treatment.

4. Neglect (NEG) is defined as isolated incidents and patterns of failure over time on the part of the parent or caretaker, when in a position to do so, to provide for the food, clothing, shelter, health, education, nutrition and safety of the child.

In the US, child abuse and neglect have sometimes distinct definitions in different professional fields and are codified under different federal and state statutes. Maltreatment, a more encompassing term which includes abuse, neglect and exploitation is often used, and several types are discussed, such as physical abuse, sexual abuse, neglect, medical care neglect and emotional/psychological maltreatment. Physical abuse can be further subdivided into abusive head trauma, abusive fractures and other skin and organ injuries, while sexual abuse is often categorized as penetrating or non-penetrating, contact or non-contact, or sexual exploitation. The broadest category, neglect, has been further classified as physical neglect (lack of appropriate food, clothing or shelter), medical care neglect (lack of appropriate medical attention, dental care or medications), and supervisional neglect (lack of developmentally appropriate surveillance and protection from environmental or other dangers). These definitions have been extended to include exploitation of children in inappropriate work settings that are likely to be hazardous or interfere with the child's education or are harmful to the child's health or physical, mental, spiritual, moral, or social development.

Sexual abuse encompasses several types of maltreatment. *Rape,* which is often reported by law enforcement and criminal justice systems, has been generally defined as forceful, penetrative contact, and is further specified in individual state penal codes. *Sexual assault* refers to a broader collection of acts, including fondling and other non-penetrating acts and also is further refined in state penal codes. Other terms imply the relationship of the offender to the victim. *Incest* refers to sexual contact between family members, which is sometimes limited to immediate family but in other contexts can extend to fifth degree relationships (second cousin, once removed). *Sexual exploitation* generally refers to acts without sexual contact, such as having children pose for sexually explicit photographic or video images, having them witness sexual acts, or by adults exposing themselves to children inappropriately for the sexual gratification of the adult. Thus, a broad definition of *child sexual abuse* (SA) has been taken as the "... involvement of dependent, developmentally immature children and adolescents in sexual activities that they do not fully comprehend, to which they are unable to give informed consent, or that violate the social taboos of family roles" (13). This has been modified for practical application to "... an act of commission, including intrusion or penetration, molestation with genital contact, or other forms of sexual acts in which children are used to provide sexual gratification for the perpetrator." This type of abuse also includes commercial sexual exploitation with acts such as prostituting children and child pornography" (14).

An additional form of child maltreatment, *medical neglect* or medical care neglect, has been defined separately from neglect in some jurisdictions. For example, seven US states specifically define medical neglect as failing to provide any special medical treatment or mental health care that a child needs while four US states define medical neglect as withholding medical treatment or nutrition from disabled infants with life-threatening conditions (15). The American Academy of Pediatrics (AAP) notes that medical neglect is usually the failure to heed obvious signs of serious illness or the failure to follow a physician's instructions once medical advice is sought. Either of these situations can be fatal or lead to chronic disability (16). Several factors are considered necessary for diagnosing medical neglect (MN):

1. A child is harmed or is at risk of harm from lack of health care.
2. The recommended health care offers significant net benefit to the child.
3. The anticipated benefit of the treatment is significantly greater than its morbidity so that reasonable caregivers would choose treatment over nontreatment.
4. It can be demonstrated that access to health care is available and not used.
5. The caregiver understands the medical advice given.

While studies of risk and protective factors across the world are problematic due to methodological and definitional differences, studies clearly confirm child maltreatment to be an international problem with common themes among countries. Recent studies found rates in resource-rich countries in line with comparable North American research; for example, rates for sexual abuse ranged from 7% to 36% for women and 3% to 29% for men (17-19). Most studies find females to be sexually abused 1 to 3 times more frequently than are males. Economic development of the country, socioeconomic status of the survivor, age, and gender are among the many factors associated with the risk of lethal violence. Studies suggest that young children are at greatest risk of physical violence, while sexual violence predominantly affects those who have reached puberty or adolescence. Boys are at greater risk of physical violence than girls, while girls face greater risk of sexual violence, neglect, and forced prostitution (20).

A recent systematic review confirmed that children with disabilities are more likely to be victims of violence than are their peers who are not disabled. However, the continued scarcity of robust evidence, due to a lack of well designed research studies, poor standards of measurement of disability and violence, and insufficient assessment of whether violence precedes the development of disability, leaves gaps in knowledge that need to be addressed (21). Stable family units can be a powerful source of protection from violence for all children in all settings, and factors that are likely to be protective in the home and other settings include good parenting, strong bonds between parents and children, and positive, nonviolent discipline. Factors that are likely to protect against violence at school include school-wide policies and effective curricula that support the development of nonviolent and nondiscriminatory attitudes and behaviors. High levels of social cohesion are shown to have a protective effect against violence in the community even when other risk factors are present.

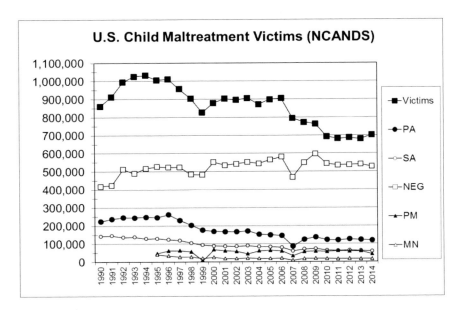

Figure 1. Child maltreatment victims by type, 1990-2014. PA= physical abuse; SA=sexual abuse; NEG=neglect; PM=psychologic maltreatment; MN=medical neglect

PHYSICAL ABUSE

The victimization of children by physical abuse remains an all-too-common occurrence around the globe (22). While international estimates vary and likely underestimate the extent of the problem, over 100,000 children were found to be physically abused in the US in 2014, at a rate of 2 children per 1,000 with an estimated 1,580 fatalities in the U.S. alone (1). Child maltreatment is associated with a variety of serious and life-threatening injuries with patterns of risk factors, with the highest risk in infants less than one years of age (23). In addition to death and physical injury, growing evidence further links child maltreatment to physical and emotional disease and disability during adulthood (24).

National estimates of the overall numbers of victims (substantiated or indicated CPS reports) as well as victims identified with physical abuse show decline over the 20+ years of nationally collected data in the US (see Figure 1). This represents a decrease from a high of 261,605 cases in 1996, following similar trends in other national crime statistics (1). Unlike the reported incidence of sexual abuse, in which it has been suggested that at least some of the decrease is real, it is not clear if or why physical abuse rates have actually declined (25). While economic indicators improved in the 1990s, the number of cases continued to fall in NCANDS during 2008-2011 during an economic recession in the US. This may indicate that states are changing how they count child maltreatment fatalities and how they are delivering that information to NCANDS as could occur with differential response systems. Further studies are needed to ascertain whether the number of physical cases is continuing to decline and the causes why this is occurring. Rates of physical abuse reportedly also fell in the United Kingdom (UK) during 1974 to 2008 (26). The Fourth National Incidence Study of Child Abuse and Neglect (NIS–4) also shows an overall decrease in the incidence of maltreatment since NIS–3, as well as decreases in some specific maltreatment categories and increases in others (9). Using the stringent Harm Standard definition during the NIS–4 study year (2005–2006), an estimated total of 553,300 were abused, and most (58%) of these abused children experienced physical abuse. "Harm standard" physical abuse cases decreased from an estimated 381,700 at the time of the NIS–3 to an estimated 323,000 in the NIS–4 (a 15% decrease in number and a 23% decline in the rate). Under "Endangerment," the estimated number of physically abused children decreased from an estimated 614,100 children to 476,600 (22% decrease in number, 29% decline in the rate) (9).

Smaller independent samples offer additional information. In the Carolinas in the US, the incidence of harsh physical discipline was found to be 4.3% of respondents (with 2.4% shaking infants), and a retrospective prevalence survey, 24% of adolescents reported being physically assaulted (27,28). The range of incidence rates of abusive head trauma (AHT) has been found to be 27.5-32.2 per 100,000 in a large US inpatient database, with an estimates rising from 6.6 to 7.4 million annually during 1997 to 2009 (27). Lane and colleagues (30) noted hospital discharge rates of 1.8 per 100k, with 25% of head trauma in infants being AHT. The ISPCAN Child Abuse Screening Tool (ICAST) has been used by experts from 40 countries to study the prevalence of childhood victimization. In one sample using the parent version, approximately 15% of children were shaken, 24% were hit on the buttocks with an object, and 37% were spanked. Two percent of parents reported choking and smothering their child (31).

Several factors have been associated with child physical abuse. Unlike previous NIS cycles, NIS–4 (9) found strong and pervasive race differences in the incidence of maltreatment with rates of maltreatment for Black children significantly higher than those for White and Hispanic children. Under the Harm Standard, children with confirmed disabilities had significantly lower rates of physical abuse and of moderate harm from maltreatment, but they had significantly higher rates of emotional neglect and serious injury or harm. NIS-4 also confirmed findings from other studies which associated increased physical abuse in poor, larger, unemployed families, with one parent and an unrelated caregiver present. Zhou and colleagues (32) found that infant maltreatment can best be predicted when there are young mothers less than 20 years old, who are unmarried, with inadequate prenatal care, who are poor or smoke during the pregnancy, or when there are three or more siblings. In an NCANDS sample, parent emotional problems, alcohol abuse, and other family violence were found to be associated with the recurrence of physical abuse before age three years (33).

Studies in the United Kingdom have shown similar rates and risk factors. In a population-based study in Wales in the late 1990s, severe physical abuse, defined as death, traumatic brain injury, intracranial hemorrhage, medical child abuse, internal injuries, fractures, burns, and bites, was seen in 54 per 100,000 infants annually. When data from both child protection registers and a pediatrician surveillance system were combined, the incidence rose to 114 per 100,000 (34). A random survey of 2,869 young adults throughout the United Kingdom noted that the prevalence of maltreatment during their childhood was 16% of the sample (35). Of these, 7% had serious physical abuse, 6% had emotional abuse, 11% had sexual abuse with contact, 6% had absence of care, and 5% had absence of supervision. Using a cohort from the Avon Longitudinal Study of Parents and Children (ALSPAC), risk factors noted to be associated with abuse were parental unemployment, public housing, overcrowding, lack of car ownership, and a poor social network. In a later analysis, the strongest risks were found to be socioeconomic deprivation and other factors in the parents' own background (26).

It has been consistently estimated that 1-2 per 100,000 US children annually are fatally maltreated (1,36). More than three-quarters (78%) of these deaths were in children under 4 years of age, and 44% were among infants. Physical abuse, alone or in combination with neglect, causes most of these deaths, but there have been persistent concerns about a systematic under ascertainment of these fatalities (37). Using an inpatient hospital database, there were 6.2 per 100,000 children with 300 deaths, with higher rates for infants and children receiving Medicaid (29). Separating abuse from deaths due to neglect is problematic (38). Family configuration, child gender, social isolation, lack of support, maternal youth, marital status, poverty, and parenting practices contribute to increased risk (39). Children residing in households with unrelated adults were significantly more likely to die from inflicted injuries than were children residing with two biologic parents, and risk was also elevated with step, foster and adoptive parents (40). Among newborns, 2.1 per 100,000 in North Carolina were killed or left to die each year, usually by their mothers, many of whom were poor, had no prenatal care, or were adolescents (41). There were more boys than girls, and infant boys had the highest rate (18.5 per 100,000). A review in the UK identified child age less than five years, non-organic failure to thrive, prior abuse or unexplained injuries, caregiver youth, inexperience, mental illness, drug and alcohol abuse, stress, and poverty as risk factors (42). Independent of these factors, a prior CPS report of maltreatment has been associated with almost six times the risk for death from later injury (43).

SEXUAL ABUSE

As with other forms of child maltreatment, child sexual abuse (SA) has likely occurred since the dawn of human history. But unlike physical abuse, neglect and psychological maltreatment, SA has been shrouded by the cloak of social taboo surrounding sexual contact with children and human sexuality in general. This has made determining the true number of SA cases difficult, leading physicians and other scientists to believe it was an uncommon problem. In the 1970s in the US, reports of SA grew dramatically as the social changes associated with the women's movement revealed the plight of sexually victimized children. Early counts of SA rose dramatically from a few thousand, to 44,700 annually in 1979 (44). SA now consistently comprises 10-15% of child maltreatment (CM) reports in the US and Canada (45). Similar patterns have been noted in other countries, with initial reports of SA being low or "non-existent" in number, and more recently increasing case identification and reporting associated with social acceptance and improved professional response. Despite improved identification and reporting, a large proportion of SA cases are thought to remain hidden from public view or investigation (8).

A variety of sources report aspects of the incidence and prevalence of child sexual victimization. Unfortunately, varying definitions of the type of sexual contact (direct or indirect, penetrative or non-penetrative, harm or endangerment) and what constitutes a 'child' can make assessment problematic. Of particular application to a population of children with disability, Herman-Giddens (46) has defined three types of aberrant genital practices which could be considered abusive: 1) ritualistic inspection, handling and cleaning of the genitals, 2) deriving sexual gratification from the application of genital crams and ointments, and 3) excessive seeking of medical care for reported conditions of the anus and genitals (46).

David Finkelhor(8) has noted that "because sexual abuse is usually a hidden offense, there are no statistics on how many cases actually occur each year. Official statistics include only the cases that are disclosed to child protection agencies or to law enforcement." There are several ways, however, that SA can be identified. Cases are most often reported by witnesses or disclosed by the child. These reports are transmitted to law enforcement and child welfare agencies (child protective services [CPS] in the US) as "suspected cases" until an investigation identifies credible evidence to make a determination that the child is a victim and/or that a crime has occurred. To identify more cases, screening has been proposed to find victims in the general pediatric population (47). Screening procedures have been devised which use information from the parents, characteristics of the child, interview or physical examination findings and other case factors. However, while some case characteristics have been found to be more predictive of SA determination, there is no single "test" that identifies a child as a SA victim (48,49). That determination usually requires a finding by an investigatory agency, and the variability of these findings leads to variations in case finding in official statistics.

There are three principle sources of data on the incidence of SA in the US. Sexual abuse is reportable in the US to CPS and cases are collected in the National Child Abuse and Neglect Data System. In NCANDS, the number of CM victims rose, fell, and then stabilized at approximately 900,000 annually since the year 2000, with rises in neglect and declines in physical abuse. The number of SA victims, while rising during the late 1980s, actually declined during much of the 1990s, declining from a peak of 144,760 cases in 1991 to 58,000 in 2014 (1).Traditional criminal justice agencies also collect information about a variety of crimes in the US, including violent crimes such as homicide and rape, as well as property crimes. In the Federal Bureau of Investigation's Uniform Crime Reports in 12 US states during 1991-1996, for example, two-thirds of the 60,991 sexual assault victims were less than 18 years of age (50). Juvenile victims accounted for 75% or more of incidents of fondling, sodomy and forcible assault with an object, but only 46% of rapes. Most offenders were male (96%) and over 18 years of age (76.8%), but only 34% were family members, suggesting that only a relatively small proportion of the cases in this dataset are true child sexual abuse.

Surveys such as the National Crime Victimization Survey (51) have estimated there were 197,000 incidents of forcible rape and 110,000 other incidents of sexual assault of victims ages 12 years and older in the US in 1996, only one-third were estimated to have been reported to law enforcement agencies. The Canadian Incidence Study (CIS) reported that 11% of confirmed CM reports were for sexual abuse, affecting 0.93 children per 1,000 in 1998 (45). In the US, the National Incidence Studies of child abuse and neglect (NIS) have provided separate, periodic estimates of a growing number of sentinel professionals in a representative group of US counties to determine the actual number of CM victims (9). Sexual abuse fell from an estimated 217,700 to 135,300 cases (1.8 per 1,000) under the 'harm standard' and from 338,900 to 180,500 cases (2.4 per 1,000) under the 'endangerment standard' in 2005-2006. While both datasets showed decreases, any absolute differences in these estimates from those reported by NCANDS are thought to be explained by: (a) the fact that NCANDS reports victims which have been investigated and determined to include SA and do not include unsubstantiated or unfounded cases; (b) NIS includes cases identified by community professionals at schools and hospitals but which have not been reported to CPS; (c) NIS includes cases under the 'endangerment standard' which do not meet CPS criteria for SA case finding: and, (d) some cases are never revealed during the child's lifetime.

Despite the variability, it does appear that overall SA numbers and rates in the US are declining (see Figures 1 and 2). A variety of explanations have been offered (52). Increased evidentiary requirements, increased caseworker caution due to new legal rights for caregivers, and increasing limitations on the types of cases that are accepted to be investigated are given as potential causes, as well as the potential effects of prevention programs, increased prosecution, and public awareness campaigns. Some of these potential causes have also been associated with SA declines outside of the US.

There are additional studies which report the prevalence of SA. Early small studies reported prevalence rates as low as 3% for males and 12% for females, but with increasing social recognition and acceptance and improved survey techniques, rates of 25% or higher have been consistently identified. Prevalence studies have historically varied greatly in their definition of SA and in their methods, but they also likely include cases that have not been reported in prospective incidence studies, creating an apparent disparity in the numbers of cases (7,53). The National Family Violence Survey in 1985 reported that 27% of adult women and 16% of adult men reported sexual contact or sexual abuse during childhood, but their relationship to the offender (a key element of SA) was not specified (16). Others later reported rates from as low as 4.5% to as high as 37%, varying by location and methodology (45). A meta-analysis (54) of 59 studies from 1974-1995 noted that there were wide variations in definitions but that, in aggregate, college students reported prevalence rates of 16% for SA with 'close' family members and 35% for total SA with 'close' and 'wider' family. These rates were 33% higher than the national studies used for comparison, but wide ranges of results were obtained depending on the sexual acts included in their definition.

In other studies completed over a wide span of years (1988-2002), there are wide variations in the self-reported rates of SA based on locality, sampling technique (convenience vs. population), victim gender, age, type of sexual contact (SA vs. rape vs. unwanted sexual contact), condition of interest (medical vs. psychological), or criminal justice status (incarceration) (55). Rates range from 1% in a population-based study in North and South Carolina to over 66% among pregnant adolescents in Washington State. Women with pregnancy and men with sexually transmitted infections (consequences of sexual activity) had higher lifetime prevalence of SA. University students, incarcerated men, and those with injection drug use also had greater rates. This does not mean that these populations are more likely to be abused; rather, it implies that a history of SA, when obtained by retrospective self-report, is more likely to be found in groups with certain medical, psychological, and social problems.

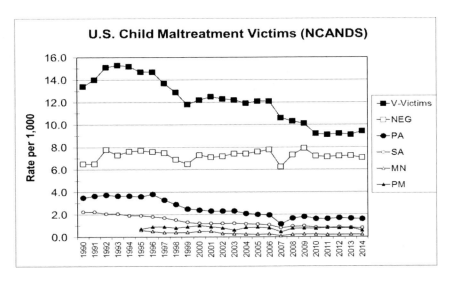

Figure 2. Child maltreatment victim rates by type, 1990-2014. PA= physical abuse; SA=sexual abuse; NEG=neglect; PM=psychologic maltreatment; MN=medical neglect

International studies offer a window into other cultures and their social acceptance and reporting of SA (55). Early reports from professionals in countries associated with the United Kingdom noted lower rates (3 per 1,000), while later reports have rates similar to those in the US. The Canadian Incidence Study mentioned previously also showed similar rates. Reports from Asia, while limited, show smaller (but increasing) numbers. Other than CIS, these studies have not included national samples and should not be interpreted as representing true population prevalence estimates, especially when done with special populations.

CM recurrence has been studied to measure program effectiveness and to identify risk factors in cases which can be addressed to prevent further harm. A wide range of recurrence rates are reported (1-66%) based on the type of maltreatment and whether re-reports or substantiated reports are used. For physical abuse, factors that increase the likelihood that children will be re-abused include younger aged children, children with more severe maltreatment, disabled children, white race, multiple CM types, multiple prior CM victimization, families with emotional problems, family abuse alcohol, and families with other violence histories (33). Data regarding SA recurrence are limited. In a longitudinal survey of 1,467 sexually victimized children in 2002-2003, 39% were revictimized by the second year, with the odds of recurrence at 6.9, higher than property crime, assault or other maltreatment (56). My own analysis of NCANDS data for 2000-2004 has identified a CM re-substantiation rate of 10% within 2 years of the first confirmed SA report, with over one-third of the new confirmed reports being SA. Factors associated with an increased risk of SA recurrence were family housing problems or other family violence; the only services associated with decreased recurrence were counseling, mental health, and juvenile court petition.

Females and certain race, origin and age groups appear consistently to have elevated risk for SA, but these are not case characteristics that are easily modified (e.g., we would not want to reduce the number of girls to reduce SA). Some factors, such as poverty and single parent households, are very difficult to address, and in many poor families with a single parent head of the household, no SA occurs. We are then left with several factors such as alcohol use, domestic violence, less than high school education, and mental illness which, if they could be reduced or prevented, could reduce the incidence (and therefore the lifetime prevalence) of SA. And while up to half of sexually or physically abused adolescents have been found to be 'resilient' or resistant to the effects of these adverse experiences, further reductions could occur by increasing protective factors such as attachment security and social supports. Unfortunately, most epidemiologic studies fail to provide the proportion of SA in the population that could be prevented by reducing a particular risk factor (the population attributable risk fraction, or PAR_f) or the specific type of intervention that could be used. And while issues regarding communication have been addressed, the evidence base and techniques needed for medical evaluations of SA among children with disabilities are still being developed and/or disseminated.

There are several factors specific to children and young people with disabilities which place them at higher risk for sexual abuse (57). Young people with disabilities can be overprotected as they grow up and are not taught to take risks in the same way as their non-disabled peers. Thus, when the time arrives for adulthood and independence, they can be more easily exploited. This lack of preparation may come from the parents' overprotection but it may also come from failures of helping professionals in schools and the community. Children with IDs and DDs may be disempowered and not involved in important decision-making about their lives. This may also contribute to their failure to disclose abuse once it has occurred because they believe they will not be heard. Actual or perceived social isolation may lead disabled young people to actually take more risk in their behavior so that they are accepted by their age-peers. In today's world, this includes electronic social networking and dangerous internet practices which are also often not discussed with them by adults. Their lack of sex and relationships education in the most basic way may lead disabled youth to not know that it is illegal for adults to have sex with children. If such basic material is given, more complicated information about relationships, consent and sexual orientation is not. Lastly, many child-helping professionals are not properly trained in recognizing and responding to sexual abuse among disabled children.

PSYCHOLOGIC MALTREATMENT

Psychologic maltreatment (PM) and has been described as a pattern of damaging parent-child interactions that becomes typical of the relationship. PM occurs when a person conveys to a child that he or she is worthless, flawed, unloved, unwanted, endangered, or only of value in meeting another's needs by spurning, terrorizing, isolating, corrupting, or ignoring the child's socialization. Emotional neglect has been further characterized as inadequate nurturance/affection, exposure to chronic intimate partner violence, permitting child substance abuse or delinquency, and inappropriate developmental expectations of a child by the parent. It can be chronic and pervasive or can occur only when triggered by certain potentiating factors (58) and encompasses emotional abuse, emotional neglect, verbal abuse, and mental abuse. PM is associated with a variety of negative and lasting effects which vary according to age, gender, and other factors, and it has strong links to depression, problems with relationships and attachment, and more rapid onset of major and minor mental illness which are dose dependent. The effects of PM in childhood and adolescence also represent important risk factors for other victimization since children with high levels of internalizing and externalizing symptoms which can result from PM are particularly likely to experience increased peer victimization, maltreatment, and sexual victimization (59). A recent systematic review by Maguire et al. noted increased externalizing and internalizing behaviours after neglect and PM in addition to Attention Deficit Hyeractivity Disorder (ADHD), depression, and poor academic performance (60).

In NCANDS, the numbers of children identified with PM have remained essentially unchanged since 1995, staying under 100,000 and hovering near 50,000 in more recent years (see Figure 1). Although 42,000 US children were found to be victims of PM after investigation by child protective services (CPS) agencies in 2014 (1), PM has received far less attention in the literature than other forms of maltreatment, leaving several knowledge gaps about its epidemiology. While the true rate of PM occurrence is unknown, the National Incidence Study (9) identified substantially more children, with 193,400 children having emotional neglect alone under its harm standard (2.6 per 1,000), with an additional 148,500 (2.0 per 1,000) under the endangerment standard in 2005-2006. For emotional abuse, there were 302,600 children (4.1 per 1,000) under the harm standard and 360,500 (4.9 per 1,000) under the endangerment standard, which were substantial increases over NIS-3 and many more than were identified in NCANDS.

In addition to its incidence, the pervasive nature of PM and its association with other forms of CM suggest that PM has increased prevalence and recurrence, especially among children with disabilities. When Trickett et al. (61) reviewed the complete files for 303 cases known to CPS, they found 48% met criteria for PM, while only 9% had been previously identified. As such, even when PM is confirmed, few families receive any services, and most services that are provided are not associated with reductions in PM recurrence. In one study, for example, Palusci and Ondersma (62) studied a sample of 11,646 children with a first CPS-confirmed report with PM, and 9.2% of them had a second confirmed PM report within 5 years. Fewer than one-fourth of families were referred for services after PM, with service referrals being more likely for families with poverty, drug or alcohol problems or other violence. Controlling for these factors, counseling referral was associated with a 54% reduction in PM recurrence, but other services were not associated with statistically significant reductions.

When definitions and practices were examined in Canada, PM was found to be included as a form of reportable maltreatment in all provincial and territorial statutes, and more than 11,000 cases were substantiated in Canada in 2008 at a rate of 1.86 cases per 1,000 children (45). While investigations were substantiated at a lower rate than were other forms of maltreatment, a higher proportion of PM cases were referred for specialized services, kept open for on-going child welfare services, lead to an out of home placement, and lead to an application to child welfare court. Using a broad definition, the number of investigations classified as emotional maltreatment in Canada, excluding Québec, nearly tripled from 1998 to 2003. In 2008, using more specific definitions focusing on caregiver definitions, the number of investigations nearly returned to their 1998 level, with nearly twice as many cases being classified as having risk for future maltreatment.

NEGLECT AND MEDICAL CARE NEGLECT

Overall, neglect is the most frequently identified form of CM, with over 500,000 children neglected in NCANDS (approximately 7 per 1,000 children), and more than two thirds of all CM fatalities have been linked to neglect (1). Neglect comprises over 60% of reports, with 1-2% of reports being separately confirmed for medical care neglect, with proportions and rates that have remained steady since 1995. NCANDS includes physical, supervisional, and educational neglect in its neglect counts but reports medical care neglect separately. Risk factors for neglect include poor parental physical and emotional health, disability, socialization, education, substance abuse, and poverty. When thinking about mechanisms, disorganized, emotionally-neglecting, and depressed types have been described. Dubowitz (63) has suggested that defining neglect is difficult, and that the degree of actual or potential harm, degree of risk of that harm occurring, contributions of parental behavior, and the acceptance of certain practices within societies and by cultures further confounds how to best identify the actual numbers of neglected children. He suggests we keep in mind several key concepts: severity, frequency, chronicity, intentionality, cultural context and poverty (63). Malnutrition due to neglect, a form of failure to thrive (FTT) in infants and children, results from inadequate nutrition to maintain physical growth and development. In its extreme form, FTT secondary to neglect may be fatal (64).

The Fourth National Incidence Study (NIS-4) (9) breaks down neglect into physical, emotional (noted above) and educational neglect. Physical neglect includes abandonment; refusal of custody; illegal transfer of custody; unstable custody arrangements; medical neglect; inadequate supervision; inadequate attention to needs for food, clothing, shelter, or personal hygiene; and other disregard for the child's physical needs or physical safety. In 2005-2006, there were 295,300 children (4 per 1,000) under the 'harm standard' and 1,192,200 children (16.2 per 1,000) under the 'endangerment standard.' For educational neglect, there were 360,500 children (4.9 per 1,000) under both standards (9).

Medical care neglect (or medical neglect, MN) can lead to serious physical harm and death, particularly when medical care is not sought for curable and/or treatable conditions such as infections, asthma and diabetes. One-third or more of CM fatalities had medical neglect contributing to or directly causing the death being investigated by CPS (65). Risk factors for MN include children with special medical needs and disabilities requiring additional medical treatments and follow-ups, including those with the complications of prematurity, low birthweight, and gestational drug exposure. MN has generally been defined to include refusal of health care, delay in health care, or failure to comply with recommended care (63). For our purposes, we will include mental health care with physical health care, although others define these separately under psychologic maltreatment. It is difficult to separate the role of the parents from the available resources in a community/society, and it is even more difficult to count cases of medical neglect for a variety of other reasons, including differences in state definitions and reporting statutes, and varying identification and thresholds for reporting among health care providers.

State reporting laws vary significantly in the US for medical neglect. Some use a standard of withholding medically indicated treatment, which is a specific form of medical neglect that is defined by CAPTA (3) as "the failure to respond to the infant's life-threatening conditions by providing treatment (including appropriate nutrition, hydration, and medication) which, in the treating physician's or physicians' reasonable medical judgment, will be most likely to be effective in ameliorating or correcting all such conditions..." In addition, CAPTA has exceptions for infants who are "chronically and irreversibly comatose"; situations when providing treatment would not save the infant's life but merely prolong dying; or when "the provision of such treatment would be virtually futile in terms of the survival of the infant and the treatment itself under such circumstances would be inhumane."

Medical neglect is usually identified in only a small proportion of child maltreatment victims identified by child welfare agencies. NIS-4 (9) reported 771,700 cases of neglect (10.5 per 1,000) in the US, of which physical neglect (which included refusal to allow or provide needed care for diagnosed condition or impairment, and unwarranted delay or failure to seek needed care) had 295,300 cases (4.0 per 1,000). These numbers were not thought to be significantly different from NIS-3 (1993) or NIS-2 (1986). In 2012 in NCANDS (1), medical neglect was found among 2.3% of child victims overall, a number less than 1/30th that of other neglect (15,705 compared to 531,241 neglect victims). MN cases confirmed by CPS have decreased by 50% since 1995 in NCANDS, but neglect has remained relatively unchanged overall (see Figures 1 and 2). In NCANDS, states with broader definitions of medical neglect (such as failing to provide needed medical/mental health care) had lower rates than those where MN was not specifically defined in statute. States with more restrictive definitions (such as withholding medical treatment or nutrition from disabled infants with life-threatening conditions) had even lower rates (66).

CHILDREN WITH DISABILITIES

Initial reports of child maltreatment in the special needs pediatric population were anecdotal rather than addressing the true population-based incidence. In the 1986 National Incidence Study for child abuse in the US, 35.5 per 1,000 children with disabilities were maltreated, compared to 21.3 per 1,000 children without disabilities, suggesting an epidemiologic connection (9). Physical abuse alone has been reported to be three times more likely among children with disabilities than among the general pediatric population (9% versus 31%). Spencer et al. (67) found similar increases in the UK. However, a systematic review concluded that the evidence base for an association of disability with increased abuse and neglect is weak (68), and another review found that physical disability did not increase the risk for any type of victimization once confounding factors and co-occurring disabilities were controlled (69).

A US crime victimization survey (70) identified that the age-adjusted rate of nonfatal violent crime against persons with disabilities was 1.5 times higher than the rate for persons without disabilities, and persons with a disability had an age-adjusted rate of rape or sexual assault that was more than twice the rate for persons without a disability. Females with a disability had a higher victimization rate than males with a disability; males had a higher rate than females among those without a disability. Persons with a cognitive functioning disability had a higher risk of violent victimization than persons with any other type of disability, and persons with more than one type of disability accounted for about 56% of all violent crime victimizations against those with any disability. This resulted in nearly 1 in 5 violent crime victims with a disability believing that they became a victim because of their disability. Looking at a variety of disabilities in a meta-analysis, Jones et al. (19) found that 26.7% of disabled children reported being the victim of any violence (OR 3.68), with 20.4% having had physical violence (OR 3.56) and 13.7% having experienced sexual violence (OR 2.88). Internationally, children with chronic conditions in Sweden had an increased risk for physical abuse only (OR 1.67) as well as in combination with exposure to intimate partner violence (IPV) (OR 2.54), but not to IPV only, compared to children without chronic conditions (71). Furthermore, when chronic conditions were combined with country of birth other than Sweden and living in low income areas, the risk for physical abuse increased even more, indicating interactive effects.

The reasons for higher rates of child maltreatment in populations with disabilities are unclear. Characteristics of children with disabilities (CWD) that alter their vulnerability include the nature of the disability itself. Those with impaired mobility have a diminished ability to escape abuse and those with impaired speech have inability to communicate about abuse. They may be targeted by predators because they are unable to disclose the abuse, delay disclosure of abuse, are unlikely to testify and/or unlikely to be viewed as credible witnesses. With respect to being sexually abused, CWD often have high dependency, which leads to excessive compliance and have diminished understanding of the motives of perpetrators (72).

Premature infants may be at increased risk due to the lack of bonding created by their prolonged neonatal stay in hospital and the prolonged stress associated with this and with separation from their parents. Infants who may be seen for assessment and referral for early intervention services have histories which include being low birth weight or small for gestational age, being one of multiple births, having other structural anomalies such as spina bifida, chronic problems such as chronic lung or heart disease, chromosomal anomalies, including Trisomy 21, and visual and hearing impairments (73). Children with hearing and visual problems have increased risk for sexual abuse because of their inability to adequately report victimization. Children receiving bowel and bladder routines due to neurologic incontinence may be accustomed to having these performed by a variety of health care professionals and their index of suspicion may be lowered. They may also have reduced access to developmentally-appropriate sex education services. There are also issues regarding normal sexuality that pose additional risks for adolescents with disabilities (57). Subtle maltreatment can also occur in hospitalized children who are physically-challenged as such children with cognitive limitations may not have procedures explained to them in a developmentally appropriate manner by staff and/or may not have their privacy as well respected as do more vocal children who are able to complain.

Spencer et al. (67) noted cerebral palsy, speech and language disorder, learning difficulties, conduct disorders, and non-conduct psychological disorders were all significantly associated with child protection registration in England before adjustment, and all but cerebral palsy retained significance after adjustment for birth weight, gestational age, and socioeconomic status among 119,729 children. Autism and sensory disabilities (vision and hearing) were not associated with an increased risk of child-protection registration. Conduct disorders and moderate/severe learning difficulty were associated with registration after adjustment for socioeconomic status, birth weight, and gestational age. Children with speech and language disorders and mild learning difficulties had increased risk for physical abuse, emotional abuse, and neglect. Non-conduct psychological disorders were associated with all categories except neglect, and cerebral palsy was associated with all categories except physical abuse and neglect.

Sullivan and Knutson's (74) study of 50,278 young- and school-age children in Omaha, Nebraska identified 4,503 maltreated children, 1,012 of whom also had an identified disability. The overall rate of maltreatment for children without disabilities was 11%. For children with disabilities, the overall rate was 31%. They found that children with disabilities were 3.4 times more likely to be neglected, or physically, emotionally, or sexually abused compared with children who do not have disabilities. Risk was not equal for all types of disabilities, with deaf and hard of hearing children having twice the risk for neglect and emotional abuse, and almost four times the risk for physical abuse than did non-disabled counterparts. Children with speech and language difficulties had five times the risk for neglect and physical abuse, and three times the risk for sexual abuse.

Children who were mentally retarded had four times the risk for all four types of maltreatment. Children with learning or orthopedic disabilities had twice the risk for all types of maltreatment. The children with highest risk were those with behavioral disorders, with a risk seven times higher for neglect, physical abuse and emotional abuse, and 5.5 times higher for sexual abuse than for children without disabilities.

In a more recent, population-based analysis of young children born with 3 birth defects: (Down syndrome, cleft lip with/without cleft palate, and spina bifida) in Texas from 2002 to 2011, the risk of maltreatment (any type) in children with cleft lip with/without cleft palate and spina bifida was increased by 40% and 58%, respectively, compared with children with no birth defects (75). The risk of any maltreatment was similar between children with Down syndrome and unaffected children. Across birth defect groups, the risk of medical neglect was 3 to 6 times higher than in the unaffected group. Child-, family-, and neighborhood-level factors predicted maltreatment in children with and without birth defects. The authors concluded that enhancement of existing maltreatment prevention and early intervention programs may be effective mechanisms to provide at-risk families additional support.

In the US child welfare system, children who were reported to child protective services with any of the following risk factors were considered as having a disability in the US National Child Abuse and Neglect Data System (1): mental retardation, emotional disturbance, visual or hearing impairment, learning disability, physical disability, behavioral problems or other medical problems. During 2005-2011, a progressively increasing proportion of children being reported had an identified disability (see Figure 3). Behavior problems and other medical problems had the greatest frequency, followed by emotional disability, and mental retardation, sensory disability, and physical disability. Approximately 3% of the children with confirmed CM in NCANDS had one or more of these disabilities, although this is thought to be an undercount.

Table 1. Disability types associated with types of child maltreatment, child and family factors and services provided, among children with first confirmed maltreatment in NCANDS, 2011

Disability Type (% of total)	% of	Mental Retardation (0.23%)		Sensory Disability (0.51%)		Physical Disability (0.41%)		Any Disability* (2.8%)	
(Total = 398,841)	Victims	OR[a]	95%CI	OR	95%CI	OR	95%CI	OR	95%CI
Physical Abuse	18.9%	NS[a]		0.79	0.70-0.90	1.48	1.32-1.66	1.46	1.40-1.53
Sexual Abuse	1.9%	2.86	2.13-3.84	2.16	1.72-2.71	3.88	3.19-4.72	3.97	3.67-4.30
Neglect	71.2%	NS		3.25	2.86-3.70	1.33	1.19-1.49	0.70	0.68-0.73
Medical Neglect	64.9%	NS		2.96	2.63-3.33	1.13[b]	1.01-1.25	0.67	0.65-0.70
Psychologic Maltreatment	5.2%	2.86	2.13-3.84	2.16	1.72-2.71	3.88	3.19-4.72	0.81	0.73-0.88
Child: Male Gender	48.4%	1.57	1.36-1.81	NS		1.38	1.25-1.54	1.23	1.19-1.28
Live with Married Parents	9.8%	NS		NS		1.44	1.25-1.66	1.33	1.25-1.41
Native American	2.2%	2.78	1.93-4.01	3.03	2.39-3.85	NS		1.32	1.18-1.48
Asian	1.0%	NS		NS		NS		0.81[b]	0.65-0.99
Black	26.0%	1.19[b]	1.02-1.39	0.78	0.69-0.87	1.34	1.99-1.50	1.04	1.00-1.08
Native Hawaiian	0.3%	NS		2.69	1.58-4.58	NS		0.89	0.62-1.26
White	63.0%	1.23[c]	1.06-1.43	1.76	1.57-1.97	NS		1.40	1.35-1.46
Hispanic	18.5%	0.51	0.42-0.63	NS		0.27	0.22-0.33	0.53	0.55-0.59
Family: Military	0.5%	NS		NS		0.12[b]	0.02-0.83	0.42	0.25-0.69
Housing Problems	19.9%	0.69	0.56-0.87	0.53	0.36-0.51	NS		0.88	0.83-0.93
Money Problems	24.6%	NS		0.55	0.47-0.63	1.89	1.68-2.13	1.62	1.54-1.70
Public Assistance	21.2%	2.37	1.96-2.87	2.41	1.96-2.96	4.54	4.05-5.09	1.18	1.12-1.23
Child: Alcohol Exposure	0.3%	5.58	3.13-9.92	17.4	13.9-21.9	7.35	5.10-10.6	3.63	3.05-4.32
Drug Exposure	1.5%	2.48	1.78-3.45	4.43	3.73-5.27	3.11	2.48-3.89	2.51	2.29-2.75
Family: Alcohol Problems	5.4%	1.49[c]	1.14-1.95	NS		0.41	0.30-0.58	1.13[c]	1.04-1.21
Drug Problems	12.1%	NS		NS		0.32	0.25-0.40	0.92[c]	0.86-0.97
Retardation	0.4%	26	19.8-34.1	2.63[c]	1.24-5.59	4.53	3.11-6.59	2.20	1.83-2.65

Disability Type (% of total)	% of	Mental Retardation (0.23%)		Sensory Disability (0.51%)		Physical Disability (0.41%)		Any Disability* (2.8%)	
Emotional Problems	6.7%	3.05	2.43-3.83	NS		1.7	1.41-2.05	1.83	1.72-1.95
Physical Disability	0.8%	4.24	2.94-6.12	2.48	1.52-4.04	NS		2.08	1.80-2.39
Violence	22.4%	0.68	0.58-0.82	0.33	0.28-0.39	0.22	0.17-0.27	0.64	0.61-0.67
Post-Investigation Services	52.1%	2.16	1.84-2.53	5.15	4.52-5.87	7.66	6.46-9.07	1.96	1.88-2.05

* Includes one or more of child mental retardation, vision/hearing, physical disability, behavior, emotional, learning, or other medical problems.

P <0.001 unless noted: [a]NS: p>0.05; [b]p<0.05; [c]p<0.01.

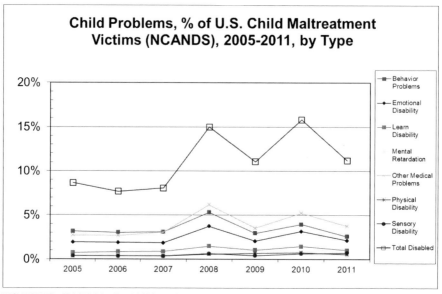

Source: US DHHS. (2007-2012). Child Maltreatment, 2005-2011.

Figure 3. Child problems recorded among child maltreatment victims in NCANDS, 2005-2011.

When demographic factors are assessed, it is apparent that not all types of disability are equally related to child, family and community factors. In 2011, for example (see Table 1), children with "any disability" in NCANDS were significantly more likely to be identified with physical or sexual abuse, but they had less neglect, medical neglect, and psychologic maltreatment. Sexual abuse was statistically significantly higher among children with confirmed maltreatment when mental retardation, sensory disability or physical disability was present. "Money problems" and receiving "public assistance" were significantly increased over all types, but there were marked differences among the different forms of disability noted in NCANDS across the child, family and community factors measured. Some demographic factors were seen more frequently in some forms of disability, as were child and family problems with drugs, alcohol and other disabilities. Interestingly, children with disabilities were actually less likely to have other family violence present and were almost twice more likely to have services provided after child protective services investigation than were non-disabled children. Using NCANDS data, Kistin et al. (76) noted that among 12,610 children with disabilities from a total of 489,176 children confirmed for neglect from 33 states, Puerto Rico, and the District of Columbia, children with vs. without disabilities were more likely to be re-referred to CPS (45% vs. 36%), experience substantiated maltreatment (16% vs. 10%), and be placed in foster care (7% vs. 3%). Experiences in foster care were also different for children with disabilities (77).

Disabled children can become disabled parents. There are 4.1 million parents with disabilities in the United States, reflecting 6.2 percent of all American parents with children under the age of 18 years (2). The rates are even higher for some subgroups of this population, with 13.9% of American Indian/Alaska Native parents and 8.8% of African American parents having a disability. Further, 6% of White, 5.5% of Latino/Hispanic, and 3.3% of Asian/Pacific Islander parents have a disability. Of the parents with disabilities, 2.8 percent have a mobility disability, 2.3 percent have a cognitive disability, 2.3 percent have a daily activity limitation, 1.4 percent have a hearing disability, and 1.2 percent have a vision disability. Many have more than one. Children of parents with intellectual disability are assumed to have increased risk for poor outcomes, but this has not been conclusively studied. In one study (76), a search from March, 2010 to March, 2011 resulted in 26 studies for review, and two groups of studies were identified. The first investigated an association between parental intellectual disability and child outcomes where there was significant disadvantage. Some studies suggested low parental intellectual capacity can negatively impact child outcomes, but others indicated child development approaches population norms. A second, small group of studies explored narrative accounts and found that social exclusion, bullying, and stigma are commonplace during the childhood of disabled children. Removal from parental care emerged as a significant risk for this group of children. They concluded there was no consensus about likely developmental or behavioral outcomes.

Beyond the physical limitations placed on them by these disabilities, it is unclear if parents with disabilities have any difference in risk for maltreating their children. Another study examined the experiences and outcomes of children in the foster care system in the United States who were removed from their homes at least partially in relation to their parent's or caretaker's disability (77). Using data for 2012 from the Adoption and Foster Care Reporting System (AFCARS), the US federal reporting system that collects case-level data on all children in foster care, the authors found that 19.0% of children in foster care had parental disability indicated as a removal reason, and 5.18% had parental disability indicated as their sole removal reason. Removal because of parental disability correlated with removal manner, type of placement, location of placement, current case plans, discharge reasons and termination of parental rights. Children who have parental disability as a removal reason had different experiences in child welfare and different child welfare outcomes than did those without parental disability as a removal reason. They concluded that there needs to be closer attention to parental disability within the child welfare system to ensure appropriate services and supports as well as fair treatment.

CONCLUSION

Several steps have been taken to improve our identification of child maltreatment, including among disabled children. In addition, international initiatives are underway to expand knowledge about the epidemiology of child maltreatment beyond currently available statistics. With mandated early intervention referrals for children with developmental delays, disabled children with maltreatment are now more readily identified and services can be initiated earlier. Formalized respite care can provide a hiatus from familial stressors. It is clinically believed that such interventions reduce the risk of abuse and neglect because of additional emotional support, which, in addition to direct benefits in enhancing child development, may be a secondary rationale for their existence.

Yet, additional steps remain. While mandatory training for health care professionals in the identification of child abuse and neglect is required in many states, little or no training is available addressing the specific issues associated with children with disabilities. Clinicians and advocates need to be able to identify and report patterns of maltreatment while excluding mimics and other confounders. Children with disabilities are seen by many subspecialists, and it is important that there is one individual or group of professionals who follow them on a consistent basis, preferably in a defined "medical home" integrated with community services which can reduce the risk of abuse or neglect and permit proactive, preventative services to be put into place. School personnel and other professionals, especially those dealing with special education populations, need additional training beyond baseline mandatory courses.

Further analyses are needed to illuminate the interrelationships between disabilities and child maltreatment. Do households with disabled children have higher incidence rates even when household socioeconomic factors are taken into account? Are differences in CM identified based on disability status or do they reflect biases in reporting or investigation? Why do the majority of maltreated children identified not receive CPS services? Have the historic reductions in physical and sexual abuse been proportionately experienced by the community of children with disabilities? How do we more accurately identify and report CM among children with disabilities?

REFERENCES

[1]   US Department of Health and Human Services (US DHHS): Child Maltreatment 1990-2014: Reports from the states to the National Child Abuse and Neglect Data System. Washington, DC: US Government Printing Office, 1992-2016.

[2]   National Council on Disability. Rising expectations: The Developmental Disabilities Act. Washington, DC: NCD, 2011;27-33.

[3]   US Child Abuse Prevention and Treatment Act (CAPTA) 42 USC 5101 et seq; 42 USC 5116 et seq; Reauthorization Act of 2010, Pub. L. 111-320, 124 Stat. 3459, Dec. 20, 2010.

[4]   UN General Assembly, Convention on the Rights of the Child. United Nations Treaty Series 1989;1577:3.URL: http://www.refworld.org/docid/3ae6b38f0.html.

[5]   UN General Assembly, Convention on the Rights of Persons with Disabilities, 2006. URL:http://www.un.org/disabilities/convention/conventionfull.shtml

[6]   World Health Organization, International Society for Prevention of Child Abuse and Neglect. Preventing child maltreatment: A guide to taking action and generating evidence. Geneva, Switzerland: World   Health   Organization,   2006.   URL: http://whqlibdoc.who.int/-publications/2006/9241594365_eng.pdf

[7]   Gray J, ed. World perspectives on child abuse, 9th ed. Aurora, CO: International Society for Prevention of Child Abuse and Neglect, 2010.

[8]   Finkelhor D. The international epidemiology of child sexual abuse. Child Abuse Negl 1994;18:409–17.

[9]   Sedlak AJ, Mettenburg J, Basena M, Petta I, McPherson K, Greene A, Li, S. Fourth National Incidence Study of Child Abuse and Neglect (NIS–4): Report to Congress. Washington, DC: US Department of Health and Human Services, Administration for Children and Families, 2010.

[10]   Nieman M, Legano L, McHugh MT, Palusci VJ. Onsite medical consultation for New York City child protective services workers. APSAC Adv 2013;25(1/2):18-24.

[11]   Collings S, Llewellyn G. Children of parents with intellectual disability: Facing poor outcomes or faring okay? J Intellect Dev Disabil 2012; 37(1): 65–82.

[12]   United Nations (2006). United Nations Secretary-General's report on violence against children. New York: Author, 2006. URL: http://www.unviolencestudy.org/

[13]   Rosenberg DA, Gary N: Sexual abuse of children. In: Briere J, Berliner L, Bulkley JA, et al, eds. The APSAC handbook on child maltreatment. Thousand Oaks, CA: Sage, 1996.

[14]   Greenbaum VJ. Commercial sexual exploitation and sex trafficking of children in the United States.Curr Probl Pediatr Adolesc Health Care 2014;44(9):245-69.

[15]   Palusci VJ, Datner E, Wilkins C. Developmental disabilities: Abuse and neglect in children and adults. Int J Child Health Hum Dev 2015;8(4):407-28.

[16]   Jenny C, American Academy of Pediatrics Section on Child Abuse and Neglect. Recognizing and responding to medical neglect. Pediatrics 2007;120:1385–9.

[17]   UNICEF. A league table of child maltreatment deaths in rich nations. Innocenti report card No.5, Florence Italy: UNICEF Innocenti Research Center, 2003.

[18]   Finkelhor D, Hoteling G, Lewis IA, et al. Sexual abuse in a national survey of adult men and women: prevalence, characteristics and risk factors. Child Abuse Negl 1990;14(1):19-28.

[19]   Akmatov KS. Child abuse in 28 developing and transitional countries—Results from the multiple indicator cluster surveys. Int J Epidemiol 2010:1(1):67-80.

[20]   Ten Bensel RW, Reinberger MM, Radbill SX. Children in a world of violence: The roots of maltreatment. In: Helfer ME, Kempe RS, Krugman RD, eds. The battered child, 5th edition. Chicago, IL: University of Chicago Press, 1997:3-28.

[21]   Jones J, Bellis MA, Wood S, Hughes K, McCoy E, Eckley L, et al. Prevalence and risk of violence against children with disabilities: A systematic review and meta-analysis of observational studies. Lancet 2012:380(9845):899-907.

[22]   Palusci VJ. Current issues in physical abuse. In: Korbin JE, Krugman, eds. Handbook of child maltreatment. Dordrecht: Springer Science, 2014:63-80.

[23]   Palusci VJ, Covington TM. Child maltreatment deaths in the US National Child Death Review Case Reporting System. Child Abuse Negl 2014;38(1):25-36.

[24]   Widom CS, Czaja SJ, Bentley, T, Johnson MS. A prospective investigation of physical health outcomes in abused and neglected children: New findings from a 30-year follow-up. Am J Pub Health 2012;102(6):1135-44.

[25]   Finkelhor D, Jones L. Why have child maltreatment and child victimization declined? J Soc Issues 2006;62:685-716.

[26]   Sidebotham P, Heron J, ALSPAC Study Team of Bristol. Child maltreatment in the 'children of the nineties': A cohort study of risk factors. Child Abuse Negl 2006;30:497-522.

[27]   Theodore AD, Chang JJ, Runyan DK, et al. Epidemiologic features of the physical and sexual maltreatment of children in the Carolinas. Pediatrics 2005;115:e331-7.

[28]   Kaplan SJ, Labruna V, Pelcovitz D, Salzinger S, Mandel F, Weiner M. Physically abused adolescents: Behavior problems, functional impairment, and comparison of informants' reports. Pediatrics 1999;104:430-49.

[29]   Hussey JM, Chang, JJ, Kotch JB. Child maltreatment in the United States: Prevalence, risk factors and adolescent health consequences. Pediatrics 2006;118:933-42.

[30]   Lane WG, Dubowitz H, Langenberg P, Dischinger P. Epidemiology of abusive abdominal trauma hospitalizations in United States children. Child Abuse Negl 2012;36:142-8.

[31]   Runyan DK, Dunne MP, Zolotor AJ, Madrid B, Jain D, Gerbaka B, et al. The development and piloting of the ISPCAN Child Abuse Screening Tool-Parent version (ICAST-P). Child Abuse Negl 2009;33(11):826-32.

[32]   Zhou Y, Hallisey EJ, Freymann GR. Identifying perinatal risk factors for infant maltreatment: An ecological approach. Int J Health Geograph 2006;5:53-63.

[33]   Palusci VJ, Smith EG, Paneth N. Predicting and responding to physical abuse in young children using NCANDS. Child Youth Serv Rev 2005;27:667-82.

[34]   34. Siebert JR, Payne EH, Kemp AM, Barber M, Rolfe K, Morgan RJ, et al. The incidence of severe physical abuse in Wales. Child Abuse Negl 2002;26:267-76.

[35]   May-Chahal C, Cawson P. Measuring child maltreatment in the United Kingdom: A study of the prevalence of child abuse and neglect. Child Abuse Negl 2005;29:969-84.

[36]   US Commission to Eliminate Child Abuse and Neglect Fatalities. Within our reach: A national strategy to eliminate child abuse and neglect fatalities. Washington, DC: US Government Printing Office, 2016.

[37]   US Government Accountability Office. Child maltreatment: Strengthening national data on child fatalities could aid in prevention (GAO-11-599). Washington, DC: U.S. Government Printing Office, 2011. URL: http://www.gao.gov/assets/ 330/320774.pdf

[38]   Palusci VJ, Wirtz SJ, Covington TM. Using capture-recapture methods to better ascertain the incidence of fatal child maltreatment. Child Abuse Negl 2010;34(6):396-402.

[39]   Jenny C, Isaac R. The relation between child death and child maltreatment. Arch Dis Child 2006;91(3):265-9.

[40]   Schnitzer PG, Ewigman BG. Child deaths resulting from inflicted injuries: Household risk factors and perpetrator characteristics. Pediatrics 2005;116(5),e687-e93.

[41]   Herman-Giddens ME, Smith JB, Manjoo Mittal M, Carlson M, Butts JD. Newborns killed or left to die by a parent: A population-based study. JAMA 2003;289(11):1425-9.

[42]   Browne KD, Lynch MA. The nature and extent of child homicide and fatal abuse. Child Abuse Rev 1995;4:309-16.

[43]   Putnam-Hornstein E. Report of maltreatment as a risk factor for injury death: A prospective birth cohort study. Child Maltreat 2011;16:163-74.

[44]   Finkelhor D. Victims. In: Finkelhor D, ed. Child sexual abuse: New theory and research. New York: Free Press, 1984.

[45]   Trocmé NM, Fallon B, MacLaurin B, Daciuk J, Felstiner C, Black Y, et al. Canadian Incidence Study of Reported Child Abuse and Neglect-2003: Major findings. Ottawa, Canada: Minister of Public Works and Government Services, 2005.

[46]   Herman-Giddens M, Berson N. Harmful genital care practices. JAMA 1989;261:577-80.

[47]   Palusci VJ, Palusci JV. Screening tools for child sexual abuse. J Pediatr (Rio J) 2006;82:409-10.

[48]   Palusci VJ, Cox EO, Cyrus TA, Heartwell SW, Vandervort FE, Pott ES. Medical assessment and legal outcome in child sexual abuse. Arch PediatrAdolesc Med 1999;153:388-92.

[49]   Palusci VJ, Cox EO, Shatz EM, Schultze JM. Urgent medical assessment after child sexual abuse. Child Abuse Negl 2006;30:367-80.

[50]   Snyder HN. Sexual assault of young children as reported to law enforcement: Victim, incident and offender characteristics. Washington, DC: US Department of Justice, Bureau of Justice Statistics, 2000.

[51]   Finkelhor D, Ormrod R, Turner H, Hamby SL. The victimization of children and youth: a comprehensive, national survey. Child Maltreat 2005;10:5-25.

[52]   Finkelhor D, Jones LM. Explanations for the decline in child sexual abuse cases. OJJDP Juvenile Justice Bull 2004;Jan:1-12. (NCJ 199298).

[53]   Finkelhor D, Jones L, Shattuck A. Updated trends in child maltreatment, 2011. Durham, NH: University of New Hampshire crimes Against Children Research Center, 2013. URL: http://www.unh.edu/ccrc/pdf/CV203_Updated%20Trends%20in%20Child%20Maltreatment%202008 _8-6-10.pdf

[54]   Rind B, Tromovitch P, Bauserman R. A meta-analytic evaluation of assumed properties of child sexual abuse using college samples. Psychol Bull 1998;124:22-53.

[55]   Palusci VJ.Epidemiology of sexual abuseIn: Jenny C, ed. Child abuse and neglect. Diagnosis, treatment and evidence. Philadelphia, PA: Elsevier Saunders, 2010:16-22.

[56]   Finkelhor D, Ormrod RK, Turner HA. Re-victimization patterns in a national longitudinal sample of children and youth. Child Abuse Negl 2007;31:479-502.

[57]   Jones C, Stalker K, Franklin A, Fry D, Cameron A, Taylor J. Enablers of help-seeking for deaf and disabled children following abuse and barriers to protection: a qualitative study. Child FamSoc Work. 2016 Apr 9. doi:10.1111/cfs.12293.

[58]   Kairys SW, Johnson CF, Committee on Child Abuse and Neglect. The psychological maltreatment of children- Technical report. Pediatrics 2002;109:e68.

[59]   Turner HA, Finkelhor D, Ormrod R. Child mental health problems as risk factors for victimization. Child Maltreat 2010;15:132-43.

[60]   Maguire SA, Williams B, Naughton AM, Cowley LE, Tempest V, Mann MK, et al. A systematic review of the emotional, behavioural and cognitive features exhibited by school-aged children experiencing neglect or emotional abuse. Child Care Health Dev 2015;41(5);641-53.

[61]   Trickett PK, Mennen FE, Kim K, Sang J. Emotional abuse in a sample of multiply maltreated urban young adolescents: Issues in definition and identification. Child Abuse Negl 2009;33:27-35.

[62]   Palusci VJ, Ondersma SJ. Services and recurrence after psychological maltreatment confirmed by child protective services. Child Maltreat 2012;17(2):153-63.

[63]   Dubowitz H. Epidemiology of child neglect. In Jenny C, et al, eds. Medical evidence in child maltreatment. Philadelphia, PA: Elsevier Publishing, 2010.

[64]   Block RW, Krebs NF, Committee on Child Abuse and Neglect, Committee on Nutrition. Failure to thrive as a manifestation of child neglect. Pediatrics 2005;116:1234–37

[65]   Palusci VJ, Yager S, Covington TM. Effects of a citizen's review panel in preventing child maltreatment fatalities. Child Abuse Negl 2010;34(5), 324-31.

[66]   Palusci VJ. Some thoughts on counting medical neglect. Maltreat Sci. 2014. URL: http://www.maltreat.info/index.php/contribution-articles?download=9:some-thoughts-on-counting-medical-neglect-reports

[67]   Spencer N, Devereux E, Wallace A, Sundrum R, Shenoy M, Bacchus C, Logan S.Disabling conditions and registration for child abuse and neglect: A population-based study. Pediatrics 2005;116:609-13.

[68]   Govindshenoy M, Spencer N. Abuse of the disabled child: A systematic review of population-based studies. Child Care Health Dev 2007;33:552-8.

[69]   Turner HA, Vanderminden J, Finkelhor D, Hamby S, Shattuck A. Disability and victimization in a national sample of children and youth. Child Maltreat 2001;16:275-86.

[70]   Rand MR, Harnell E. Crimes against people with disabilities. Washington, DC: US Department Justice, Office of Justice Programs, Bureau of Justice Statistics (NCJ 227814), 2011.

[71]   Svensson B, Bornehag C-G, Janson S. Chronic conditions in children increase the risk for physical abuse–but vary with socio-economic circumstances. Acta Paediatrica 2011;100(3):407-12.

[72]   Nowak CB.Recognition and prevention of child abuse in the child with disability. Am J Med Gen 2015;169C:293–301.

[73]   Hibbard RA, Desch LW, Committee on Child Abuse and Neglect, Council on Children with Disabilities. Maltreatment of children with disabilities. Pediatrics 2007;119:1018-25.

[74]   Sullivan PM, Knutson JF. Maltreatment and disabilities: A population-based epidemiological study. Child Abuse Negl 2000;24:1257-74.

[75]   Van Horne BS, Moffitt KB, Canfield MA, Case AP, Greeley CS, Morgan R, Mitchell LE. Maltreatment of children under age 2 with specific birth defects: A population-based study. Pediatrics 2015;136(6):e1504-12.

[76]   Kistin CJ, Tompson MC, Cabral HJ, Sege RD, Winter MR, Silverstein M. Subsequent maltreatment in children with disabilities after an unsubstantiated report for neglect. JAMA 2016;315(1):86-7.

[77]   Lightfoot E,DeZelar S. The experiences and outcomes of children in foster care who were removed because of a parental disability. Child Youth Serv Rev 2016;62:22-28.

In: Child Abuse: Children with Disabilities
Editors: V. J Palusci, D. Nazer et al.

ISBN: 978-1-53612-035-6
© 2017 Nova Science Publishers, Inc.

Chapter 4

CONCEPTUAL FRAMEWORK AND DEFINITIONS OF DISABILITY: AN OVERVIEW

Dilip R Patel*, MD, MBA, MPH
and Kelly A Brown, MD
Department of Pediatric and Adolescent Medicine,
Western Michigan University Homer Stryker MD School of Medicine, Kalamazoo,
Michigan, US

Disability is variably defined because of its significant political, policy, societal and economic implications. Various models of disability have been described; the predominant ones being a medical model and a social model. Various agencies and institutions define disability differently serving their explicit narrow purpose. A more widely used construct of disability is that of World Health Organization, called the International Classification of Functioning, Disability, and Health. Physical disability and intellectual disability also differ in terms of their conceptualization and implications. The definition of intellectual disability has evolved significantly over the past decade. Intellectual disability is characterized by deficits in cognitive and adaptive abilities that initially manifest before 18 years of age.

* Correspondence: Professor Dilip R Patel, MD, MBA, MPH, Chair, Department of Pediatric and Adolescent Medicine, Western Michigan University Homer Stryker MD School of Medicine, 1000 Oakland Drive, D48G, Kalamazoo, MI 49008-1284, United States. E-mail dilip.patel@med.wmich.edu.

INTRODUCTION

The conceptual framework and definition of disability has evolved over the years from a predominantly medical model to a broader social model. Because the definition of disability has significant individual, societal, economic, and political and policy implications, it is difficult to construct an all-encompassing, unifying definition (1).

Table 1. Spectrum of developmental disabilities

Intellectual disability
Specific learning disability
Communication disorders
Autism spectrum disorder
Neurobehavioral disorders
Neurogenetic disorders
Neurometabolic disorders
Neuromuscular disorders
Cerebral palsy
Other neuromotor disorders
Sensory impairments
Disabilities associated with chronic diseases
Traumatic brain injury
Spinal cord injury

In the medical model of disability, the individual is considered disabled based on a disease or health condition that limits his or her ability to carry out expected individual and societal obligations (2-4). Many conditions are associated with disability (see Table 1). The person with a disability is in a sick role. The medical model attributes problems with disability to the individual and if his or her condition is cured, then the disability could be remediated (2). There is no consideration of environmental or societal factors in the medical model. On the other hand, the social model of disability takes in to consideration, the role of the environmental and societal factors in the construct of disability (2-6). Disability is based on the fact that by itself any functional impairment at an individual level may not create disability, but sociocultural expectations and built environment together limit person's ability to engage in a productive role. It is important to distinguish impairment, handicap and disability (5-7). An impairment is any psychological, structural, or functional abnormality at an individual level. Impairment by itself may or may not cause a person to be disabled. Rather, any limitation of ability to perform an activity as expected because of an impairment results in disability. When a person is at a relative disadvantage in terms of leading a productive life, and fulfilling his or her social role, because of impairment or disability, he or she is considered handicapped.

Table 2. World Health Organization International Classification of Functioning, Disability and Health

NORMAL FUNCTION	LACK OF NORMAL FUNCTION
Body function The physiological functions of the body	Impairment Problems with the body function as a significant deviation or loss
Body structures Anatomic parts of the body	Impairments Problems in structure as a significant deviation or loss
Activity The execution of a task or action by an individual	Activity limitation Difficulties an individual may have in executing activities
Participation Involvement in a life situation	Participation restrictions Problems an individual may have in involvement in life situation
Functioning A global term used to encompass body functions, body structures, activities, and participation	Disability A global term used to encompass problems with body functions, body structures, activity limitations, and participation restrictions

The definition of disability has direct implications for access to medical care and funding of various programs by the public and private health plans (4, 5). It is therefore useful to understand the conceptual definitions as used by various health and regulatory entities. The World Health Organization has developed the International Classification of Functioning, Disability, and Health, which comprises three key components, 1) body function and structure, 2) activity, and 3) participation (see Table 2) (5, 7). The general WHO classification provides a framework for delineating specific disabilities. It is important to note that the three key components of the WHO classification are interrelated and may interact with a given health condition and personal or individual and environmental factors.

In the United States, according to the Individuals with Disability Education Improvement Act (IDEA, 2004), the term child with disability means a child with intellectual disability, hearing impairments (including deafness), speech and language impairments, visual impairments (including blindness), serious emotional disturbance, orthopedic impairments, autism, traumatic brain injury, other health impairments, or specific learning disabilities (LDs) (8). A child with disability as defined by the IDEA needs special education and related services (see Table 3), as may be required to assist a child with disability to benefit from special education and includes the early identification and assessment of disabling conditions in children. Related services do not include a medical device that is surgically implanted, or the replacement of such a device.

The term infant or toddler with a disability, as defined by IDEA, means a child under the age 3 years who needs early intervention (EI) services because she or he is experiencing developmental delays, as measured by appropriate diagnostic instruments and procedures in one or more of the areas of cognitive development, physical development, communication development, social or emotional development, and adaptive development; or has a diagnosed physical or mental condition that has a high probability of resulting in developmental delay.

Table 3. Related services provided under the IDEA

Audiology services
Corrective services
Counseling services, including rehabilitation counseling
Developmental services
Interpreting services
Medical services (diagnostic and evaluation only)
Orientation and mobility services
Physical and occupational therapy
Psychologic services
Recreation, including therapeutic recreation
School nurse services
Social work services
Speech-language pathology
Transportation

Under the American with Disabilities Act (ADA), in the United States, the term "disability" means, with respect to an individual, a physical or mental impairment that substantially limits one or more major life activities of such individual; a record of such an impairment; or being regarded as having such an impairment (9). For the purpose of ADA, major life activities include, but are not limited to, caring for oneself, performing manual tasks, seeing, hearing, eating, sleeping, walking, standing, lifting, bending, speaking, breathing, learning, reading, concentrating, thinking, communicating, and working. A major life activity also includes the operation of a major bodily function, including but not limited to, functions of the immune system, normal cell growth, digestive, bowel, bladder, neurologic, brain, respiratory, circulatory, endocrine, and reproductive functions.

Based on the ADA, and individual is considered to meet the requirement of "being regarded as having such an impairment" if the individual established that he or she has been subjected to an action prohibited under ADA because of an actual or perceived physical or mental impairment whether the impairment limits or is perceived to limit a major life activity. The impairment must not be transitory and minor. A transitory impairment is an impairment with an actual or expected duration of 6 months or less.

According to the United States Social Security Administration (SSA), the definition of disability is based on an individual's inability to work (10). An individual is considered to have a disability if the individual cannot do the work that he or she did before; he or she cannot adjust to other work because of the medical condition (s); and the disability has lasted or is expected to last for at least 1 year or to result in death. Social security programs rules assume that working families have access to other resources to provide support during periods of short-term disabilities, including workers' compensation, insurance, savings, and investments.

INTELLECTUAL DISABILITY

According to the American Association on Intellectual and Developmental Disabilities (AAIDD), intellectual disability "is a disability characterized by significant limitations both in intellectual functioning and in adaptive behavior as expressed in conceptual, social, and practical adaptive skills" (11). The assessment of intellectual functioning and adaptive behavior must take into consideration the expectations based on individual's age and culture. The influence on cognitive assessment of sensory, motor, communication, or behavioral factors should also be appropriately considered in the administration of assessment instruments, and interpretation of their results.

In the United States, a widely used definition is the one from the Individuals with Disabilities Education Act that defines intellectual disability as "significantly sub-average general intellectual functioning, existing concurrently with deficits in adaptive behavior and manifested during the developmental period that adversely affects a child's educational performance" (8).

According to the Diagnostic and Statistical Manual of Mental Disorders (12), intellectual disability (intellectual developmental disorder) is defined as an intelligence quotient (IQ) of approximately 70 or below on an individually administered standardized test of intelligence concurrent with deficits in adaptive functioning in two of the following areas: communication, self-care, home living, social or interpersonal skills, use of community resources, self-direction, functional academic skills, work, leisure, health, and safety. All definitions stipulate that the onset of disability must occur before the age of 18 years or during the developmental period.

It is generally agreed that, although not perfect, appropriately measured IQ provides the best estimate of intellectual functioning. Based on the mean value for IQ of 100, the upper limit of 70 as the cut off represents the value that is two standard deviations below the mean. Because there is a five-point standard error of measurement, it is argued that a range of 70-75 should be considered as the upper limit of IQ as the cut off value for intellectual disability. Based on the typical bell shaped curve of distribution of IQ scores, raising the IQ score from 70 to 75 as the upper limit of cut off, will double the number of individuals with intellectual disability from 2.27% to 4.85% of the population. An individual with an IQ score of 75 with significant adaptive disability will be considered to have intellectual disability, whereas an individual with no adaptive disability and an IQ score of 65 may not be considered to have intellectual disability.

The severity of intellectual disability is further categorized based on intellectual functioning, adaptive functioning, and intensity of supports needed (see Table 4) (11, 12). When the severity of intellectual disability cannot be reliably assessed, but there is a high level of confidence based on clinical judgment, a diagnosis of intellectual disability is made without specifying the severity.

Table 4. Classification of intellectual disability severity

Severity level	Percent of individuals who have intellectual disability	Intelligence quotient range	Intensity of supports needed in daily living activities such as school, work, or home.
Mild	85	From 50-55 to 70	Intermittent: Support on as needed basis, episodic or short-term
Moderate	10	From 35-49 to 50-55	Limited: Consistent over time, but time limited
Severe	4	From 20-25 to 35-40	Extensive: Regular, consistent, lifetime support. Regular support in at least one aspect such as school, work or home
Profound	1	Less than 20-25	Pervasive: High intensity, across all environments, lifetime, and potentially life-sustaining

[Based on American Psychiatric Association. DSM-IV-TR, 2000; American Association of Intellectual and Developmental Disabilities. Mental Retardation, 2002].

The reported prevalence of intellectual disability reflects consideration of the definition used, method of ascertainment of the data, and the characteristics of the population studied (4, 13-15). Based on the typical bell shaped distribution of intelligence in the general population and 2 standard deviations below the mean as a cutoff point, approximately 2.5% of the population is expected to have intellectual disability. Most epidemiological studies consider those with an IQ score of 50 or less as having severe and those above that as having mild intellectual disability. Eighty-five percent of individuals with intellectual disability have mild intellectual disability. The prevalence of severe intellectual disability has remained the same over several decades at 0.3%-0.5% of the population in the United States (16). Based on the United States National Center for Health Statistics 1997-2003 National Health Interview Survey, the prevalence of intellectual disability among children ages 5-17 years is estimated to be 7.5 per 1,000 (16).

Table 5. Severity of intellectual disability and adult age functioning

Level	Mental age as adult	Adult adaptation
Mild	9-11 y	Reads at 4th-5th grade level; simple multiplications/ divisions; writes simple letters, lists; completes job application; basic independent job skills (arrive on time, stay at task, interact with co-workers); uses public transportation; may qualify for recipes
Moderate	6-8 y	Sight-word reading; copies information e.g., address from card to job application; matches written number to number of items; recognizes time on clock; communicates; some independence in self-care; housekeeping with supervision or cue cards; meal preparation, can follow picture recipe cards; job skills learned with much repetition; uses public transportation with some supervision
Severe	3-5 y	Needs continuous support and supervision; may communicate wants and needs, sometimes with augmentative communication techniques
Profound	Less than 3 y	Limitations of self-care, continence, communication, and mobility; may need complete custodial or nursing care

[Used with permission from Shapiro BK, Batshaw M. Mental retardation (intellectual disability), In: Kliegman RM, Behrman RE, Jenson HB, Stanton BF, eds. Nelson textbook of pediatrics, 18th ed. Philadelphia, PA: Saunders/Elsevier, 2008:191-7, Table 38-6, page 197].

Intellectual disability is reported to be twice as common in males compared to females. The recurrence risk of intellectual disability in families with one previous child with severe intellectual disability is reported to be between 3% and 9% (13, 14).

Mild intellectual disability is associated predominantly with environmental risk factors and a specific etiology can be identified in less than half of affected individuals (16, 18). On the other hand, underlying biological or neurological etiology can be identified in more than two-thirds of affected individuals who have severe disability (16, 18). The most common identified conditions in children with severe intellectual disability include chromosomal disorders, genetic syndromes, congenital brain malformations, neurodegenerative diseases, congenital infections, inborn errors of metabolism, and birth injury (13-18). The severity of intellectual disability and adult age functioning are summarized in Table 5.

CONCLUSION

Disability has been defined differently by different agencies and organizations to serve specific purpose. However, most definitions include the concept of physical or intellectual disability at an individual level combined with inability to fulfill social role or expectations because of environmental factors. A medical and a social model are the two widely described models of disability. A more encompassing and widely used model is that developed by the World Health Organization. While in general, a disability is more readily associated with apparent physical disability, the implications of intellectual disability are equally important to consider.

Intellectual disability is defined as significant limitations in cognitive functioning characterized by an intelligence quotient of about 70 or below and concurrent deficits in adaptive functioning. The severity is classified as mild, moderate, severe, and profound, based on the IQ scores and the intensity of supports needed. Eighty-five percent of individuals who have intellectual disability have mild deficits. Environmental factors are predominant risk factors for mild intellectual disability whereas biologic factors are predominant risk factors for severe intellectual disability. The age at initial presentation depends up on the severity of the deficits. Intellectual deficits can be identified in most children by 3 to 5 years of age. The diagnosis is based on clinical evaluation and psychometric testing for cognitive and adaptive functioning. The need to search for the cause of intellectual disability in all cases is debatable. The main strategies for management of individual who have intellectual disability are general medical care, treatment of co-morbid conditions, treatment of behavioral symptoms, special education, vocational training, and community based supports.

ACKNOWLEDGMENTS

Section on intellectual disability is adapted with permission from Patel DR, Merrick J. Siuba M. Intellectual developmental disorder, In: Greydanus DE, Patel DR, Pratt HD, Calles J Jr, Merrick J, eds. Behavioral pediatrics, 4rd edition. New York: Nova Science, 2015.

REFERENCES

[1]   Patel DR, Greydanus DE, Merrick J, Rubin IL. Introduction to intellectual and developmental disabilities. In : Rubin IL, Merrick J, Greydanus DE, Patel DR, eds. Health care for people with intellectual and developmental disabilities acroos the lifespan. Cham: Springer, 2016:5-12.

[2]   Smart JF, Smart DW. Models of disability: implications for the counseling profession. J Couns Dev 2006;84:29-40.

[3]   Mitra S. The capability approach and disability. J Disabil Policy Stud 2006;16(4):236-47.

[4]   Patel DR, Merrick J. Neurodevelopmental disabilities: Introduction and epidemiology. In: Patel DR, Greydanus DE, Omar HA, Merrick J, eds. Neurodevelopmental disabilities, New York: Springer, 2011:1-13.

[5]   Patel DR, Greydanus DE, Calles JL Jr, Pratt HD. Developmental disabilities across the lifespan. Disease-a-Month 2010;56(6):299-398.

[6]   Iezzoni LI, Freedman VA. Turning the disability tide : the importance of definitions. JAMA 2008;299(8):332-4.

[7]   Kyrkou MR. International classification of function, In : Rubin IL, Merrick J, Greydanus DE, Patel DR, eds. Health care for people with intellectual and developmental disabilities acroos the lifespan. Cham: Springer, 2016:137-48.

[8]   Building the legacy: IDEA 2004. URL: http://idea.ed.gov/.

[9]   Information and techical assistance on the Americans with Disabilities Act. URL: http://www.ada.gov/.

[10]   Social Security. Benefits for people with disabilities. URL: https://www.ssa.gov/disability/.

[11]   Schalock RL, Borthwick-Duffy SA, Buntinx WHE, Coulter DL, eds. Intellectual disability: Definition, classification, and systems of supports, 11th ed. Washington, DC: AAIDD, 2009.

[12]   American Psychiatric Association. Diagnostic and statistical manual of mental disorders, 5th ed, text rev. Washington, DC: APA, 2013:33-40.

[13]   Curry CJ, Stevenson RE, Aughton D, Byrne J, Carey JC, Cassidy S, et al. Evaluation of mental retardation: recommendations of a consensus conference: American College of Medical Genetics. Am J Med Genet 1997;72(4):468-77.

[14]   Moeschler JB, Shevell MI and Committee on Genetics. Clinical genetic evaluation of the child with mental retardation or developmental delays. Pediatrics 2006;117:2304-16.

[15]   Pratt HD, Greydanus DE. Intellectual disability (mental retardation) in children and adolescents. Prim Care 2007;34:375-86.

[16]   Shapiro B, Batshaw M. Intellectual disability. In: Kliegman RM, Stanton BF, St Geme JW III, Schor NF, eds. Nelson textbook of pediatrics, 20th ed. Philadelphia, PA: Elsevier Saunders, 2016:216-22.

[17]   Shevell MI, Ashwal S, Donley D, Flint J, Gingold M, Hirtz D, et al. Practice parameter: Evaluation of the child with global developmental delay. Neurology 2003;60:367-79.

[18]   VanKarnebeck CDH, Janswiejer MCE, Leenders AGE, Offringa M, Hennekam RC. Diagnostic investigation in individuals with mental retardation: A systematic literature review of their usefulness. Eur J Human Genet 2005;13(1):6-25.

In: Child Abuse: Children with Disabilities
Editors: V. J Palusci, D. Nazer et al.

ISBN: 978-1-53612-035-6
© 2017 Nova Science Publishers, Inc.

Chapter 5

ABUSE AND NEGLECT AS CAUSE FOR DISABILITY

Anastasia Feifer[*], MD* *and Ingrid Walker-Descartes, MD, MPH*

David Geffen School of Medicine at UCLA, Los Angeles, California, and Albert Einstein College of Medicine/Maimonides Infants and Children's Hospital of Brooklyn, New York, US

This chapter will present the evidence for physical abuse and child neglect as contributors to disability statistics in the United States and worldwide. We will explore the epidemiology, mechanism, and overall costs of abuse-related sequelae. The injury best studied in the context of pervasive disability is abusive head trauma (AHT), but we will also explore the limited research around other forms of physical abuse as etiologies for short- and long-term disability. In addition, we will explore the effects of child neglect in the form of failure to thrive and how this impairs intellectual development and social functioning.

INTRODUCTION

Child maltreatment encompasses abuse and neglect diagnoses, which can cause disability. Abuse and neglect's contribution to lifetime physical and intellectual disability is difficult to quantify for multiple reasons: underdiagnosis, misdiagnosis, and the paucity

---

[*] Correspondence: Anastasia Feifer, MD, Harbor-UCLA Medical Center, 1000 W Carson Street, Box 460, Torrance, California, United States. E-mail: afeifer@dhs.lacounty.gov.

of longitudinal data collection among them (1). Several discrete abusive etiologies have shown good evidence of causing long-term disability. Physical trauma in the pediatric population, whether it be from maltreatment or from accidental etiologies, is a major cause of long-term morbidity (2). In fact, injury is the leading cause in preventable morbidity and limitation of function in the pediatric age group (3).

MEASURING DISABILITY AFTER TRAUMA IN GENERAL

Several systems have been devised to quantify and qualify severity of acute trauma; similarly, classifications have also been developed to measure long-term functional outcomes in morbid conditions following trauma. Trauma classification systems are used less in the delivery of immediate clinical care, but they give us information for the prediction of morbidity, mortality, and resource utilization (including triage support) (4). In assessing severity of acute trauma, more than a dozen classification systems rely on either anatomic or physiologic criteria to categorize severity–among them the Glasgow Coma Scale (GCS), Pediatric Trauma Score (PTS), Abbreviated Injury Scale (AIS), Injury Severity Score (ISS), Acute Trauma Index (ATI), Shock Index (SI), Trauma Score (TS), Revised Trauma Score (RTS), Modified Injury Severity Score (MISS), and the Trauma and Injury Severity Score (TRISS), to name a few. Description of the measures of each of these classification systems is beyond the scope of this chapter.

Disability is also measured by various data-driven classification systems. They include measurement tools such as the Glasgow Outcome Scale (GOS), the Pediatric Evaluation of Disability Inventory (PEDI), the World Health Organization's International Classification of Functioning, Disability, and Health Children and Youth Version (ICF-CY), the Pediatric Overall Performance Category (POPC), the Functional Independence Measure (FIM™), and the WeeFIM™ for children (5). Gofin et al. (6) proposed a trauma-specific disability measure in 1995, using just seven domains, designed to be cross-cultural with specificity highest in diagnosing long-term disability. Other validated tools assess for health-related quality of life (HRQOL), a measure which queries patients' perceptions about how health status affects quality of life (7). These include tools such as the Child Health Questionnaire (CHQ) and the Pediatric Quality of Life Inventory (PedsQL), among others. A large body of additional evidence-based tools assess for developmental and neurocognitive disability, among them the Vineland Adaptive Behavior Scales, the Battelle Developmental Inventory, Bayley Scales of Infant Development in younger children, and many additional modalities. Some studies link the objective measures of injury classification with disability classification, though they are few in number (3, 8). A lack of uniformity in examining disability outcome measures further limits our ability to fully evaluate its impact (9, 10).

Existing research has sought to objectively quantify disability caused by trauma in the pediatric population. Generally, these objective outcome measures help us understand that most pediatric trauma patients have either short- or long-term functional sequelae, although results are mixed. It is important to recognize that most research exploring long term effects of pediatric trauma do not focus on child maltreatment as cause of injury. Nevertheless, the disability measures utilized by some researchers indicate that serious injury from trauma has been shown to most frequently cause short-term disability (3, 11), but more far-reaching longitudinal studies are needed to investigate permanent disability. Winthrop and colleagues studied children discharged from a Level 1 pediatric trauma center sustaining multisystem injuries (excluding CNS). The majority of these patients suffered motor vehicle accidents, falls, and sports injuries; the trauma was mostly femur fracture, abdominal injury, or burn. The study found that after 1 and 6 months, physical functioning was still below that of peers; quality of life measures in multiple domains (including physical, social-emotional, and inter-familial) also scaled lower compared to normative data (3). Mobility and self-care were greatest affected, with behavioral outcomes being more moderate in severity. The higher Injury Severity Scale (ISS) scores correlated with poorer functioning (3). Gabbe et al. (12) demonstrated that their cohort of children ages 0-16 who suffered injuries with an Injury Severity Score >15 had both functional and quality-of-life impairments as long as 12 years out from the event. The sample included 2.7% deemed to be intentional injuries (others being falls, motor vehicle accidents (MVA), burns, and bicycle injuries). Their subjects were scaled using multiple functional and HRQOL tools. Some measurement tools showed over half of patients had disability and poorer HRQOL even 1 year after injury; other tools (notable the FIM) resulted in a much lower number. This study underscores the variability in measurement of pediatric disability.

Another survey by Valadka and colleagues (8) reported on longer-term outcomes (mean 4.4 years post-injury) in pediatric trauma patients with a mean age of 13 (much older than victims of serious abuse-related trauma). Their study found that just over half of respondents had no functional debility after a range of injuries (MVA, sports, falls, or "other" inclusive of child abuse). 47% had limitations affecting age appropriate functioning (9). In these and other studies, the majority of impairments were in mobility, age-appropriate role activities, self-care, cognitive-behavioral domains, and in effects on family functioning/stress (3, 9, 10-16). In most research, including the above, it has been found that presence and severity post injury correlates both with initial injury severity and with presence and acuity of head injury (12, 15, 16). It is important to note that though research in pediatric trauma recognizes the need to measure long-term functional outcomes, most of the literature focuses on trauma as a whole without a focus on abusive injury. As we will explore, injury from abuse (particularly abusive head trauma or AHT) comprises a subset of pediatric trauma with more evidence of longer term and more severe sequelae contributing more significantly to pediatric disability.

DISABILITY FROM CHILD PHYSICAL ABUSE: ABUSIVE HEAD TRAUMA

Pediatric abusive head trauma (AHT) survivors currently account for 8.6 per 100,000 population hospitalizations annually (17). The decision to use this nomenclature for a highly complex pediatric injury was undertaken by both the American Academy of Pediatrics (AAP) as well as the Centers for Disease Control (CDC). The CDC defines abusive head trauma as: "an injury to the skull or intracranial contents of an infant or young child (< 5 years of age) due to inflicted blunt impact and/or violent shaking" (18). The AAP issued a statement in 2009 recommending the use of the term "abusive head trauma" based on multi-disciplinary consensus that this language best describes the complex injury mechanism. Older terminology has referred to inflicted head injury as "shaken baby syndrome" or "shaken impact syndrome," among others. The current term was established not to refute that shaking likely plays a major role in clinical manifestations of AHT, but rather to reflect that AHT may consist of a heterogeneous constellation of injury mechanisms inclusive of acceleration/deceleration, impact, or both (19). Based on a voluminous body of peer-reviewed literature on the subject, the most commonly encountered manifestations of AHT include subdural hematoma, retinal hemorrhage, and hypoxic-ischemic encephalopathy. Infants and children suffering from AHT may also sustain spinal cord injury, cutaneous injury, fractures, abdominal trauma, or maxillofacial trauma. Though the latter are not diagnostic of AHT, they aid in diagnosing physical abuse (5). AHT victims are most commonly young infants under the age of two years. There has been shown to be a male predominance (20).

Abusive head trauma in infants and children requires an understanding of the unique qualities of the young brain as well as particulars of infant anatomy. Firstly, infants and young children do not possess the musculature supporting the cervical spine to withstand acceleration-deceleration type forces. This coupled with a head that is proportionally larger in size to the trunk makes for a stronger acting force on the intracranial contents (20). Secondly, brains typically under the age of 18 months lack sufficient myelination to moderate the affects of inertial forces, so affects of shearing are more severe (21). The ratio of lipid to water in the immature brain also leads to a greater impact against the adjacent skull. These phenomena can be seen in the acceleration-deceleration forces that come from shaking and/or impact. Edema from neuronal necrosis then leads to local parenchymal hypoxic injury, at times together with infarction (22). Hypoxia can then be exacerbated by seizure activity from local parenchymal irritation, usually a subdural bleed. Local parenchymal injury is also sustained by tears (23) or contusion. Subdural hematoma, the most common finding in abusive head trauma (24), occurs from tearing of the bridging veins that puncture the dura mater and drain to the dural sinuses. Rupture of these vessels is again from acceleration-deceleration, in the form of shaking **or** impact (including a severe fall injury). These injury modalities have been described in clinical research both prospectively and retrospectively, and a more limited body of literature describes trials in animal studies (21).

Retinal hemorrhage (RH) is seen in 74% to 82% of AHT cases (25). In contrast, RH has been shown to appear in fewer than 3% of severe accidental injuries such as motor vehicle collisions or falls from great heights (26). Although retinal hemorrhage resulting from abusive head trauma can have any appearance, the classic pattern of AHT-related retinal hemorrhage is diffuse (extending outwardly from the posterior pole), and bleeding is seen within many layers of the retina (pre-retinal, intraretinal, sub-retinal) (26). The RH may be unilateral or bilateral. Retinoschisis (the peeling of superficial layers of retina away from deeper layers, creating a ridge-like effect) is also highly specific of abusive head trauma (27). Again, mechanisms of both RH and retinoschisis in abusive head trauma have been researched in clinical settings and with animal models, and the most likely mechanism is acceleration-deceleration forces acting on the eye, agitating vitreous fluid away from the retinal surface (26). These complex injuries have a spectrum of long-term disabilities on children. Some cases of abusive head trauma result in few long-term effects, though studies show a variable prevalence of those with good outcomes ranging from 4%-48% (28).

COMMON SEQUELAE OF ABUSIVE HEAD TRAUMA (AHT)

Given the complexity and magnitude of forces acting on the intracranial contents of AHT victims, outcomes can often be severe. It should be noted that despite inflicted head trauma being the most fatal form of child abuse, claiming 0.74 per 100,000 annually in children aged 0-4 years in the United States, the patients who survive AHT number 8.6 per 100,000 (29). Therefore, the vast majority of these patients survive with significant implications for the clinicians and guardians who care for them. Several studies have followed these patients and are able to give longitudinal data on functional impairments.

Visual impairment is among the more common results of AHT, including visual field defects and acuity loss, visual agnosia, and even cortical blindness (30-32). Abnormal extra-ocular movements have also been described as a result of inflicted head trauma (29). Interestingly, visual deficiency is usually not caused by ocular manifestations of AHT (as retinal hemorrhage, in most cases, resolves within the time-frame of weeks) but rather parenchymal brain injury (31, 33).

Not surprisingly, given the presence of subdural hemorrhage, encephalopathy, and diffuse and local brain ischemia often resulting from AHT, motor debility can be significant (29, 30, 34, 35). Permanent motor deficits including hypotonia or spasticity, hemiparesis and hemi, tetra-, and quadriplegia, among other permanent disturbances, are seen in about 60-65% of patients (29, 33). About 20-40% have been found to have ongoing epilepsy. Both micro- and macrocephaly have also been results of AHT, with 17% of survivors relying on intracranial shunts (39). 37% of age-appropriate patients require either a feeding tube or other assistive eating device as a result of AHT-related disability (36).

Cognitive and behavioral consequences are highly prevalent in those children who have suffered inflicted traumatic brain injury (TBI). These children exhibit significant behavioral disturbances, both in descriptive studies and when compared with peers (29, 34, 37) described as self-injurious behaviors, irritability, rage, impulsivity, sleep disturbance, and poor attention (29). Ewings-Cobb et al. studied post-AHT patients in comparison with matched controls and found persistent cognitive deficits up to 3 months using Bayley Scales of Infant Development. The authors noted the 'ceiling effect' of the improvement from baseline to 3 months as compared to non-inflicted TBI patients showing more significant improvement (37). In fact, nearly all research examining cognitive-behavioral problems after AHT demonstrate either significant deviation from normative scores (29, 33, 34) or impairment in comparison with matched groups (37-40, 43).

FUNCTIONAL OUTCOMES OF ABUSIVE HEAD TRAUMA VERSUS NON-ABUSIVE HEAD TRAUMA

Several important studies have demonstrated important differences in functional outcomes for patients who have sustained AHT as compared to pediatric patients with head trauma determined to be non-inflicted. Overall, the picture is less favorable for AHT patients in short-term and long-term disability outcomes. At time of discharge post-injury, Keenan and colleagues (39) demonstrated a significant propensity for "poor outcome" (Pediatric Overall Performance Category [POPC] score of 3 or 4) in children sustaining head injury from maltreatment (75.7%) as opposed to accident (24.3%) (39).

Keenan et al. (40, 41) also examined a cohort of children aged 0-23 months who sustained intracranial injuries by both abuse and by other mechanisms, in a series of prospective longitudinal studies. The authors persistently identified more significant impairments at 1 year and 2 years post-injury in the AHT cohort. Also, at the 1- to 2-year interval, there was no significant change in status between the two groups. At one year, 27% of the AHT group was classified as "severely disabled" per POPC scoring, as opposed to 6.5% of the non-abusive head injuries. The disabilities were measured by utilization of rehabilitative therapies as well as resource use (high versus low resource utilization). When the same cohort was again evaluated at age 3, the Mullen Scales of Early Learning (validated to measure gross and fine motor skills and cognitive ability) were significantly lower for the AHT group as opposed to the non-AHT cohort (first percentile vs. fourteenth percentile, respectively) (42). In another small prospective study conducted at a large, urban children's hospital, short-term disability outcomes were found to be less favorable in the cohort of children sustaining inflicted traumatic brain injury as opposed to accidental. Using the Glasgow Outcome Scale at the time of the baseline evaluation, fewer than half of the inflicted group were deemed to have "good recovery" as compared with accidental. The children categorized as being "moderately" or "severely" disabled was 1.7 times higher in the maltreatment cohort (46). These groups were again evaluated an average of 1.3 months post-injury, where cognitive test scores differed greatly between cohorts. 45% of children with inflicted injury scored in the "mentally deficient" range, versus just 5% of children with non-inflicted trauma (using Bayley Scales of Infant Development in younger children and Stanford-Binet Intelligence Scale and the McCarthy Scales of Children's Abilities motor scales for older subjects) (43). Hymel and colleagues also followed small cohorts of patients in AHT and non-AHT groups 6 months post-injury. They found that while none of the subjects in the accidental cohort had mental developmental index (MDI) and gross motor quotient (GMQ) scores below 60, 75% of the AHT group had MDIs <60, with 67% suffering GMQ <60. (Scoring was done using Bayley Scales of Infant Development and the Peabody Developmental Motor Scales, both of which utilize standardized scores with mean values of 100) (44). Overall, although measurement tools are many and without standardization between studies, results demonstrate that children with head injuries resulting from abuse fare poorly in multiple domains. As we will explore, the relatively high prevalence coupled with the high costs of disability from abuse should prompt an urgent push for maltreatment prevention in our communities.

BURNS

Little is known about the long-term disability caused by abusive burns. However, given our knowledge of what types of burns carry a high specificity for maltreatment, we can extrapolate results of burn-sequelae studies to patients who suffered inflicted burns. Here, we will focus on scalding, which is the most common type of abusive burn (45). Furthermore, scald injuries tend to cover greater surface area than other forms of inflicted burn (with the exception home fires from arson), and often overlie joint surfaces, contributing to long-term complications. Scald burns without adequate history that have a certain burn pattern and characteristics carry a higher specificity for abuse:

- circumferential scalds of extremities
- bilateral uniform-appearing burns of extremities
- stocking-glove distribution (on lower and upper extremities, respectively)
- sparing of the palmar/plantar surfaces of hands/feet where immersed extremities may have been in contact with cooler surfaces
- burns of the truck and buttocks with sparing of the flexor surfaces of the trunk and groins
- sharp demarcation on skin and absence of splash marks, suggesting forced immersion
- uniform depth of injury, also suggesting a child being held in contact with hot liquid
- a history incompatible with the child's developmental capabilities
- delay in seeking care

The child most at risk for scald injuries is a toddler 2-4 years old, with a male predominance (46). Although there is no empiric evidence, it could be suggested that scalding occurs as a punishment for children transitioning out of diapers who have accidents, or for active toddlers with exploratory play who become dirty as a result of their developmentally appropriate curiosity.

Literature on disability from pediatric burn injuries best illuminates abuse when it examines hand burns. For reasons outlines above, bilateral hand burns carry high specificity for intentional injuries. We can extrapolate information from studies which include analysis of disability from bilateral hand burns to give us a perspective on sequelae from abusive burns. In a study by Sheridan and colleagues, 41% of their subjects suffered bilateral hand burns; 22% were scald injuries, and average age was 2.3 ± 5.4 years. Although abuse as etiology was not explored in their research, it is likely from these demographics that a significant portion suffered maltreatment. Of their study sample, 32% required a total of 94 reconstructive operations during the follow-up period of >5 years (0.6 operations per child). These included web space releases, finger extension contracture releases, finger flexion contracture releases, wrist extension contracture releases, wrist flexion contracture releases, and several smaller numbers of other procedures (47). Needless to say, disability and serious compromise in mobility from scar tissue formation are a significant risk in children with burn injuries (48). The hand in particular, a known target of inflicted scald burn, limits normal gross and fine motor development; when other areas of burn are involved (notably the feet and face), outcomes are worse (49).

Scald burns from neglect are more common than inflicted burns, often involving lack of supervision in handling of hot liquids that spill onto a child's skin (50). Since these injuries far more commonly affect the trunk and head and neck (51), the same complex contracture-related disability is less common than that found in abusive burns. Mental health sequelae are best described in severe burns with and in adult populations, where rates of anxiety, depressions, and PTSD post-injury are higher (52-54). In pediatric patients, psychological sequelae appear to be more modest, with mixed results, but still showing prevalence in the form of anxiety, PTSD, self-esteem problems, and social functioning (55, 56). It should be noted that these studies explore the psychological sequelae of burns outside of the context of child abuse.

ABDOMINAL TRAUMA

Abusive abdominal trauma (AAT) is the second deadliest form of child maltreatment (57). Young children have relatively short rib cages with respect to adult truncal anatomy, more pliant and cartilaginous ribs, and under-developed abdominal musculature–all of which leads to more serious visceral injury when force is applied (58). AAT is rare, though difficult to quantify. Various sources estimate a 2-3% rate among all abuse cases, but outliers show rates as high as 14-20% (59).

Although mortality from AAT is cited as being as high as 40-50% (52), when children do not die, outcomes are quite good and surgical management is less common that conservative management (60). Complications leading to more severe illness, including death, include shock (septic or hypovolemic); peritonitis; obstruction due to small bowel hematoma; and pancreatic pseudocyst (61).

In a study by Trokel and colleagues (62), abdominal injury data culled from the National Pediatric Trauma Registry® (NPTR) showed that about 16% of visceral trauma was abusive. Their research showed that if abdominal injury was isolated, recovery was excellent and mortality was 4.5 times lower than abdominal injury associated with other findings (head/skeletal involvement). In terms of morbidity, a surprising 0.2% (just one patient) required rehabilitation facility care if the visceral damage was isolated. The child abuse group had the highest prevalence of isolated abdominal injury at 8.8%. The AAT group also had highest mortality in isolated and non-isolated gut trauma (6.45% adjusted odds ratio compared to fall injury); authors concluded that abuse is independently associated with increased mortality. However, apart from mention of post-discharge needs, disability was not studied. It was not stated whether a higher percentage of the abuse subset required ongoing rehabilitative care (62).

Another data set (KIDS Inpatient Database of the U.S. Agency for Healthcare Research and Quality) was queried on whether abusive mechanism in abdominal injury was associated with poorer outcomes in a study by Lane and colleagues. The researchers found longer hospitalizations and higher mortality rates in the AAT group. (Interestingly, this excluded infants under 1 year of age, in whom mortality rates were not significantly different for inflicted versus noninflicted abdominal injury) (63).

Information about longer-term disability is lacking. An important future direction for disability-related research is a longitudinal perspective on isolated pediatric abdominal trauma, inclusive of abuse and non-abusive causes. In summary, though abusive visceral injury carries a high mortality burden, it is overall relatively rare and outcomes are generally favorable. However, abdominal injury is so often concomitant with other forms of more debilitating trauma–and the more multi-system the involvement, the more prevalent the long-term functional limitation.

COST OF ABUSE-RELATED DISABILITY

Pediatric injury is costly. Presently, the expenditure for medical care of pediatric injuries in general is well over $350 billion or 3.8% of the gross domestic product (64). Abused children tend to have the highest costs coupled with worse overall outcomes, including higher mortality (65). In the United States overall, Fang and colleagues discovered astonishingly high costs related not just to medical care, but also to many other infrastructure costs related to the social and legal spheres involved in child maltreatment. They calculate an average lifetime cost per victim of $210,012 in 2010 dollars, including $32,648 in childhood health care costs; $10,530 in adult medical costs; $144,360 in productivity losses; $7,728 in child welfare costs; $6,747 in criminal justice costs; and $7,999 in special education costs. The estimated average lifetime cost per death is $1,272,900, including $14,100 in medical costs and $1,258,800 in productivity losses.

The 2008 burden resulting from fatal and nonfatal child maltreatment in the United States was calculated at $124 billion (66).

Abusive head trauma is also fairly well-studied in terms of cost-analysis of child abuse. In a study by Peterson et al., acute costs were calculated in overall nationwide as well as event-costs for both emergency department and inpatient hospitalizations for AHT. The researchers found that ED visits cost an average of $2,612 per visit; admissions $31,901 (67). As compared to Fang et al., who found that the average *lifetime* medical cost of child maltreatment in general is $43,178 in living patients, we can see that acute costs of AHT are substantial (61). Using their data set from the US Department of Health and Human Services' Healthcare Cost and Utilization Project (HCUP), Peterson and colleagues calculated a $69.6 million annual AHT acute medical cost-burden between 2006-2011 (62).

In terms of associated lifetime costs in life- and productivity loss, Miller and colleagues undertook to study the disability-adjusted life-year (DALY) burden of small children who suffered AHT. DALYs are calculated by summing years of productive life that survivors lost to disability plus life-years lost to premature death (40). It is a measure of overall disease burden, expressed as the number of years lost due to ill-health, disability or early death. In Miller's study, estimated mean lifetime loss per case was 4.7 DALYs for minor AHT, 5.4 for moderate AHT, 24.1 for severe AHT; to clarify, the latter score correlated to a DALY burden for a severe AHT case equaling 80% of the burden of death (37). They found that even a mild AHT case with lasting functional effects exceed the DALY burden of a severe burn. Economic costs of abuse are staggering, but more sobering is the cost of a lifetime of compromise from such early childhood events.

It should also be noted that exact numbers are often elusive. Corso and colleagues outlined multiple barriers to exacting a true estimate of both medical and societal cost of child abuse. They cite intangible costs such as acute trauma of the maltreatment that results in pain and suffering, mental anguish, and social stigma. They also note that potential societal costs of abuse such as future violence victimization and perpetration represent weak causal links to maltreatment (68). Adding to this, a review of the literature by Brown et al. reveals that actual dollar estimates in health expenditures for child maltreatment vary widely because of differences in research designs, metrics used, and study quality. As one example, per-episode estimates of child costs ranged from $0 to >$24,000 across studies at the time of their publication (69).

DISABILITY FROM FAILURE TO THRIVE
AND CHILD NEGLECT

Failure to thrive (FTT) is a common problem in infancy and can extend into childhood if the underlying etiology remains elusive. It is defined as the prolonged cessation of weight gain in comparison to the norms recognized for age and gender matched peers after having achieved a stable growth pattern. This insult to the growth trajectory causes the weight-for-age to decrease across 2 major percentile channels from the previously established growth pattern, while the weight for length is less than 80% of what would be considered ideal weight for the child (70-72). Despite the acceptance of these definitions and the wide spectrum of normal growth variations, diagnoses based on percentile shifts must be scrutinized closely (73). As a general rule, actual weight that is 70% of predicted weight-for-length requires urgency in evaluation given the importance of nutrition for the maintenance of physical growth and development (74).

Initially, FTT was differentiated into two forms: "organic FTT" in which the child's growth failure was attributed to a medical condition, and "non-organic FTT" where the insult was attributed to psychosocial causes such as psychological neglect or "maternal deprivation." It is now accepted that this approach to dichotomizing FTT etiologies is an oversimplification. This generalization is thought to complicate the clinical approach to finding the correct underlying etiology as many children exhibit components of both types. FTT has come to be understood as a chronic condition that is the final common pathway of the interaction of diverse medical, nutritional, developmental and social stresses (70). A myopic approach to the FTT diagnosis may result in a missed opportunity to effectively address the biopsychosocial needs for the child in question and by extension, the needs of the family.

THE IMPACT OF POVERTY AND NEGLECT AS IT RELATES TO
IMPAIRMENT FROM FTT

It is important to remember that the nutritional deficiency causing failure to thrive can stem from poverty and food insecurity, defined as any household not supplied with enough food on a consistent basis to support an active and healthy lifestyle for all family members (70). Although not all children with a diagnosis of FTT come from food insecure households, the significant impact of poverty and its undeniable relationship to lack of resources should not be overlooked. In the United States in 2014, 15.3 million children lived in food-insecure households. Even more concerning, households with children reported food insecurity at a significantly higher rate than those without children, 19 percent compared to 12 percent (76). The cumulative effect of this nutritional deprivation resulting in FTT not only impairs growth but is also linked to long-term deficits in intellectual, social, and psychological functioning (77,78). However, in spite of the high prevalence of child poverty, children may fail to thrive in homes of any social class; layered dynamics ultimately contribute to FTT. Dysfunctional environments caused by disorders of parent-child interactions, parental mental illness or substance abuse, organic pathology, developmental impairment–all of which are on top of financial stressors–creates children at risk for FTT (70).

Although poverty remains the most significant social risk factor for developing FTT worldwide and within the United States (74, 79), caregiver behaviors, including neglect, are strong contributors to the intellectual and developmental disabilities observed in children with FTT. When the underlying etiology for FTT is child neglect, there are often coexisting risk factors. Each risk factor should be evaluated in the context of each child's presentation and their associated family dynamics. The parents(s) of an infant with FTT may exhibit inadequate adaptive social interactional behavior and less positive affective behavior. They may also have their own histories of trauma (80, 81). A preterm infant with FTT may have been separated from caregivers due to complications in their perinatal course. In these cases, complex family dynamics and social factors that contribute to neglect include: lack of available extended family to help with child care, social isolation of the family, substance abuse, family violence, single parenthood, and employment instability. On the other hand, parents in affluent circumstances or parents engaged in career development or activities away from home also may lack the emotional strength or maturity to nurture their infant appropriately (50,51). Any of these parental behaviors have the potential to impact a child's intellectual and developmental abilities secondary to the development of FTT. The development of intellectual and developmental disabilities are thus multifactorial with no metric to clearly delineate what is attributable to FTT or the omissions on the part of the caregivers leading to this presentation.

INTELLECTUAL DEVELOPMENT AS IT RELATES TO IMPAIRMENT FROM FTT

Children who experience prolonged malnutrition and/or FTT appear to be at risk for intellectual deficits severe enough to affect their learning potential (82, 83). The severity of the developmental impairments can vary substantially among pre-school and school aged children with histories of early FTT (84-88). Studies have underscored the central importance of a history of serious malnutrition as well as the quality of the home environment and educational experience in predicting the cognitive development of the affected child later in life (55-58, 89-91). The requirement to evaluate both of all of these factors highlights the complexity of untangling their effects on later cognitive development.

It was once thought that under-nutrition linearly affected brain development. Undoubtedly, adequate protein and fat sources are crucial to neuronal development and myelination (92). However, multiple complex models have since been proposed to link FTT to intellectual disability. For example, in animal models as early as the 1970s, malnourished rats performed more poorly in maze studies not because of poor nutrition *per se*, but rather because they withdrew from social contact with their mates (93). From then, the intricacies of biological impairment from caloric insufficiency coupled with environmental factors have become partially understood (94).

In the evaluation of pre-school and school aged children with histories of early FTT, the clinician is advised to pay careful attention to the potential effects of a child's nutritional state on his or her response to test items in the early phases of the evaluation. Meanwhile, in a younger age group, the infants who have experienced nutritional and/or stimulus deprivation are also often withdrawn, which may severely limit their capacity to respond at least initially during similar evaluation (95). As a result, intellectual tests given early during the hospitalization when a child is apathetic from undernutrition may underestimate the intellectual potential in the long term (96). It is advised to conduct the assessment soon after the hospital admission and repeating it once nutritional recovery is well underway which should provide a more predictive estimate of the intellectual potential than one assessment in the early phase of recovery (63).

SOCIOEMOTIONAL DEVELOPMENT

Children with FTT are at risk for suboptimal development. Although no one pattern of behavioral disturbance a pathognomonic sign of past FTT, deficits in social responsiveness, affect, activity level and avoidance of social contact have been noted by observers (97-99). In one study, Polan and colleagues found that children with FTT consistently demonstrated less positive affect in a range of situations than did normally growing children, while acute and chronic malnutrition were associated with heightened negative affect (100). Due to multiple areas of the psychological development that may be affected, a comprehensive assessment of several behavioral domains, including social responsiveness, affect, and response to feeding, is generally necessary for children with

FTT (101). Again, the impact of environment on these same domains makes it difficult to attribute challenges in these developmental areas to the single diagnosis of FTT.

TREATMENT

Due to the complex interplay of several factors randomized intervention trials in the United States and abroad have demonstrated that nutrition interventions alone are not sufficient to minimize long-term development/behavioral sequelae of malnutrition, but weekly home-based developmental interventions sustained for several years into early childhood are associated with decreased academic and behavioral deficits into young adulthood (107, 108). In the case of socioemotional development, one would expect improvement in the social responsiveness of a child with FTT after nutritional treatment. On the contrary, some children continue to demonstrate significant deficits in responsiveness which requires additional specialized interventions.

There is a complicated interplay between the secondary effects of poverty and neglect together with familial psychodynamics associated with FTT. This complexity has posed a challenge to researchers to clearly delineate how a diagnosis of FTT contributes or distracts from the clinical picture when a child presents with a developmental or intellectual disability. As a result, researchers can so far conclude that although FTT is associated with reduction in IQ and possibly minimal reduction in childhood weight and height, there is little evidence that identifying this diagnosis is predictive of any damaging consequences for both growth and intellectual development in the long term (104).

CONCLUSION

The contribution of child maltreatment to disability is far-reaching, complicated, expensive, and damaging. This chapter has outlined only some aspects of abuse and neglect as they contribute to childhood disability burden; perhaps it can be extrapolated that *all* abusive events carry the potential to cause some form of long-term debility even into adulthood. Indeed, the landmark work of Fellitti and colleagues shows us that even one adverse childhood experience (ACE) sets us up for the potential to have any number of impairments in the future (105). As medical care advances and mortality from abuse injuries drops, we can expect to provide care to more and more of those who survive.

Abuse and neglect prevention and careful, consistent involvement with at-risk patients is our path to slowing the tide.

REFERENCES

[1]   Chadwick DL, Chin S., Salerno C, Landsverk, J, Kitchen L. Deaths from falls in children: How far is fatal? J Trauma 1991;31(10):1353-5.

[2]   Letts M, Davidson D, Lapner P. Multiple trauma in children: predicting outcome and long-term results. Can J Surg 2002;45(2):126.

[3]   Winthrop AL, Brasel KJ, Stahovic L, Paulson J, Schneeberger B, Kuhn EM. Quality of life and functional outcome after pediatric trauma. J Trauma Acute Care Surg 2002;58(3):468-74.

[4]   Marcin JP, Pollack MM. Triage scoring systems, severity of illness measures, and mortality prediction models in pediatric trauma. Critical care medicine 2002;30(11):S457-67.

[5]   Willis CD, Gabbe BJ, Butt W, Cameron PA. Assessing outcomes in paediatric trauma populations. Injury 2006;37(12):1185-96.

[6]   Gofin R, Adler B. A seven item scale for the assessment of disabilities after child and adolescent injuries. Inj Prev 1997;3(2):120-3.

[7]   Health-related Quality of Life (HRQOL). Centers for Disease Control and Prevention, 2016. URL: www.cdc.gov/hrqol/.

[8]   Valadka S, Poenaru D, Dueck A. Long-term disability after trauma in children. J Pediatr Surg 2000;35(5):684-7.

[9]   Van Beeck EF, Larsen CF, Lyons RA, Meerding WJ, Mulder S, Essink-Bot ML. Guidelines for the conduction of follow-up studies measuring injury-related disability. J Trauma Acute Care Surg 2007;62(2):534-50.

[10]   Chawda MN, Hildebrand F, Pape HC, Giannoudis PV. Predicting outcome after multiple trauma: Which scoring system? Injury 2004;35(4):347-58.

[11]   van der Sluis CK, Kingma J, Eisma WH, Ten Duis HJ. Pediatric polytrauma: Short-term and long-term outcomes. J Trauma Acute Care Surg 1997;43(3):501-6.

[12]   Gabbe BJ, Simpson PM, Sutherland AM, Palmer CS, Williamson OD, Butt W, et al. Functional and health-related quality of life outcomes after pediatric trauma. J Trauma Acute Care Surg 2011;70(6):1532-8.

[13]   Polinder S, Meerding WJ, Toet H, Mulder S, Essink-Bot ML, van Beeck EF. Prevalence and prognostic factors of disability after childhood injury. Pediatrics 2005;116(6):e810-7.

[14]   Aitken ME, Tilford JM, Barrett KW, Parker JG, Simpson P, Landgraf J, et al. Health status of children after admission for injury. Pediatrics 2002;110(2):337-42.

[15]   Schalamon J, Bismarck SV, Schober PH, Höllwarth ME. Multiple trauma in pediatric patients. Pediatr Surg Int 2003;19(6):417-23.

[16]   Wesson DE, Scorpio RJ, Spence LJ, Kenney BD, Chipman ML, Netley CT, et al. The physical, psychological, and socioeconomic costs of pediatric trauma. J Trauma Acute Care Surg 1992;33(2):252-7.

[17] Parks SE, Sugerman D, Xu L, Coronado V. Characteristics of non-fatal abusive head trauma among children in the USA, 2003–2008: Application of the CDC operational case definition to national hospital inpatient data. Inj Prev 2012;18(6):392–8.

[18] Parks SE, Annest JL, Hill HA, Karch DL. Pediatric abusive head trauma: recommended definitions for public health surveillance and research. Atlanta, GA: US Centers for Disease Control and Prevention, 2012. URL:www.cdc.gov/violence prevention/pdf/pedheadtrauma-a.pdf.

[19] Christian CW, Block R, and the American Academy of Pediatrics. Abusive head trauma in infants and children. Pediatrics 2009;123(5):1409-11.

[20] Kemp A, Joshi A, Mann M, Tempest V, Liu A, Holden S, Maguire S. What are the clinical and radiological characteristics of spinal injuries from physical abuse: A systematic review. Arch Dis Child 2009;95(5):355-60.

[21] Margulies S, Coats B. Biomechanics of head trauma in infants and young children, In C. Jenny (ed). Child abuse and neglect: Diagnosis, treatment, and evidence. St. Louis, MO: Elsevier, 2011:360.

[22] Ewing-Cobbs L, Prasad M, Kramer L, Louis PT, Baumgartner J, Fletcher JM, Alpert B. Acute neuroradiologic findings in young children with inflicted or noninflicted traumatic brain injury. Child Nerv Syst 2000;16(1):25-34.

[23] Palifka LA, Frasier LD, Metzger RR, Hedlund GL. Parenchymal brain laceration as a predictor of abusive head trauma. Am J Neuroradiol 2016;37(1):163-8.

[24] Christian CW. Understanding abusive head trauma in infants and children. Elk Grove Village, IL: American Academy of Pediatrics, 2015.

[25] Narang S, Clarke J. Abusive head trauma: Past, present, and future. J Child Neurol 2014;29(12):1747-56.

[26] Levin AV. Ophthalmology of shaken baby syndrome. Neurosurg Clin North Amer 2002;13(2):201-11.

[27] Levin AV. Retinal hemorrhage in abusive head trauma. Pediatrics 2010;126(5):961-70.

[28] Ewing-Cobbs L, Prasad M. Outcome of abusive head trauma. In: Jenny C, ed. Child abuse and neglect: Diagnosis, treatment, and evidence. St. Louis, MO: Elsevier, 2011:452.

[29] Parks SE, Kegler SR, Annest JL, Mercy JA. Characteristics of fatal abusive head trauma among children in the USA: 2003–2007: An application of the CDC operational case definition to national vital statistics data. Inj Prev 2012;18(3):193-9.

[30] Barlow KM, Thomson E, Johnson D, Minns RA. Late neurologic and cognitive sequelae of inflicted traumatic brain injury in infancy. Pediatrics 2005;116(2):e174-85.

[31] Chiesa A, Duhaime AC. Abusive head trauma. Pediatric Clin North Am 2009;56(2):317-31.

[32] Jayawant S, Parr J. Outcome following subdural haemorrhages in infancy. Arch Dis Child 2007;92(4):343-7.

[33] Levin AV. Retinal hemorrhage and child abuse. In: David TJ, ed. Recent advances in paediatrics. London: Churchill Livingstone, 2000;18:151-219.

[34] Bonnier C, Nassogne MC, Saint-Martin C, Mesples B, Kadhim H, Sébire G. Neuroimaging of intraparenchymal lesions predicts outcome in shaken baby syndrome. Pediatrics 2003;112(4):808-14.

[35] Duhaime AC, Christian C, Moss E, Seidl T. Long-term outcome in infants with the shaking-impact syndrome. Pediatric Neurosurg 1996;24(6):292-8.

[36] Miller TR, Steinbeigle R, Wicks A, Lawrence BA, Barr M, Barr RG. Disability-adjusted life-year burden of abusive head trauma at ages 0–4. Pediatrics 2014;134(6):e1545-50.

[37] Ewing-Cobbs L, Prasad M, Kramer L, Landry S. Inflicted traumatic brain injury: Relationship of developmental outcome to severity of injury. Pediatric Neurosurg 2000;31(5):251-8.

[38]   Beers SR, Berger RP, Adelson PD. Neurocognitive outcome and serum biomarkers in inflicted versus non-inflicted traumatic brain injury in young children. J Neurotrauma 2007;24(1):97-105.

[39]   Keenan HT, Runyan DK, Marshall SW, Nocera MA, Merten DF. A population-based comparison of clinical and outcome characteristics of young children with serious inflicted and noninflicted traumatic brain injury. Pediatrics 2004;114(3):633-9.

[40]   Keenan HT, Runyan DK, Nocera M. Child outcomes and family characteristics 1 year after severe inflicted or noninflicted traumatic brain injury. Pediatrics 2006;117(2):317-24.

[41]   Keenan HT, Runyan DK, Nocera M. Longitudinal follow-up of families and young children with traumatic brain injury. Pediatrics 2006;117(4):1291-7.

[42]   Keenan HT, Hooper SR, Wetherington CE, Nocera M, Runyan DK. Neurodevelopmental consequences of early traumatic brain injury in 3-year-old children. Pediatrics 2007;119(3):e616-23.

[43]   Ewing-Cobbs L, Kramer L, Prasad M, Canales DN, Louis PT, Fletcher JM, et al. Neuroimaging, physical, and developmental findings after inflicted and noninflicted traumatic brain injury in young children. Pediatrics 1998;102(2):300-7.

[44]   Hymel KP, Makoroff KL, Laskey AL, Conaway MR, Blackman JA. Mechanisms, clinical presentations, injuries, and outcomes from inflicted versus noninflicted head trauma during infancy: Results of a prospective, multicentered, comparative study. Pediatrics 2007;119(5):922-9.

[45]   Thombs BD. Patient and injury characteristics, mortality risk, and length of stay related to child abuse by burning: Evidence from a national sample of 15,802 pediatric admissions. Ann Surg 2008;247(3):519-23.

[46]   Keen JH, Lendrum J, Wolman B. Inflicted burns and scalds in children. BMJ 1975;4(5991):268-9.

[47]   Sheridan RL, Baryza MJ, Pessina MA, O'Neill KM, Cipullo HM, Donelan MB, Ryan CM, Schulz JT, Schnitzer JJ, Tompkins RG. Acute hand burns in children: management and long-term outcome based on a 10-year experience with 698 injured hands. Ann Surg 1999;229(4):558.

[48]   Schneider JC, Holavanahalli R, Helm P, O'Neil C, Goldstein R, Kowalske K. Contractures in burn injury, part II: Investigating joints of the hand. J Burn Care Res 2008;29(4):606-13.

[49]   Palmieri TL, Nelson-Mooney K, Kagan RJ, Stubbs TK, Meyer WJ, Herndon DN, et al. Impact of hand burns on health-related quality of life in children younger than 5 years. J Trauma Acute Care Surg 2012;73(3):S197-204.

[50]   Chester DL, Jose RM, Aldlyami E, King H, Moiemen NS. Non-accidental burns in children—are we neglecting neglect? Burns 2006;32(2):222-8.

[51]   Daria S, Sugar NF, Feldman KW, Boos SC, Benton SA, Ornstein A. Into hot water head first: distribution of intentional and unintentional immersion burns. Pediatr Emerg Care 2004;20(5):302-10.

[52]   Williams EE, Griffiths TA. Psychological consequences of burn injury. Burns 1991;17(6):478-80.

[53]   Partridge J, Robinson E. Psychological and social aspects of burns. Burns 1995;21(6):453-7.

[54]   Altier N, Malenfant A, Forget R, Choiniere M. Long-term adjustment in burn victims: A matched-control study. Psychol Med 2002;32(04):677-85.

[55]   Bakker A, Maertens KJ, Van Son MJ, Van Loey NE. Psychological consequences of pediatric burns from a child and family perspective: A review of the empirical literature. Clin Psychol Rev 2013;33(3):361-71.

[56]   Zeitlin REK. Long-term psychosocial sequelae of paediatric burns. Burns 1997;23(6):467-72.

[57]   Lane WG, Dubowitz H, Langenberg P, Dischinger P. Epidemiology of abusive abdominal trauma hospitalizations in United States children. Child Abuse Negl 2012;36(2):142-8.

[58]   Maguire SA, Upadhyaya M, Evans A, Mann MK, Haroon MM, Tempest V, Lumb RC, Kemp AM. A systematic review of abusive visceral injuries in childhood—their range and recognition. Child Abuse Negl 2013;37(7):430-45.

[59] Herr SM. Abdominal and Chest Injuries in Abused Children. In: Jenny C, ed. Child abuse and neglect: Diagnosis, treatment, and evidence. St. Louis, MO: Elsevier, 2011:326.

[60] Canty TG, Brown C. Injuries of the gastrointestinal tract from blunt trauma in children: A 12-year experience at a designated pediatric trauma center. J Trauma Acute Care Surg 1999;46(2):234-40.

[61] Cooper A, Floyd T, Barlow B, Niemerska M, Ludwig S, Seidl T, et al. Major blunt abdominal trauma due to child abuse. J Trauma Acute Care Surg 1988;28(10):1483-7.

[62] Trokel M, DiScala C, Terrin NC, Sege RD. Blunt abdominal injury in the young pediatric patient: Child abuse and patient outcomes. Child Maltreat 2004;9(1):111-7.

[63] Lane WG, Lotwin I, Dubowitz H, Langenberg P, Dischinger P. Outcomes for children hospitalized with abusive versus noninflicted abdominal trauma. Pediatrics 2011;127(6):e1400-5.

[64] Segui-Gomez M, Chang DC, Paidas CN, Jurkovich GJ, MacKenzie EJ, Rivara FP. Pediatric trauma care: An overview of pediatric trauma systems and their practices in 18 US states. J Pediatr Surg 2003;38(8):1162-9.

[65] Irazuzta J, McJunkin JE, Danadian K, Arnold F, Zhang J. Outcome and cost of child abuse. Child Abuse Negl 1997;21(8):751-7.

[66] Fang X, Brown DS, Florence CS, Mercy JA. The economic burden of child maltreatment in the United States and implications for prevention. Child Abuse Negl 2012;36(2):156-65.

[67] Peterson C, Xu L, Florence C, Parks SE. Annual cost of US hospital visits for pediatric abusive head trauma. Child Maltreat 2015; 20(3):162-9.

[68] Corso PS, Fertig AR. The economic impact of child maltreatment in the United States: Are the estimates credible? Child Abuse Negl 2010;34(5):296-304.

[69] Brown DS, Fang X, Florence CS. Medical costs attributable to child maltreatment: A systematic review of short-and long-term effects. Am J Prev Med 2011;41(6):627-35.

[70] Zenel JA. Failure to thrive: A general pediatrician's perspective. Pediatr Rev 1997;18:371-8.

[71] Kleinman RE. Failure to thrive (pediatric undernutrition). In: Kleinman RE, ed. Pediatric nutrition handbook, 5th ed. Elk Grove Village, IL: American Academy of Pediatrics 2003:443-57.

[72] Block RW, Krebs NF, and the American Academy of Pediatrics. Clinical report on failure to thrive as a manifestation of child neglect. Pediatrics 2005;116;1234.

[73] Mei Z, Grummer-Strawn LM, Thompson D, Dietz W. Shifts in percentiles of growth during early childhood: Analysis of longitudinal data from the California Child Health and Development Study. Pediatrics 2004;113(6):e617-27.

[74] Frank DA, Zeisel SH. Failure to thrive. Pediatr Clin North Am 1988;35:1187-1206.

[75] Kleinman RE. Failure to thrive. In: Kleinman RE, ed. Pediatric nutrition handbook, 7th ed. Elk Grove Village, IL: American Academy of Pediatrics 2013:664-700.

[76] Coleman-Jensen A, Rabbitt MP, Gregory C, Singh A. Household food security in the United States in 2014, ERR-194, US Department of Agriculture, Economic Research Service, 2015. URL: www.ers.usda.gov/media/1896841/err194.pdf.

[77] Drotar D, Sturm L. Prediction of intellectual development in young children with early histories of nonorganic failure-to-thrive. J Pediatr Psychol 1988;13:281-96.

[78] Skuse D, Pickles A, Wolke D, Reilly S. Postnatal growth and mental development: Evidence for a "sensitive period." J Child Psychol Psychiatry 1994;35:521-45.

[79] Frank DA, Silva M, Needlman R. Failure to thrive: Mystery, myth, and method. Contemp Pediatr 1993;10:114-33.

[80] Weston JA, Colloton M, Halsey S, Covington S, Gilbert J, Sorrentino-Kelly L, et al. A legacy of violence in nonorganic failure to thrive. Child Abuse Negl 1993;17:709-14.

[81] Oates RK, Kempe RS. Growth failure in infants. In: Helfer ME, Kempe RS, Krugman RD, eds. The battered child, 5th ed. Chicago, IL: University of Chicago Press, 1997:374-91.

[82] Galler JR, Ramsey F, Solimano G, Lowell WE, Mason E. The influence of early malnutrition on subsequent behavioral development I. Degree of impairment in intellectual performance. J Am Acad Child Psychiatry 1982;22(1):8-15.

[83] Silver J, DiLorenzo P, Zukoski M, Ross PE, Amster BJ, Schlegel D. Starting young: Improving the health and development outcomes of infants and toddlers in the child welfare system. Child Welfare 1999;78(1):148-65.

[84] Drewett RF, Corbett SS, Wright CM. Cognitive and educational attainments at school age of children who failed to thrive in infancy: A population-based study. J Child Psychol Psychiatry 1999;40(4):551-61.

[85] Galler JR, Ramsey F, Solimano G. The influence of early malnutrition on subsequent behavioral development III: Learning disabilities as a sequel of malnutrition. Pediatr Res 1984;18(4):309-13.

[86] Galler JR, Ramsey F, Solimano G. A follow-up study of the effects of early malnutrition on subsequent behavioral development II: Fine motor skills in adolescence. Pediatr Res 1985;19(6):524-7.

[87] Mendez MA, Adair LS. Severity and timing of stunting on the first two years of life affect performance on cognitive tests in late childhood. J Nutr 1999;129(8):1555-62.

[88] Black MM, Hutcheson JJ, Dubowitz H, Berenson-Howard J. Parenting style and developmental status among children with nonorganic failure to thrive. J Pediatr Psychol 1994;19(6):689-707.

[89] Drotar D, Eckerle D. The Family environment in nonorganic failure to thrive: a controlled study. J Pediatr Psychol 1989;14(2):245-57.

[90] McKay H, Sinisterra L, McKay A, Gomez H, Lloreda P. Improving cognitive ability in chronically deprived children. Science 1978;200(4339):270-8.

[91] Zeskind PS, Ramey CT. Fetal malnutrition: An experimental study of its consequences on infant development in two caregiving environment. Child Dev 1978;49(4):1155-62.

[92] Prado EL, Dewey KG. Nutrition and brain development in early life. Nutr Rev 2014;72(4):267-84.

[93] Levitsky DA, Barnes RH. Nutritional and environmental interactions in the behavioral development of the rat: Long-term effects. Science 1972;176(4030);68-71.

[94] Brown JL, Pollitt E. Malnutrition, poverty and intellectual development. Scientific American 1996;274(2):38-43.

[95] Dobbing J. Infant nutrition and later achievement. Nutr Rev 1984;42(1):1-7.

[96] Drotar D, Sturm LA. Psychological assessment and intervention with failure to thrive infants and their families. In: Olson M, Mullins L, Gillman P, eds. Sourcebook of pediatric psychology. Baltimore, MD: Johns Hopkins Press, 1994:26-41.

[97] Drotar D, Sturm LA. Personality development, problem solving, and behavior problems among preschool children with early histories of nonorganic failure-to-thrive: A controlled study. J Dev Behav Pediatr 1992;13(4):266-273.

[98] Powell GF, Low J. Behavior in nonorganic failure to thrive. J Dev Behav Pediatr 1983;4(1):26-33.

[99] Ramey CT, Yeates KO, Short EJ. The plasticity of intellectual development: Insights from preventative intervention. Child Dev 1984;55(5):1913-25.

[100] Polan HJ, Leon A, Kaplan MD, Kessler DB, Stern DN, Ward MJ, Disturbances of affect expression in failure-to-thrive. J Am Acad Child Adolesc Psychiatry 1991;30(6):897-903.

[101] Wolke D, Skuse D, Mathisen B. Behavioral style in failure to thrive infants: A preliminary communication. J Pediatr Psychol 1990;15(2):237-54.

[102] Black MM, Dubowitz H, Krishnakumar A, Starr RH. Early intervention and recovery among children with failure to thrive: Follow-up at age 8. Pediatrics 2007;120(1):59-69.

[103] Walker SP, Chang SM, Vera-Hernandez M, Grantham-McGregor S. Early childhood stimulation benefits adult competence and reduces violent behavior. Pediatrics 2011;127(5):849-57.

[104] Rudolf MCJ, Logan S. What is the long term outcome for children who fail to thrive? A systematic review. Arch Dis Child 2005;90:925-31.

[105] Dube SR, Felitti VJ, Dong M, Giles WH, Anda RF. The impact of adverse childhood experiences on health problems: evidence from four birth cohorts dating back to 1900. Prev Med 2003;37(3):268-277.

In: Child Abuse: Children with Disabilities
Editors: V. J Palusci, D. Nazer et al.

ISBN: 978-1-53612-035-6
© 2017 Nova Science Publishers, Inc.

Chapter 6

TRAGEDY OF SIBLING ABUSE OF CHILDREN WITH DISABILITIES

Donald E Greydanus[1],, MD, DrHC(Athens),FAAP*
Elizabeth K Hawver[2], MSW
and Joav Merrick[3-7], MD, MMedSc, DMSc

[1]Department of Pediatric and Adolescent Medicine,
Western Michigan University Homer Stryker MD
School of Medicine, Kalamazoo, Michigan, United States
[2]Private Practice Behavioral Therapy, Kalamazoo, Michigan, US
[3]National Institute of Child Health and Human Development, Jerusalem
[4]Office of the Medical Director, Health Services,
Division for Intellectual and Developmental Disabilities,
Ministry of Social Affairs and Social Services, Jerusalem
[5]Division of Pediatrics, Hadassah Hebrew University Medical Center,
Mt Scopus Campus, Jerusalem, Israel
[6]Kentucky Children's Hospital, University of Kentucky
School of Medicine, Lexington, Kentucky, US
[7]Center for Healthy Development, School of Public Health,
Georgia State University, Atlanta, US

---

* Correspondence: Professor Donald E Greydanus, MD, DrHC(Athens), Department of Pediatrics and Adolescent Medicine, Western Michigan University Homer Stryker MD School of Medicine, 1000 Oakland Drive, Oakland Drive Campus, Kalamazoo, MI, 49008-8048, United States.
E-mail: donald.greydanus@med.wmich.edu.

The literature of Homo sapiens and research by scientists have attested to the high frequency and the severe consequences of sibling abuse seen in families around the world. Often hidden or ignored by society, such exploitation is the most common form of abuse found in humans. Underpinnings to this phenomenon of desecration of our children are many, but tend to focus on family dysfunction, lack of education in parenting provided to most parents, and the underlying violent nature of humankind. This discussion presents concepts of sibling abuse found in all societies for thousands of years that has been hinted at in children's fables and finally studied by research in the 20th and 21st centuries.

INTRODUCTION

Now Cain said to his brother Abel, "Let's go out to the field." While they were in the field, Cain attacked his brother Abel and killed him (Genesis 4:8).

> Genesis 37:3
> Jacob loved Joseph more than any of his other children because Joseph had been born to him in his old age. So one day Jacob had a special gift made for Joseph--a beautiful robe.

> Genesis: 37:17-20, 26-28: So Joseph went after his brothers and found them near Dothan. But they saw him in the distance, and before he reached them, they plotted to kill him. "Here comes that dreamer!" they said to each other. "Come now, let's kill him and throw him into one of these cisterns and say that a ferocious animal devoured him. Then we'll see what comes of his dreams."

Judah said to his brothers, "What will we gain if we kill our brother and cover up his blood? Come, let's sell him to the Ishmaelites and not lay our hands on him; after all, he is our brother, our own flesh and blood." His brothers agreed. So when the Midianite merchants came by, his brothers pulled Joseph up out of the cistern and sold him for twenty shekels[a] of silver to the Ishmaelites, who took him to Egypt.

The world's first murder was recorded in Genesis (Greek for "origin"), the first book of the Pentateuch, that perhaps was written in the 6th century BCE. In the story of the world's first family, Cain kills his brother Abel over perceived favoritism by God for Abel versus Cain (Genesis 4:3-8). This represents the first example in the culture of the Middle East and Western civilization of sibling abuse and the underlying factor of perceived favoritism of one sibling over another. Another example of sibling abuse is found in the Old Testament story of Joseph, favored by his father Jacob (Israel), causing much anger and resentment by Joseph's many brothers who at first were plotting to kill their youngest brother but then decided to get rid of him by selling 17 year old Joseph into slavery perhaps around 2000 BC (Genesis 37:3-27).

FREQUENCY OF SIBLING ABUSE

Such stories are a harbinger to the high frequency of sibling to sibling abuse that has been seen in many families in all cultures throughout the history of human beings. Research in the 20th and 21st centuries have confirmed that such stories, including classic childhood fables, have hinted at for thousands of years. Though society often ignores the phenomenon of sibling abuse, this tragic reality has occurred and continues to occur with dramatically negative consequences for all our children, especially those with disabilities.

In the last decade of the 20th century researchers stunned the scientific community with their data that 37% of 498 studied children noted they had executed one or more "serious" act (s) of aggression against one or more of their siblings; these families were described as being "non-pervasively" abusive (1). In families identified as "pervasively" abusive, such sibling abuse was found in 100% (1). Researchers Straus and Gelles have reported that 3 in 100 siblings are "dangerously violent" toward a sibling (2, 3).

The idea of one sibling killing another has continued from the Cain-Abel story to the present. For example, a 2006 publication detailed the killing of a 6 month old female infant by her 10 year old sister who threw her out of a window (4). The older sibling was described as having a diagnosis of autism spectrum disorder complicated by epilepsy and family dysfunction that included limited supervision of these siblings (4). Another group published a paper in 2015 about an 8 year old brother who killed his 18 month old sister also by defenestration; the older sibling had a history of violence and autism spectrum disorder (5).

Most of the aggressive acts between siblings, fortunately, does not result in death of a child. The aggression is usually the older and large sibling (s) on younger and smaller sibling (s). The 2006 published research by Straus Gelles, and Steinmetz noted that 74% of siblings are aggressive toward other siblings at some time that involved pushing or shoving (6). In this same study it was noted that 42% bite and/or punch their siblings and 85% of siblings are verbally abusive to other siblings on a regular basis (6). The University of Kentucky researcher, Vernon Wiehe, has noted that as many as 53% of children perform one or more severe acts of aggression against one or more siblings and that sibling to sibling abuse is more common than abuse found in spouse to spouse abuse and parent to child abuse (3).

Such aggression by older siblings can result in variable injury to younger sibling(s) (7). If an 18 month old girl (21 pounds, 31 inches) is attacked by a 3 year old brother (30 pounds, 36 inches), a 5 year old brother (45 pounds, 43 inches), a 7 year old sister (58 pounds, 50 inches), and a 9 year old brother (63 pounds, 52 inches), their combined weight of nearly 200 pounds can do considerable damage to this 18 month old which can include bone or organ fractures, severe hemorrhaging, and even death (7). Such behavior could be intentional and/or reflect modeling behavior seen in the world of these children that includes family violence and aggression seen in movies, television and one's internet as well as one's neighborhood (7).

Sexual violence between siblings is another form of sibling to sibling abuse and is discussed in chapter 5. In 1978 Finkelhor published his research noting that 15% of female college females indicated they had been raped by a sibling and 10% of male college students reported they had suffered rape by a sibling (8). Sexual abuse between siblings can be repeated over many years and can result in catastrophic damage to the victim as noted in chapter 5 (9-12).

ETIOLOGIC FACTORS BEHIND SIBLING ABUSE

Reasons for siblings abusing their sibling (s) are many and complex but often reflect underlying family dysfunction (7). The stories of Cain killing Abel or the Pentateuch figure, Joseph, being sold into slavery by his older brothers reflect the paradox of jealousy. For example, Joseph was the favorite son of his father, Jacob, who may have had good reason to love his youngest son the most; however, this was not appreciated by the older brothers. Joseph's story turned out favorable in the end. Many other victim of sibling abuse do not turn out so well.

The childhood fable of Cinderella deals with jealousy of a step-mother for the beautiful Cinderella. It was originally written by 17th century French writer Charles Perrault (1628-1703) (13). Though this step-mother seeks great harm for this young girl, fate has a better ending for Cinderella as she is granted a better destiny by her Prince Charming at the end of the story. Parental anger or jealousy at an offspring, whether biological or novercal, is not an unusual story in human history, and can fuel direct harm to a child or secondary harm via siblings. Study of childhood fables can teach much about human nature. As noted by Albert Einstein (1879-1955): "If you want your children to be intelligent, read them fairy tales. If you want them to be more intelligent, read them more fairy tales."

Family dysfunction can include the abuse of one spouse toward another that may or may not also include parental abuse of one or more of the children in the house. A father or stepfather may sexual abuse one of the children and move to others over time. Siblings can also model abusive behavior and older siblings may abuse younger ones after seeing such abuse by adults in their household. Researchers Pfout, Schopler and Henley published data in 1982 that indicated 60% of children abused younger siblings after observing their father abuse their mother; this pattern was called "second hand abuse (14)."

Family dysfunction can reflect absent parents that includes parents or stepparents who do not bond with the children in the house for various reasons. They may reflect the parenting that they received when they were children. This may also be complicated by the reality that few parents receive comprehensive training in parenting skills before they biologically become parents and/or marry into a family with children biologically belong to other adults. Such families are quite complex and considerable family and individual therapy is necessary to deal with the potential damage that children in such settings suffer (11, 12).

Another factor contributing to violence seen between siblings is that it reflects the underlying violent and aggressive nature of Homo sapiens who emerged from a violent evolution over many millennia and perhaps emerged successfully because of being a successfully violent species (15). Weak, disabled children are especially targeted as a tool to increase evolutionally efficiency. The violence of humans reflected in the aggression found in some children was dramatically reflected in the 1954 novel by Nobel Prize winning British author William Golding called "Lord of the flies." Boys are isolated on a tropical island during a mythical nuclear war. In the absent of parents or adult supervision, the author depicts the aggressive nature of children in which older children (10-12 years of age) abuse younger ones (6 years of age) that includes the killing of two of the children. The story concludes with the saving of another child about to be killed because an adult arrives on the island to save this child from the other children who have turned into aggressive, savage, frightened persons.

> [Jack] tried to convey the compulsion to track down and
> kill that was swallowing him up.
> "I went on. I thought, by myself—"
> The madness came into his eyes again.
> "I thought I might kill"
> Lord of the Flies (William Golding, 1954)

CONCLUSION

Research notes that sibling abuse is the most common form of abuse seen in families. Siblings attacking their siblings whether in childhood or even adulthood has been noted in fiction such as classic fable tales or novels and such stories are collaborated by scientists studying human behavior. It is typically older and stronger siblings abusing younger brothers or sisters and includes physical as well as sexual abuse in single or repeated events and in a single occurrence or a repeated pattern.

> The rock struck Piggy a glancing blow from chin to knee; the conch exploded into a thousand white fragments and ceased to exist. Piggy, saying nothing, with no time for even a grunt, traveled through the air sideways from the rock, turning over as he went [...]. Piggy fell forty feet and landed on his back across the square red rock in the sea. His head opened and stuff came out and turned red. Piggy's arms and legs twitched a bit, like a pig's after it has been killed
> Lord of the Flies (William Golding, 1954)

Causes are many and include family dysfunction complicated by limited education in parenting skills as well as an underlying milieu in human history of extreme violence and aggression. Children can model behavior seen in their adult supervisors. Improvement in such a vitriolic violation of children begins with recognition of this common pattern of aggression and intense therapy for those who are victims of sibling abuse. Religious works, fiction, and research all agree and converge on this tragic phenomenon of human existence.

> All at once, Robert was screaming and struggling with the strength of frenzy. Jack had him by the hair and was brandishing his knife.
> Behind him was Roger, fighting to get close. The chant rose ritually, as at the last moment of a dance or a hunt. "Kill the pig! Cut his throat! Kill the pig! Bash him in!" Ralph too was fighting to get near, to get a handful of that brown, vulnerable flesh. The desire to squeeze and hurt was over-mastering
> Lord of the Flies (William Golding, 1954)

REFERENCES

[1]	Hotaling GT, Straus MA, Lincoln A. Intrafamily violence and crime and violence outside the family. In: Straus MA, Gelles RJ, eds. Physical violence in American families: Risk factors and adaptions to violence in 8,145 familes. New Brunswick, NY: Transaction Publishers, 1990:431- 70.

[2]	Straus MA, Gelles RJ. Physical violence in American families: Risk factors and adaptions to violence in 8,145 families. New Brunswick, NY: Transaction Publishers, 1990.

[3]	Sibling abuse. URL: https://en.wikipedia-org/wiki/Sibling_abuse.

[4]	Mukaddes NM, Topcu Z. Case report: Homicide by a 10-year-old girl with autistic disorder. J Autism Dev Dis 2006;36(4):471-4.

[5]	Sabuncuoglu O, Irmak MY, Demir NU, Murat D, Tumba C, Yilmaz Y. Sibling death after being thrown from window by brother with autism: defenestration, an emerging high-risk behavior. Case Rep Psychiatry 2015. Article ID 463694. doi.org/10.1155/2015/463694.

[6]	Straus MA, Gelles RJ, Steinmetz SK. Behind closed doors: Violence in the American family. Piscataway, NJ: Transaction Publishers, 2006.

[7]	Apple R, Greydanus D, White K. Sibling abuse: an often unrecognized family history. Clin Pediatr Open Access 2016;1(2):10-6.

[8]   Finkelhor D. Psychological, cultural, and family factors in incest and family sexual abuse. J Marriage Fam Couns 1978;4:41-79.

[9]   Dunn J. Sibling influences on childhood development. J Child Psychol Psychiatry 1988;29(2):119-27.

[10]   Katz C, Hammama L. From my own brother in my own home: children's experiences and perceptions following alleged sibling incest. J Internpers Violence 2015 Aug 30. pii: 0886260515600876.

[11]   Caffaro J, Conn-Carraro A. Treating sibling abuse families. Aggression Violent Behav 2005;10(5):604-23.

[12]   Caffaro J. Sibling abuse trauma, 2nd ed. New York: Routledge, 2013.

[13]   Charles Perrault. URL: htts//en.wikipedia.org/wiki/Charles.Perrault.

[14]   Pfouts J, Schopler J, Henley C. Forgotten victims of family violence. Soc Work 1982;27(3):367.

[15]   Archer J. Can evolutionary principles explain patterns of family violence? Psychol Bull 2013;139(2):403-40.

In: Child Abuse: Children with Disabilities
Editors: V. J Palusci, D. Nazer et al.

ISBN: 978-1-53612-035-6
© 2017 Nova Science Publishers, Inc.

Chapter 7

DISABILITY AND ABUSE: SOME INTERNATIONAL ASPECTS

Joav Merrick[1-5],*, *MD, MMedSc, DMSc*

[1]National Institute of Child Health and Human Development, Jerusalem
[2]Office of the Medical Director, Health Services,
[3]Division for Intellectual and Developmental Disabilities,
Ministry of Social Affairs and Social Services, Jerusalem
Division of Pediatrics, Hadassah Hebrew University Medical Center, Mt Scopus
Campus, Jerusalem, Israel
[4]Kentucky Children's Hospital, University of Kentucky School of Medicine,
Lexington, Kentucky, United States of America
[5]Center for Healthy Development, School of Public Health,
Georgia State University, Atlanta, US

Children and adults with disabilities are at risk of neglect and maltreatment, and studies have linked adverse childhood experiences to leading causes of adult morbidity and mortality. Abuse and neglect does have a long term effect, and it appears that disabilities associated with interpersonal and behavioral difficulties are most strongly associated with victimization risks. In this discussion. International disability prevalence is reviewed and the connection between disability and maltreatment. Stigma, discrimination and ignorance about disability are factors which place people with disabilities at higher risk of violence. Prevention and early detection is therefore important public health aspects.

* Correspondence: Professor Joav Merrick, MD, MMedSci, DMSc, Medical Director, Health Services, Division for Intellectual and Developmental Disabilities, Ministry of Social Affairs and Social Services, POBox 1260, IL-91012 Jerusalem, Israel. E-mail: jmerrick@zahav.net.il.

INTRODUCTION

Children and adults with disabilities have for a very long time, even back to pre-historic times, been subject to abuse and neglect or even in the extreme to murder.

Disability abuse is when a person with a disability is abused physically, financially, sexually or psychologically due to the person having a disability (1). Since some disabled people are in need of additional support from others throughout their lives, they are also vulnerable to neglect (1). The abuse is not limited to those who are visibly disabled, such as wheelchair-users or physically deformed such as those with a cleft lip, but also those with learning disabilities or difficulties such as dyslexia and dysgraphia and other disabilities, including Asperger's syndrome, Down syndrome and developmental coordination disorder (1).

Disability is something that can happen to any of us and almost everyone will be temporarily or permanently impaired or disabled during their lifetime or at the end of our lifespan.

Disability is the umbrella term for impairments, activity limitations and participation restrictions, referring to the negative aspects of the interaction between an individual (with a health condition) and that individual's contextual factors (environmental and personal factors) (2).

DISABILITY AROUND THE WORLD

It is not easy to get a clear picture of the scope of disability around the world. This is due to the multidimensional scope of the issue at hand, definition issues and data collection methods, which vary from country to country.

There are two international surveys that can be used to estimate the burden of disability in the world: The WHO (World Health Organization) "World health survey" from 2002-2004 and the WHO "Global burden of disease study" from 2004 (2).

The "World health survey" was a face-to-face household survey in 70 countries, where 59 countries had weighted data sets that were used to estimate the prevalence of disability in adults aged 18 years and older (2). The average prevalence rate in the adult population aged 18 years and older from these 59 countries was 15.6% or some 650 million people in 2004 ranging from 11.8% in higher income countries to 18% in lower income countries for adults with significant difficulties in function in their everyday life and 2.2% (or 92 million people) with very significant difficulties (2). If the estimate went to cover 15 years and older the numbers were 720 million for significant and 100 million for very significant disabilities (2).

The "Global burden of disease" study started in 1990 on the initiative of the World Bank in order to assess the relative burden of premature mortality and disability from different diseases, injuries and risk factors (2). The analysis of the "Global burden of disease" 2004 data estimated that 15.3% of the world population (some 978 million people in 2004) had "moderate or severe disability," while 2.9% (185 million) experienced "severe disability." Among those aged 0–14 years, the figures were 5.1% and 0.7% or 93 million and 13 million children, respectively. Among those 15 years and older, the figures were 19.4% and 3.8% or 892 million and 175 million, respectively (2).

In the "World report on disability" from 2011 (2) and estimates for the 2010 population based on the "World health survey" and the "Global burden of disease" it was postulated that 785 (15.6%) to 975 (19.4%) million persons 15 years and older were living with disability. Of these, around 110 (2.2%) to 190 (3.8%) million experienced significant difficulties in functioning. Including children, over a billion people (or about 15% of the world's population) were estimated to be living with disability (2).

DISABILITY AND ABUSE AROUND THE WORLD

If it is hard to get data on disability prevalence around the world, then it is even harder to get data on abuse prevalence and people with a disability (3).

One study (4) in 2012 from the United States using an online questionnaire included 7,289 people from 50 states and the District of Columbia with 20.2% having a disability themselves and 47.4% having an immediate family member with a disability. Over 70% of people with disabilities who took the survey reported they had been victims of abuse. More than 63% of parents and immediate family members reported that their loved one with a disability had experienced abuse (4).

Some disability types had a higher incidence of abuse than others. For example, 74.8% of people with mental health conditions reported they had been victims of abuse, while 67.1% of those with a speech disability, 66.5% of those with autism, 62.5% of those with an intellectual or developmental disability and 55.2% of those with a mobility disability reported having experienced such abuse (4).

The people with disabilities in 87.2% reported verbal-emotional abuse, 50.6% physical abuse, 41.6% sexual abuse, 37.3% neglect and 31.5% financial abuse (4). The rate of sexual abuse varied greatly among victims depending on the type of disabilities they had with 47.4% of people with mental health conditions reported they had been victims of sexual abuse, whereas 34.2% of those with intellectual or developmental disabilities, 31.6% of those with a mobility disability and 24.9% of those with autism reported they had experienced sexual abuse (4).

Studies published in the English language during 1995-2005 were reviewed for the prevalence of maltreatment of people with intellectual disabilities (5) and found results from Australia, England, Spain and the United States. Only five studies provided maltreatment prevalence estimates and the limited data suggested that maltreatment was more prevalent for people with intellectual disabilities than for people with certain other disabilities

A recent report from Mexico (6) based on the results of a year-long study carried out by Disability Rights International (DRI) together with the Women's Group of the Colectivo Chuhcan –the first organization in Mexico directed by persons with psychosocial disabilities. This research included the application of a questionnaire to fifty-one women with psychosocial disabilities who were either members of the Colectivo Chuhcan or received outpatient services at four different health clinics and psychiatric institutions in Mexico City. The report found that an appalling 40% of the women interviewed – all with psychosocial or psychiatric disabilities – had been forcibly, surgically sterilized or had been coerced by their families to undergo the procedure. Additionally, over 40% also reported being abused by their gynecologist, which included sexual assault and rape (6).

In a large British study (7) of 14,256 children participating, 115 had been identified as having been placed on local child protection registers prior to their 6th birthday. Data on the children have been obtained from obstetric data and from a series of parental questionnaires administered during pregnancy and the first three years of life. Significant relationships were found between low birthweight, unintended pregnancies, poor health and developmental problems in infancy and subsequent maltreatment (7).

Dating violence is another topic of interest in this context and one study (8) examined associations of dating violence with health risks by disability status among high school girls' data from the 2009 Massachusetts Youth Health Survey. Among high school students who had ever been on a date, girls (25.9%) and boys (9.1%) with disabilities were more likely than girls (8.8%) and boys (4.5%) without disabilities to report dating violence (8). The study indicated that high school girls with disabilities who experienced dating violence were more likely to report feeling sad or hopeless for two weeks or more in the past year, suicide ideation in the past 12 months and drug use in the past 30 days compared to those with disabilities who did not report dating violence and those without disabilities who reported and did not report dating violence.

A study from Uganda (9) of 3,706 children and young adolescents aged 11-14 years were randomly sampled from 42 primary schools and 8.8% of boys and 7.6% of girls reported a disability. Levels of violence against both disabled and non-disabled children were extremely high. Disabled girls report slightly more physical (99.1% versus 94.6%) and considerably more sexual violence (23.6% versus 12.3%) than non-disabled girls, while for disabled and non-disabled boys, levels are not statistically different (9).

A study from Hong Kong (10) with 5,841 school-aged children aged 9-18 years found the prevalence of disability among children at 6% and children with disability were more likely to report victimization than those without disability: 32% to 60% of the former had experienced child maltreatment and 12% to 46% of them had witnessed inter-personal violence between parents or in-law conflict. Disability increased the risk of lifetime physical maltreatment by 1.6 times.

RISK FACTORS

Stigma, discrimination and ignorance about disability are factors which place people with disabilities at higher risk of violence. Placement of people with disabilities in institutions or supported care can increase their vulnerability to violence. Safe Place (11) have listed some risk factors in this population:

- Persons with physical disabilities may rely on others to meet some of their basic needs. Care providers may be involved in the most intimate and personal parts of the individual's life, which can increase the opportunity for abusive acts. Persons with physical disabilities may also be less likely to defend themselves or to escape violent situations.
- Persons with cognitive disabilities may be overly trusting of others and easier to trick, bribe or coerce. The individual may not understand the differences between sexual and non-sexual touches.
- Persons with cognitive disabilities who are abused may not understand that the violation is not alright, especially in cases of sexual abuse.
- Persons who are deaf may not be able to report due to barriers with communication (including lack of an interpreter and/or assistive devices).
- Persons with disabilities that impact articulation may have limited vocabulary or communication skills that can pose barriers to disclosing abuse. The individual may be misunderstood or viewed as intoxicated or making a prank call when making a report. Communication boards need to include vocabulary for reporting abuse and neglect.
- Many people with disabilities are taught to be obedient, passive, and to control difficult behaviors.

- This compliance training may teach the individual to be a "good victim" of abuse.
- Many persons with disabilities grow up without receiving sexuality education, abuse prevention information or self-defense training. Individuals may lack knowledge about their bodies, healthy relationships, and how to protect themselves.
- A person who has a mental illness can be at risk for victimization if they have difficulty discerning between reality and fantasy, are dependent on others for their mental and physical care, view themselves as unworthy, do not trust their instincts, and/or misinterpret the intentions of others.
- Persons with disabilities may be perceived by offenders as easy targets based on a perceived lack of credibility within society, and a lower likelihood that the person will not speak out.
- Society generally views people with disabilities as non-sexual, lacking intelligence, and not credible witnesses.
- In general, social isolation is associated with higher risk for sexual abuse. Unfortunately, many people with disabilities still face barriers to fully participate in the community and remain socially isolated.

This is just some of the risk factors that we must have in mind when providing care to people with disabilities in order to prevent maltreatment.

In a representative national sample of 4,046 children aged 2-17 years of age from the 2008 National Survey of Children's Exposure to Violence, the associations between several different types of disability and past-year exposure to multiple forms of child victimization were examined (12). It was found that attention-deficit disorder/attention-deficit with hyperactivity disorder elevated the risk for peer victimization and property crime, internalizing psychological disorders increased risk for both child maltreatment and sexual victimization, and developmental/learning disorders heighten risk only for property crime. Physical disability did not increase the risk for any type of victimization (12).

RIGHTS

The convention on the rights of persons with disabilities (CRPD), adopted in 2006 with its comprehensive new model of care, has created an opportunity for change, which over time should provide better integration, inclusion, quality of life and health for this group of people. The convention is also a tool or instrument for health care professionals to use in order to create and demand better healthcare and services from their government or ministries (13).

Articles 15, 16 and 17 are important and relevant in the context of this discussion:

Article 15: Freedom from torture or cruel, inhuman or degrading treatment or punishment

1. No one shall be subjected to torture or to cruel, inhuman or degrading treatment or punishment. In particular, no one shall be subjected without his or her free consent to medical or scientific experimentation.
2. States Parties shall take all effective legislative, administrative, judicial or other measures to prevent persons with disabilities, on an equal basis with others, from being subjected to torture or cruel, inhuman or degrading treatment or punishment.

Article 16: Freedom from exploitation, violence and abuse

1. States Parties shall take all appropriate legislative, administrative, social, educational and other measures to protect persons with disabilities, both within and outside the home, from all forms of exploitation, violence and abuse, including their gender-based aspects.
2. States Parties shall also take all appropriate measures to prevent all forms of exploitation, violence and abuse by ensuring, inter alia, appropriate forms of gender- and age-sensitive assistance and support for persons with disabilities and their families and caregivers, including through the provision of information and education on how to avoid, recognize and report instances of exploitation, violence and abuse. States Parties shall ensure that protection services are age-, gender- and disability-sensitive.
3. In order to prevent the occurrence of all forms of exploitation, violence and abuse, States Parties shall ensure that all facilities and programmes designed to serve persons with disabilities are effectively monitored by independent authorities.
4. States Parties shall take all appropriate measures to promote the physical, cognitive and psychological recovery, rehabilitation and social reintegration of persons with disabilities who become victims of any form of exploitation, violence or abuse, including through the provision of protection services. Such recovery and reintegration shall take place in an environment that fosters the

health, welfare, self-respect, dignity and autonomy of the person and takes into account gender- and age-specific needs.

5. States Parties shall put in place effective legislation and policies, including women- and child-focused legislation and policies, to ensure that instances of exploitation, violence and abuse against persons with disabilities are identified, investigated and, where appropriate, prosecuted.

Article 17: Protecting the integrity of the person

Every person with disabilities has a right to respect for his or her physical and mental integrity on an equal basis with others.

This convention and its more comprehensive and multidisciplinary model for care, service and rights will ensure that people with a disability have the right to be full and effective members of society and live a life without neglect or maltreatment.

CONCLUSION

Children and adults with disabilities are at risk of maltreatment and are often not noticed or detected by the professionals or systems taking care of them. Early intervention and prevention are important public health issues in this context.

A recent study (14) linked adverse childhood experiences to leading causes of adult morbidity and mortality. Compared to those who reported no adverse childhood experiences exposure, the adjusted odds of reporting myocardial infarction, asthma, fair/poor health, frequent mental distress, and disability were higher for those reporting one to three, four to six, or seven to nine adverse childhood experiences. Odds of reporting coronary heart disease and stroke were higher for those who reported four to six and seven to nine adverse childhood experiences, while odds of diabetes were higher for those reporting one to three and four to six adverse childhood experiences. So abuse and neglect does have a long term effect and it appears that disabilities associated with interpersonal and behavioral difficulties are most strongly associated with victimization risks.

REFERENCES

[1]   Wikipedia. Disability abuse. URL: https://en.wikipedia.org/wiki/Disability_abuse.
[2]   Officer A, Posarac A, eds. World report on disability. Geneva: World Health Organization, 2011.

[3]   Palusci VJ, Datner EL, Wilkins C. Abuse and neglect. In: Rubin IL, Merrick J, Greydanus DE, Patel DR, eds. Rubin-Crocker 3rd edition. Health care for people with intellectual and developmental disabilities across the lifespan. Cham, CH: Springer International, 2016:2011-32.

[4]   Baladerian NJ, Coleman TF, Stream J. A report on the 2012 National Survey on Abuse of People with Disabilities. Los Angeles, CA: Spectrum Institute, 2013.

[5]   Horner-Johnson W, Drum CE. Prevalence of maltreatment of people with intellectual disabilities: A review of recently published research. Ment Retard DeV Disabil Res Rev 2006;12:57-69.

[6]   Rodriguez P, Rosenthal E, Ahern L, Santos N, Cancino I, Chuhcan C, et al. Twice violated. Abuse and denial of sexual and reproductive rights of women with psychosocial disabilities in Mexico. Washington, DC: Disability Rights International, 2015.

[7]   Sidebotham P, Heron J, ALSPAC study team. Child maltreatment in the "children of the nineties": The role of the child. Child Abuse Negl 2003;27(3):337-52.

[8]   Mitra M, Mouradian VE, McKenna M. Dating violence and associated health risks among high school students with disabilities. Matern Child Health J 2013;17(6):1088-94.

[9]   Devries KM, Kyegombe N, Zuurmond M, Parkes J, Child JC, Walakira E, et al. Violence against primary school children with disabilities in Uganda: A cross-sectional study. BMC Public Health 2014;14:1017.

[10]   Chan KL, Emery CR, Ip P. Children with disability are more at risk of violence victimization: Evidence from a study of school-aged Chinese children. J Interpers Violence 2016;31(6):1026-46.

[11]   SafePlace. Risk factors to abuse/neglect faced by many people with disabilities. Austin, TX: Disability Services, 2012.

[12]   Turner HA, Vanderminden J, Finkelhor D, Hamby S, Shattuck A. Disability and victimization in a national sample of children and youth. Child Maltreat 2011;16(4):275-86.

[13]   Merrick J, Morad M. Health and the UN convention on the rights of persons with disabilities. In: Rubin IL, Merrick J, Greydanus DE, Patel DR, eds. Rubin-Crocker 3rd edition. Health care for people with intellectual and developmental disabilities across the lifespan. Cham, CH: Springer International, 2016:2267-88.

[14]   Gilbert LK, Breiding MJ, Merrick MT, Thompson WW, Ford DC, Dhingra SS, et al. Childhood adversity and adults chronic disease: An update from ten states and the District of Columbia, 2010. Am J Prev Med 2015;48(30:345-9.

SECTION TWO: ASSESSMENT, TREATMENT, REPORTING AND PREVENTION

In: Child Abuse: Children with Disabilities
Editors: V. J Palusci, D. Nazer et al.

ISBN: 978-1-53612-035-6
© 2017 Nova Science Publishers, Inc.

Chapter 8

EVALUATION OF PHYSICAL ABUSE AND NEGLECT IN CHILDREN WITH DISABILITIES

Dena Nazer[*], *MD, FAAP*

Wayne State University School of Medicine, Children's Hospital of Michigan, Kids-TALK Children's Advocacy Center, Detroit,
Michigan, US

Children with disabilities are at a much higher risk for physical abuse and neglect, as compared to those with no disabilities. Both these forms of child maltreatment may result in severe injury and ultimately in death with neglect being more associated with maltreatment deaths than any other kind of maltreatment. Not only should severe cases of physical abuse and neglect be recognized, but subtle indicators of abuse and sentinel injuries need to be identified by the different professionals caring for the child to identify children at risk and prevent further abuse. In addition, recognition of the child's needs and the multiple contributors to neglect at the level of the child, parents, family, community, and society is essential to address the child's needs and increase collaboration between the families and the different professionals caring for the child to prevent neglect. This article focuses on the medical evaluation of children who are suspected of being physically abused or neglected.

---

[*] Correspondence: Dena Nazer, MD, Kids-TALK Children's Advocacy Center Medical Clinic, 40 East Ferry St, Detroit, Michigan 48202, United States. E-mail: dnazer@med.wayne.edu.

INTRODUCTION

In the United States alone, child protective services (CPS) agencies received an estimated 3.6 million referrals involving approximately 6.6 million children in 2014 (1). The highest rate of victimization was in children less than 1 year of age with the most common type of maltreatment overall being neglect (75%) followed by physical abuse (17%). A nationally estimated number of 1580 children died as a result of maltreatment in 2014, mostly as a result of neglect and most of whom were younger than 3 years of age. When looking at these numbers, one realizes the increased vulnerability of children especially those that are younger than 3 years of age, and especially when coupled with disability and the increased demands placed on caregivers.

Reporting an accurate number of children with disability who are victims of child maltreatment is challenging due to disability not always being reported. In addition, not all children who are maltreated are assessed for the presence of a developmental disability. Further adding to the complexity are the diverse definitions of disability, the diverse definitions of child neglect, and what constitutes physical abuse. According to the American Association on Intellectual and Developmental Disabilities (AAIDD), developmental disabilities are severe chronic disabilities that can be cognitive (intellectual) or physical or both. The disabilities appear in childhood and are likely to be lifelong. Intellectual disability is a disability characterized by three essential elements: limitations in intellectual functioning (such as learning and reasoning), limitations in adaptive behavior, which covers many everyday social and practical skills, and onset originating before the age of 18 years. The term intellectual disability has replaced the previously used "mental retardation" term. Intellectual disability affects about one percent of the population, and of those about 85% have mild intellectual disability. Some disorders include both physical and intellectual disability such as fetal alcohol syndrome while others are mainly physical like cerebral palsy.

Children with disabilities are at a higher risk of child maltreatment as compared to children with no disability and providers need to be aware of this risk (2). The health care provider should be able to recognize injuries suspicious for physical abuse and differentiate abusive injuries from accidental injuries and those that result from conditions that mimic child abuse. Neglect also should be addressed with a focus on the needs of the child especially when the needs of children with disabilities are increased compared to other children. The health care provider is also tasked with the responsibility of coordinating the medical services needed to treat the underlying disability, consequences of the maltreatment, and collaborate with community agencies. In addition, the health care provider is mandated to report cases of physical abuse and neglect to the appropriate authorities to prevent the detrimental lifelong consequences including death resulting from these types of maltreatment.

PHYSICAL ABUSE

The World Health Organization (WHO) defines Child maltreatment as the abuse and neglect that occurs in children under 18 years of age. It includes all types of physical and/or emotional ill-treatment, sexual abuse, neglect, negligence and commercial or other exploitation, which results in actual or potential harm to the child's health, survival, development or dignity in the context of a relationship of responsibility, trust or power. Exposure to intimate partner violence is also sometimes included as a form of child maltreatment and may result in physical injuries to the child.

Although the exact definition of physical abuse may vary from one country to another and even in between States in the US, it commonly includes the presence of a non-accidental or inflicted injury that the child sustains by a caregiver. The definition of what constitutes physical abuse is influenced by one's professional experience and personal and cultural background (3).

Physical abuse results in both physical and mental health problems in children that may exacerbate the child's underlying medical condition and disability. It is also considered one of the adverse childhood experiences that leads to long term health consequences, chronic diseases and early death (4).

NEGLECT

Neglect is the most common reported form of child maltreatment in the US. Neglect is commonly defined in state law as the failure of a parent or other person with responsibility for the child to provide needed food, shelter, clothing, medical care, or supervision to the degree that the child's safety, health, and well-being are threatened with harm. Some states specifically mention types of neglect in their statutes such as medical neglect, educational neglect, and abandonment; in addition, some States include exceptions for determining neglect, such as financial considerations for physical neglect and religious exemptions for medical neglect. However, a more child focused definition of neglect as a condition when the child's needs are not met draws attention to the child's basic needs and allows a more collaborative approach between health providers and parents (5).

RISK FACTORS FOR PHYSICAL ABUSE AND NEGLECT

It is essential to identify the risk factors of child abuse when evaluating children with disabilities. Identifying the risk factors assists in identifying and creating prevention programs for families especially those that are identified as high risk. However, one has to remember that child abuse affects all children of different socioeconomic, religious, and ethnic backgrounds and the mere presence of these risk factors is not diagnostic. Infants and toddlers are at greatest risk for abuse, proving age of the child as the most significant risk factor for abuse. Children with disabilities--whether intellectual or physical--are at higher risk for physical abuse.

Risk factors for abuse and neglect include those that are parent-related (mental health disease, substance abuse, and interpersonal violence) and those that are child related (disability, prematurity, and low birth weight). Families who live in poverty, are socially isolated, and have lower level of education are at further risk for abuse. There are certain types of abusive injuries associated with specific developmental stages which may vary depending on the developmental abilities of the child. For example, abusive head trauma is associated with excessive crying and scald burns are associated with toilet training.

In addition, children with disabilities may place additional financial, social, physical, and emotional demands on their caregivers (6). A child may require closer supervision and assistance with performing daily routines such as hygiene which may overwhelm a caregiver who has limited support. Poverty and the lack of available services in the area the child resides in may further contribute to neglect and the child's needs not being met such as the lack of mental health services, affordable dental care, and the lack of a medical home which ensures comprehensive care is provided for a child.

CORPORAL PUNISHMENT

Parents of children with disability may struggle with discipline as children may not cognitively understand recommended methods of behavioral modification such as loss of privileges and time out. The American Academy of Pediatrics strongly opposes the use of physical punishment in children. Spanking, especially in infants, may be harmful and result in physical injuries especially when on sensitive areas such as the face (7). Laws differ in relation to what is acceptable and what constitutes acceptable physical discipline so one should be familiar with the laws and sensitive to the cultural norms and perspectives.

Appropriate discipline is a main concern for families with children especially for those who have children with disabilities. It is much harder to discipline a child with disability as the child may not comprehend loss of privileges or the reason for the discipline. However, parents of all children including those with disabilities need more guidance on acceptable and effective modes of discipline that do not result in injuries, physical or mental.

PRESENTATION OF PHYSICAL ABUSE AND NEGLECT

Children who are victims of physical abuse have various presentations depending on their age, developmental ability, type of injury and severity. The child may be brought in for routine care when a provider notices the presence of an injury, for example, a bruise or a burn on the child's body or the parent may bring the child in for care due to an injury for example pain and decreased mobility in an extremity. The child may also present with severe life-threatening manifestations. Making the diagnosis of physical abuse is difficult as one has to accept that the child's caregivers, who in many cases have a long standing relationship with the medical provider, injured the child (8). In addition, the highest risk of physical abuse is in the younger children who are nonverbal because of their age, disability, or as a complication of the physical injury. Caregivers may also not provide an accurate history and the presentation may be similar to other medical problems diverting the physician from making a diagnosis of physical abuse.

When evaluating a child for neglect, the provider needs to be sensitive, avoid blame, and engage the family in an active treatment plan (9). Proper communication is essential when evaluating any child especially when maltreatment is suspected. Families need to understand the concerns, the proposed plan of evaluation and the necessity to report certain cases to the appropriate organizations. The medical evaluation is a part of the multidisciplinary evaluation needed in cases of abuse and neglect and complements the additional assessments done by other services.

There are several elements in the history and physical examination that prompt the physician to initiate a child abuse physical assessment. Concerning factors include injury in a nonmobile or nonverbal child, inconsistent or changing history, unexplained delay in seeking medical care and a disclosure of physical abuse by a verbal child (8). As in other medical conditions, an evaluation consists of a medical history, physical examination, imaging and laboratory testing when needed.

MEDICAL HISTORY

Medical history is an important component of assessment of injuries and one should answer the question of whether a particular injury is consistent with the history provided.

Injuries may be different due to developmental abilities, verbal skills and how pain is felt and expressed. One should attempt to obtain a history from the child alone and from each caregiver separately. However, for nonverbal children, a history from the child of how the injury occurred would be lacking. Questions that may help include asking about the events that lead to the injury, details of the fall or injury, supervision, when was the child last well, and development and progression of symptoms.

All assessments of children with disabilities should include a developmental assessment in order to better understand the abilities of the child and whether the history is consistent with the injury. For example, while a healthy 1-year-old child may pull to stand and fall resulting in a bruise on his forehead, a developmentally delayed 4-year-old may not be able to do so, making a bruise suspicious in the latter case. Intellectual disability also needs to be considered; for example, a 16-year-old with intellectual disability may still need supervision around electric outlets, stoves and other potentially dangerous house hold objects.

Additional important elements in the history include information regarding the child's past medical history (hospitalizations, surgeries, and medical conditions), child's birth, and dietary history. An assessment of the child's needs as a result of these medical illnesses and disabilities helps determine the needs of the child and the challenges facing the family in securing these needs. It also provides a child's needs approach to child neglect vs. a parental omission approach which is less blaming, offers a broader response to contributing factors to the child's condition and is more constructive (5, 9).

A complete social history is crucial as it is the child's social environment that is a key determinant of the child's current and future health (10). A social history serves to identify both strengths to reinforce and weaknesses to address specifically in cases where neglect is suspected and a treatment plan is being formulated with the family. Adverse childhood experiences are directly linked to risky health behaviors, chronic health conditions, and early death. A comprehensive social history may help in prevention of these adverse experiences and thus decreasing their negative outcome (4).

Due to the significant overlap of child maltreatment and intimate partner violence (IPV), the medical provider should also screen for and detect IPV in the family when evaluating the child (11). As mentioned above, IPV is sometimes included in the definition of child maltreatment. Not only do children who live in violent environments have a higher risk for child maltreatment, but children who witness IPV are at a higher risk of behavioral, psychological and adverse health problems. Victimization resulting from IPV starts even prior to the child's birth with several poor health outcomes related to abuse during pregnancy such as preterm labor and low birth weight. IPV may also result in physical injuries to the child, whether from a direct hit when being held by the parent or in older children when trying to intervene in the fight (12). Thus, identifying IPV in the clinical setting has a role in both preventing child maltreatment and better detection of high-risk families where abuse may be occurring. The American Academy of Pediatrics recognized the unique role of the pediatrician in identifying and addressing IPV and how this identification may be one of the most effective means of preventing child maltreatment (13). When IPV is recognized, the health care provider should be able to address the various health needs and refer to appropriate services for assessment and intervention.

PHYSICAL EXAMINATION

Children who are suspected of being physically abused or neglected need a complete thorough physical examination. The medical provider needs to be attentive to the general hygiene of the child, the bonding between the child and the parent, and the appropriateness of the clothing to the season during the examination.

The medical provider also needs to measure and plot the growth parameters (height, weight, and head circumference) to assess for proper growth and detect any concerns of failure to thrive (lack of appropriate growth and weight gain) whether due to neglect, an underlying medical condition or food insecurity (14). Children with certain medical conditions are also at risk for being overweight as a result of excessive food intake relative to the expenditure of energy (lower metabolic rates and lack of ambulation and exercise). Neglect needs to be considered in cases of obesity when it results in increased risk of harm and medical complications and there is noncompliance with the medical weight management plan (15). Although the measurement may be difficult especially if the child is unable to stand, has contractures, or scoliosis, these measurements need to be accurate and done regularly and plotted over time.

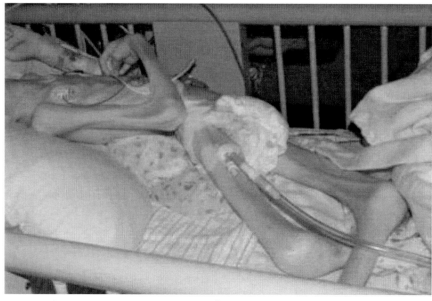

A

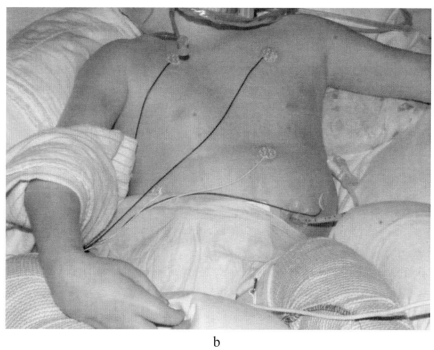

b

Figures 1a,1b. A 16-year-old with cerebral palsy who presented with failure to thrive.

Case 1

A 16-year-old child with a medical diagnosis of cerebral palsy presented with severe failure to thrive and weight loss (1a). On admission to the hospital, he weighed 9 kg (the average weight of a 9 month old infant). He was not receiving the full amount of the nutritional supplement prescribed by his pediatrician resulting in weight loss. Other elements of neglect were assessed and he had not attended school or followed up with physical therapy resulting in severe contractures. After 6 months of appropriate nutrition and corrective surgeries, he doubled his weight and the contractures had improved dramatically (1b).

Growth in children is influenced by several factors including nutrient intake, environmental circumstances, and genetics. In children with special health care needs, additional factors may impact growth such as congenital abnormalities, the medical condition, medications, and the degree of developmental disability. There are conditions that alter the growth of the child for example chromosomal disorders (e.g., trisomy 21) and genetic disorders. In addition, some conditions have the potential to alter growth such as conditions with feeding problems and those that impair ambulation.

Any problem with feeding that results in insufficient nutrient intake may affect the child's growth. Children with disabilities may have structural abnormalities of the oral area, oral-motor dysfunction, swallowing difficulties, or gastroesophageal reflux. They may also have feeding problems as a result of emotional or behavioral issues. Other than feeding difficulties, children who are non-ambulatory as a result of their medical condition lack the weight bearing which provides physical stress on the long bones of the leg required to stimulate bone growth.

Depending on the medical cause of the developmental disability, the child may need to be plotted on a special growth chart such as for children with trisomy 21, Prader-Willi syndrome, Williams syndrome, Turner syndrome, and Achondroplasia. For example, children with trisomy 21 (also called Down syndrome) have a different pattern of growth and generally have a shorter stature and a smaller head circumference. Thus, these children need to be plotted on an alternate growth chart for this patient population (16). It is not recommended to use these charts however for those children with neurologic disorders without known underlying genetic or medical conditions.

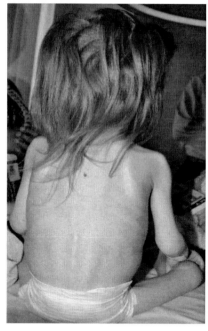

a

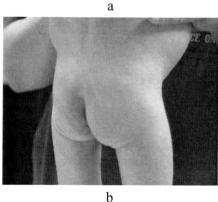

b

Figures 2a,2b. A 3-year-old girl who presented with failure to thrive. Notice the thin extremities, the protruding ribs, and the loss of subcutaneous fat in the buttocks.

Case 2

A 3-year-old child presents to the emergency department after her sister died from complications of pneumonia and failure to thrive. She had lost weight and upon reviewing her records weighed less at 3 years of age than she did when she was 9 months old. She was noted to be weak and unable to walk which resolved with optimal nutrition. An extensive medical workup was done and no medical cause was found to explain the failure to thrive other than neglect. She had missed follow up appointments with her pediatrician.

CUTANEOUS INJURIES

A thorough skin exam is required when evaluating children for suspected child maltreatment. It is also necessary when examining children for other health care needs as well. The skin needs to be examined from head to toe and bruises, and injuries found need to be documented. The child needs to be undressed when evaluated and areas that may be overlooked need to be examined for example the ears and inside the oral cavity. The genitals, and anus should also be examined (8).

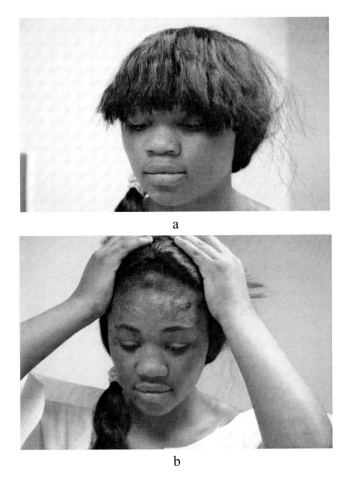

a

b

Figures 3a,3b. A child who has a history of an old burn on her forehead.

Case 3
The scar on her forehead would have been easily missed with her hair style and without conducting a full medical exam and looking under her hair. Figure 3a shows the child with her hair covering her forehead. Figure 3b shows the child exposing the forehead to show the burn.

The presence and location of bruises are linked to the developmental stage and ability of the child. As children become more mobile, they bruise more often as the number of accidental injuries increases with ambulation. However, these bruises are typically on bony prominences. In Sugar's study, those "who do not cruise rarely bruise" (17), and any bruise in a nonambulatory child needs a full evaluation as to the etiology and whether there is an explainable mechanism of injury consistent with the development of the child (see figures 4 and 5). Physicians need to be more aware of sentinel injuries when present. The presence of a bruise or an intra-oral injury in a nonmobile infant without a history even when minor needs to prompt an evaluation for physical abuse. Even when the remainder of the evaluation is negative, one should still report these injuries to the appropriate authorities to prevent future more severe abuse in the infant.

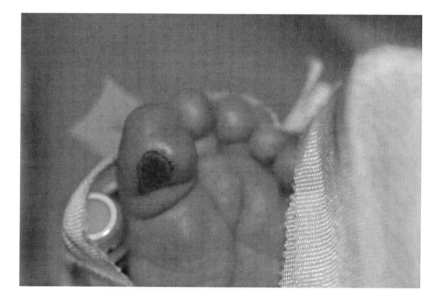

Figure 4. A 2-month old who presented with an abrasion on his big toe with an inconsistent history.

Case 4

This 2-month old baby who was born prematurely and has a history of developmental delay presented with an abrasion to his big toe with a history of the infant self-inflicting the abrasion by friction resulting from trying to move his foot on a carpeted floor he was placed on. The infant developmentally was barely able to move his extremities let alone move his foot with enough force to create a carpet friction burn on his toe. This injury was not consistent with the history provided because it is an injury in a pre-mobile infant which is inconsistent with his developmental age. This injury despite being small and heals with little medical treatment should alert professionals to perform a full medical assessment looking for other signs of physical abuse and identifying this family as a high risk family which needs further assessment and follow up.

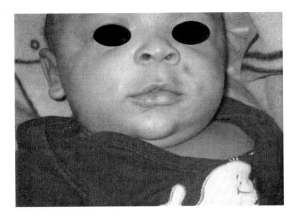

Figure 5. Infant with sentinel injury.

Case 5
Infants may present with sentinel injuries such as this bruise on the face of a 3-month old infant. These injuries need to prompt an evaluation to detect associated injuries and prevent further more severe abuse. In this infant, a skeletal survey was performed and showed multiple rib fractures.

Bruises as a result of abuse have certain discriminating factors that distinguish them from accidental bruises (18, 19). The mnemonic 'TEN 4' is an easy way to identify bruises that are of concern for abuse: T-torso; E-ear; N-neck; and 4-in children less than 4 years of age and any bruise in an infant under 4 months of age (see figures 6a and 6b). There are also certain patterns of injuries that may identify the inflicting agent for example loop marks from extension cords, ropes or strings and small double bruises from pinch marks.

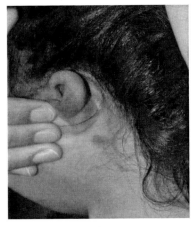

a

Figures 6a,6b. (Continued).

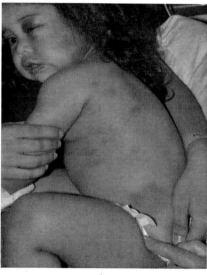

b

Figures 6a,6b. A 1-year-old child with multiple bruises.

Case 6

This 1-year-old child presented with multiple bruises with no history of how the injury happened. Multiple concerns in this child included the age of the child (less than 4), the location of the bruises (torso, ear, and neck) and the absence of a history to explain the injury.

Burn injuries make up about 10% of all child abuse cases, and about 10% of hospital admissions of children to burn units are the result of child abuse. It is crucial to identify abusive burns to protect the child from further injury as well as other children in the home. Children with abusive burns may also have other associated abusive injuries, have a higher mortality, and have longer hospitalizations as compared to those children with accidental burns.

Children presenting with burns require a thorough and complete medical evaluation (see figure 7). The evaluation includes a history from the child if the child is verbal as well as a history from the parent and any other witnesses who were present when the burn occurred (20). Specific questions in cases of burns include:

1. What was the child wearing when the burn occurred?
2. How long was the child in contact with the hot water or the hot object?
3. Does the child have any medical condition that impairs consciousness or the child's ability to move or sense pain?
4. What are the child's developmental capabilities and motor skills?

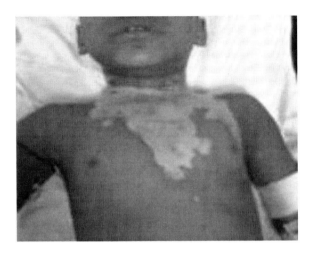

Figure 7. A 2-year-old with an accidental burn.

Case 7

This 2-year-old child presented with a burn after running in the kitchen and bumping into his mother who was holding a pot of hot water. The burn is consistent with the mechanism; however parental education was conducted regarding safety and supervision. The case was not reported to child protective services as no further concerns of abuse were present.

As with other injuries resulting from physical abuse, abusive burns are more frequent in younger children. Most are less than 10 years of age with the majority younger than 2 years of age. They are also associated with certain developmental stages. For example, abusive immersion burns are more commonly associated with toilet training as a form of punishment and immersion in hot pots is associated with children playing near a stove. Abusive burns may result from hot liquid, grease, chemicals, hot objects, microwave ovens, or electricity. Concerning characteristics of burns include children who reported inflicted injury, absent or inadequate explanation, hot water as agent, immersion scald, a bilateral/symmetric burn pattern, total body surface area >/=10%, full thickness burns, and co-existent injuries (21).

Scald burns are the most common type of abusive burns in childhood with immersion being the most frequent reported mechanism. Immersion scald burns are characterized by the presence of well-demarcated areas and the absence of splash or flow marks (see figure 8). The depth and the pattern of immersion burns reflect the position that the child was held in, with "glove" and "stocking" distributions occurring when the burns are circumferential and involve the hands and/or feet respectively. After completing the medical history, the medical physician should perform a thorough head to toe examination documenting the burns and looking for any other associated injuries.

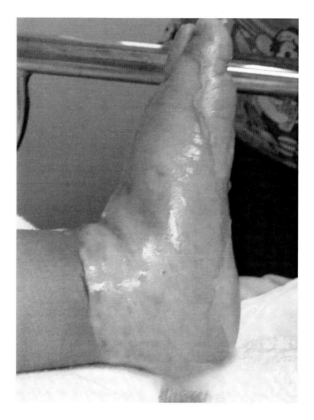

Figure 8. A 2-year old boy with an immersion burn to his left foot.

Case 8
A 2-year-old boy was left with the mother's boyfriend during the time the mother
was at work. When the mother of the child came back home, she noticed the child to be
in extreme pain and was crying. She then noticed the burns and was not provided with
any history of how the burns occurred. The child was not able to provide a history of how
the burn occurred. This burn is concerning not only because of the absence of a history
but also because of the clear line of demarcation separating the burned skin from the
normal skin and is consistent with an immersion burn.

Developmental disability and paralysis may contribute to the extent of the injury. For
example, a child with paralysis in the lower extremities may not withdraw from the pain
of hot water. Thus this child may have more significant burns and may also have an
absence of splash marks. Children may not feel the pain or express it as other children
may with no disabilities (see figure 9). However, these children would need closer
supervision and more attention when bathing especially with burns being preventable.

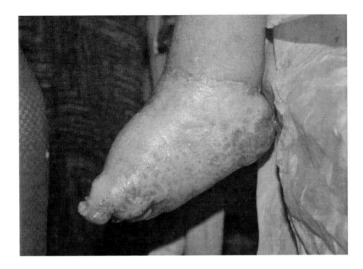

Figure 9. A 6-year-old with meningomyelocele who presented with a burn to her right foot.

Case 9

A 6-year-old child with a medical history of meningomyelocele and paralysis and absent sensation in both her lower extremities presents with a burn to her right foot. Her father was helping her bathe. He seated her in her bathtub seat and had heated up the water in a bucket then placed her foot in the bucket not realizing how hot the water was. The child did not withdraw from pain due to her paralysis and she did not perceive pain. The burn appears to be an immersion burn and has the characteristics of an immersion burn with the clear line of demarcation. In this case the child was not able to provide a history due to her developmental delay making the diagnosis rather difficult considering her medical condition. However, neglect is a serious consideration in this case as the father should have been more careful when warming the water and placing her foot in the bucket of water to wash it. This case was reported to child protective services with concerns of neglect resulting in serious injury. Abuse could not be ruled out in this case.

SKELETAL INJURIES, FRACTURES AND IMAGING

As with other injuries, child abuse is suspected when a child presents with a fracture with no underlying bone fragility and no mechanism to explain the fracture especially in non-ambulatory children (19). Physical abuse is also suspected when the child presents with multiple fractures, or with fractures that have a high specificity for child abuse such as fractures of the ribs, scapulae, classic metaphyseal lesions of the long bones, vertebrae, and sternum. The most important risk factor for skeletal injuries is age, with younger children and infants at a higher risk for abusive fractures as compared to older children. The radiologist plays a critical role in the evaluation and diagnosis of fractures (22).

Imaging in cases of suspected physical abuse is used to identify injuries present, including those that may be clinically silent and to demonstrate other radiological evidence of an associated or an alternative diagnosis as to the causation of injury (22). The American College of Radiology currently recommends a 21 dedicated view skeletal survey in children when physical abuse is suspected in children less than 2 years of age. A follow up skeletal survey is also indicated in 2 weeks when the abuse is suspected clinically or the initial findings are equivocal or abnormal.

Abusive head trauma is the leading cause of death from physical abuse and results in significant mortality and morbidity. Professionals caring for children need to consider the diagnosis of abusive head trauma in children who present with nonspecific symptoms such as vomiting, lethargy, apnea or seizures so that cases are not missed (23). Head imaging (CT or MRI) would be indicated in these cases as well as a funduscopic exam for detection of retinal hemorrhages.

FURTHER INVESTIGATIONS

After a comprehensive history and a detailed physical examination, certain investigations are needed to further evaluate for the presence of injuries in children suspected of being victims of physical abuse. Some injuries may be subtle and may not be detected on physical examination, necessitating further work up to identify the injuries and assist in reaching a diagnosis of abuse or another medical condition that explains the presentation. The investigations depend on the initial injury, its severity, and the age of the child. These investigations include laboratory tests: a complete blood count and liver function tests. Imaging is indicated in certain cases and includes imaging of the head and a skeletal survey. An ophthalmologic examination in cases of head trauma is needed. It is best to consult a child abuse pediatrician and a trauma specialist when evaluating these injuries to ensure a full evaluation is conducted and injuries are managed appropriately.

CONCLUSION

Child maltreatment in general including physical abuse and neglect is more common in children with disabilities as compared to those with no disabilities. However, evaluation is more difficult in non-verbal children due to the absence of a history of how the injury occurred. In addition, children with paralysis or loss of sensation, development disabilities may react differently to pain from physical injuries and hot liquids or objects. The evaluation requires a multidisciplinary approach including a scene investigation in certain cases of suspected abuse. The evaluation also requires a comprehensive assessment of the child's needs and the family's risk factors to prevent abuse and neglect prior to its occurrence. Professionals should also be aware of certain injuries and subtle warning signs of abuse and initiate a medical evaluation when necessary. The medical provider needs to initiate an evaluation for siblings, especially for those less than 2 years of age and twins, who are at higher risk. Medical care providers are also mandated reporters and are obligated by law to report cases of suspected child maltreatment to the appropriate authorities.

REFERENCES

[1]   US Department of Health and Human Services, Administration for Children and Families, Administration on Children, Youth and Families, Children's Bureau. Child maltreatment 2014. Washington, DC: Author, 2016. URL: http://www.acf.hhs.gov/ sites/default/files/cb/cm2014.pdf.

[2]   Hibbard RA, Desch LW, American Academy of Pediatrics Committee on Child Abuse and Neglect, American Academy of Pediatrics Council on Children with Disabilities. Maltreatment of children with disabilities. Pediatrics 2007;119(5):1018-25.

[3]   Ferrari AM. The impact of culture upon child rearing practices and definitions of maltreatment. Child Abuse Negl 2002;26(8):793-813.

[4]   Felitti VJ, Anda RF, Nordenberg D, Williamson DF, Spitz AM, Edwards V, et al. Relationship of childhood abuse and household dysfunction to many of the leading causes of death in adults. The Adverse Childhood Experiences (ACE) Study. Am J Prev Med 1998;14(4):245-58.

[5]   Dubowitz H, Newton RR, Litrownik AJ, Lewis T, Briggs EC, Thompson R, et al. Examination of a conceptual model of child neglect. Child Maltreat 2005;10(2):173-89.

[6]   American Academy of Pediatrics Committee on Child Abuse and Neglect and Committee on Children With Disabilities. Assessment of maltreatment of children with disabilities. Pediatrics 2001;108(2):508-12.

[7]   American Academy of Pediatrics Committee on Psychosocial Aspects of Child and Family Health. Guidance for effective discipline. Pediatrics 1998;101(4 Pt 1):723-8.

[8]   Glick JC, Lorand MA, and Bilka KR. Physical abuse of children. Pediatr Rev 2016;37(4):146-56;quiz 157.

[9]   Dubowitz H. Neglect in children. Pediatr Ann 2013;42(4):73-7.

[10]   Pierce MC, Kaczor K, and Thompson R. Bringing back the social history. Pediatr Clin North Am 2014;61(5):889-905.

[11]   American Academy of Pediatrics Committee on Child Abuse and Neglect. The role of the pediatrician in recognizing and intervening on behalf of abused women. Pediatrics 1998;101(6):1091-2.

[12]   Christian CW, Scribano P, Seidl T, Pinto-Martin JA. Pediatric injury resulting from family violence. Pediatrics 1997;99(2):e8.

[13]   Thackeray JD, Hibbard R, Dowd MD, Committee on Child Abuse and Neglect, Committee on Injury, Violence and Poison Prevention. Intimate partner violence: The role of the pediatrician. Pediatrics 2010;125(5):1094-100.

[14]   Homan GJ. Failure to thrive: A practical guide. Am Fam Physician 2016;94(4):295-9.

[15]   Harper NS. Neglect: failure to thrive and obesity. Pediatr Clin North Am 2014;61(5):937-57.

[16]   Cronk C, Crocker AC, Pueschel SM, Shea AM, Zackai E, Pickens G, et al. Growth charts for children with Down syndrome: 1 month to 18 years of age. Pediatrics 1988;81(1):102-10.

[17]   Sugar NF, Taylor JA, and Feldman KW. Bruises in infants and toddlers: Those who don't cruise rarely bruise. Puget Sound Pediatric Research Network. Arch Pediatr Adolesc Med 1999;153(4):399-403.

[18]   Pierce MC, Kaczor K, Aldridge S, O'Flynn J, Lorenz DJ. Bruising characteristics discriminating physical child abuse from accidental trauma. Pediatrics 2010;125(1):67-74.

[19]   Christian CW, American Academy of Pediatrics Committee on Child Abuse and Neglect. The evaluation of suspected child physical abuse. Pediatrics 2015;135(5):e1337-54.

[20]   Toon MH, Maybauer DM, Arceneaux LL, Fraser JF, Meyer W, Runge A, et al. Children with burn injuries--assessment of trauma, neglect, violence and abuse. J Inj Violence Res 2011;3(2):98-110.

[21]   Pawlik MC, Kemp A, Maguire, S, Nuttall D, Feldman KW, Lindberg, DM, et al. Children with burns referred for child abuse evaluation: Burn characteristics and co-existent injuries. Child Abuse Negl 2016;55:52-61.

[22]   American Academy of Pediatrics Section on Radiology. Diagnostic imaging of child abuse. Pediatrics 2009;123(5):1430-5.

[23]   Jenny C, Hymel KP, Ritzen A, Reinert SE, Hay TC. Analysis of missed cases of abusive head trauma. JAMA 1999;281(7):621–6.

In: Child Abuse: Children with Disabilities
Editors: V. J Palusci, D. Nazer et al.

ISBN: 978-1-53612-035-6
© 2017 Nova Science Publishers, Inc.

Chapter 9

SEXUAL ABUSE: MEDICAL EVALUATION AND MANAGEMENT IN CHILDREN WITH DISABILITIES

Dena Nazer[*], *MD, FAAP*

Wayne State University School of Medicine,
Children's Hospital of Michigan,
Kids TALK Children's Advocacy Center, Detroit, Michigan, US

Child sexual abuse is a public health problem with grave consequences affecting the child and the community. Children are vulnerable merely because of their age; furthermore, the presence of disability increases their vulnerability making children with disabilities at a greater risk for abuse as compared to children with no disabilities. This article will focus on child sexual abuse and its medical evaluation and management in children with disabilities.

INTRODUCTION

When discussing the issues surrounding children with disabilities and their risk for child abuse, the absence of a universally accepted definition of disabilities adds to the complexity of accurately assessing the problem. Disability has variable definitions making it hard to identify its true incidence and characteristics in maltreated children.

[*] Corresponding author: Dena Nazer, MD, Kids TALK Children's Advocacy Center Medical Clinic, 40 East Ferry St, Detroit, Michigan, 48202, United States. E-mail: dnazer@med.wayne.edu.

The Centers for Disease Control and Prevention (CDC) describes developmental disabilities as a group of conditions due to an impairment in physical, language, learning, or behavior areas which begins during the developmental period, usually lasts throughout the person's life time and may impact the daily life.

Intellectual disability, according to the American Association on Intellectual and Developmental Disabilities (AAIDD), is a disability characterized by three essential elements: limitations in intellectual functioning (such as learning and reasoning), limitations in adaptive behavior, which covers many everyday social and practical skills, and an onset originating before the age of 18 years. The term intellectual disability has replaced the previously used "mental retardation" term.

In the United States, about one in six, or about 15%, of children aged 3 through 17 years have one or more developmental disability. Intellectual disability affects about one percent of the population, and of those about 85 percent have mild intellectual disability. Diagnosis and identification of these children is essential as they are more vulnerable and subsequently at higher risk to be victims of abuse and neglect. Not only do medical providers need to be aware of the increased risk of maltreatment in this patient population but they also need to evaluate any child who is maltreated for the presence of developmental disabilities (1).

Child maltreatment includes all forms of physical and emotional ill-treatment, sexual abuse, neglect, and exploitation that result in actual or potential harm to the child's health, development or dignity. Within this broad definition, five subtypes can be distinguished–physical abuse; sexual abuse; neglect and negligent treatment; emotional abuse; and exploitation.

Sexual abuse occurs when a child is engaged in sexual activities that he or she cannot comprehend, for which he or she is developmentally unprepared and cannot give consent, and/or that violate the law or social taboos of society (2). The sexual activities may include all forms of oral, genital, or anal contact by or to the child or abuse that does not involve contact, such as exhibitionism, voyeurism, or using the child in the production of pornography. Thus the spectrum of sexual abuse includes activities ranging from physically less intrusive sexual abuse to rape.

Risk factors for sexual abuse in general include gender with girls reporting more sexual abuse than boys. Age is also a factor with teenagers having the highest rates of sexual assault as compared to other age groups. Other potential risk factors include absence of protective parent, prior sexual victimization, and physical disability.

There are many factors that increase the risk of sexual abuse in a child with disability in addition to the condition itself. Children with disabilities may be viewed as unable to comprehend sexual education thus they miss out on learning opportunities at schools and from parents on how to protect themselves from sexual abuse.

There is also a lack of awareness from parents and society that children with disabilities are potential victims of sexual abuse at even higher rates than other children, and they are less diligent with safety measures around these children. Depending on the severity of the disability, these children may become increasingly isolated from the general community and more dependent on the caregiver to provide assistance in daily activities that may include intimate care. This makes the child accustomed to certain activities and less likely to differentiate intrusive behaviors from those of routine daily care. As the child becomes more dependent on the caregiver, the child becomes more compliant with adults who assume an authoritative role in the child's life and becomes less likely to resist and less likely to report sexual abuse. Even when children try to communicate and disclose, their disability may prevent them communicating or describing effectively with a clear credible statement the sequence of events and care givers may explain what happened as part of the child's routine.

PRESENTATION OF CHILD SEXUAL ABUSE

Children who are victims of sexual abuse present in a multitude of ways depending on their age, developmental level, and the nature of the sexual abuse. They may present after making a disclosure of sexual abuse to a parent, teacher, social worker or another trusted individual. These disclosures and the circumstances and questions that lead to the disclosures need to be documented. Children may also present with physical or behavioral symptoms which necessitate further evaluation for sexual abuse.

Physical signs and symptoms include nonspecific complaints such as abdominal pain, headaches, and fatigue. Children may also complain of genital pain, itching, discharge or other genitourinary symptoms related to the sexual abuse.

Behavioral changes include aggression, withdrawal, problems in school, regression (e.g., return to thumb sucking), sleep disturbances, fear of people or certain locations, depression and eating disturbances. The problem with these behaviors is that although they may indicate sexual abuse, they are nonspecific and may be a result of the child acting out to other stressors. In addition, the behavior may be attributed to the child's disability or underlying condition.

Sexual Behaviors

Most children engage in sexual behaviors at a certain time in their childhood that is mostly age appropriate, transient and only requires guidance and monitoring. Some children however may exhibit sexual behavior which may initiate a sexual abuse evaluation or be both concerning to caregivers and distressing at school.

A broad range of sexual behaviors are exhibited by both children who have a history of sexual abuse and those where there is no concern of sexual abuse. This behavior is related to the child's age, maternal education, family sexuality, family stress, and family violence (3, 4). These behaviors are exhibited at a varying level of frequency with the most frequent including self-stimulating behaviors, exhibitionism, and behaviors related to personal boundaries. Self-stimulating behaviors include the child masturbating, or touching or rubbing different parts of the body to induce pleasure. Examples for behavior related to personal boundaries may include children standing too close, rubbing against people, or casually touching their mother's breasts or father's genitals. This behavior is mostly seen in the younger children who are still learning the culturally acceptable interpersonal distance between people. The less frequent behaviors are the more intrusive behaviors. This may pose a challenge for children with disabilities as they may not fully comprehend personal boundaries or understand what is hurtful for others and not accepted socially.

Children with disabilities may exhibit behaviors that correspond to their development vs. their chronological age. When assessing these behaviors, one should consider the developmental age vs. the chronological age. For example, a 16-year-old boy who functions at a developmental level of a 2-year-old may display sexualized behavior that is considered normal for a 2-year-old but not a developmentally normal 16-year-old.

Sexual behaviors appear to be inversely related to age with a peak frequency at age 5 for both boys and girls followed by a decrease in frequency over the next 7 years. Sexually abused children exhibit sexual behavior at a greater rate when compared to children who were not abused (5). However there is not a single sexual behavior that is indicative of sexual abuse.

Evaluation of Child Sexual Abuse

The evaluation all children who are suspected of being sexually abused requires a multidisciplinary team approach, and this requirement is no different in children with disabilities. Each team member has a unique perspective and an area of expertise that is essential in the full comprehensive evaluation of children. Depending on the community, a child advocacy center or a sexual abuse response team may take the lead in addressing and evaluating the child's special needs in these cases. These teams include law enforcement, a child protective services worker, a medical provider, a forensic interviewer and other personnel for example a child advocate depending on the community where the child is being evaluated.

All victims of sexual abuse should be offered a medical examination by a medical professional trained in sexual abuse evaluations. The medical exam is necessary and helpful for all survivors of violence, regardless of the level of abuse disclosed. The role of the physician also includes the assessment of the physical, emotional, and behavioral consequences of sexual abuse, and coordination with other professionals to provide comprehensive treatment and follow-up of victims (6). In the US, the physician is also mandated to report cases of child maltreatment including cases of suspected sexual abuse to the appropriate authorities. The medical evaluation includes as in the assessment of other conditions obtaining a medical history, conducting a physical examination, collecting appropriate laboratory data, and in some cases forensic evidence depending on the nature of disclosure and the time since the last incidence of suspected sexual abuse.

The timing of the medical evaluation requires consideration of multiple factors including the medical, therapeutic and evidentiary purpose of such an evaluation (7). It also requires the consideration of where the best location for the assessment is as well as who is the most qualified provider who is able to evaluate children who are suspected of being sexually abused and is experienced in evaluating children with disabilities.

There are cases when the medical examination may be an emergency and needs to be performed without delay, or the need may be less urgent. These are cases where emergency contraception or post exposure prophylaxis for sexually transmitted infections (STIs) including human immunodeficiency virus (HIV) is needed. It is also emergent when there are medical, psychological, or safety concerns such as acute pain or bleeding, suicidal ideation, or suspected human trafficking. The need for forensic evidence collection may require the medical evaluation to be done emergently if the sexual assault may have occurred within the previous 72 hours (or other state-mandated time interval). This collection needs to consider the timing of when the sexual abuse took place and not depend on the presence of physical findings. The medical provider needs to become familiar with the laws as some jurisdictions have expanded the time frame of when the evidence collection is recommended (7).

A medical evaluation is urgent but not emergent in cases where the suspected sexual abuse occurred within the previous two weeks, without immediate medical, psychological, or safety needs identified. In cases where the suspected sexual abuse occurred more than two weeks prior without urgent medical, psychological, or safety needs and in cases where sexual abuse is suspected because of other symptoms, the medical examination is non-urgent (8).

MEDICAL HISTORY

The medical history is a key component of the evaluation of sexually abused children and is in many cases the strongest evidence of abuse (9). The medical history focuses on the health and well-being of the child and complements the forensic interview and other interviews conducted by other professionals. It serves the purpose of collecting information relevant to the health of the child and also serves to help address the effects the abuse has on the family and the child's perceptions of the problem.

To effectively obtain a history, the medical provider must be familiar with communicating with children and those with developmental delay and impaired communication skills and seek the help of an interpreter when needed. Children of different ages interact and express themselves differently and that needs to be taken into account when obtaining the medical history. The medical provider also needs to be compassionate, objective, and nonjudgmental. The disclosure needs to be preserved and documented along with the circumstances of how and why the child disclosed.

It is best to obtain the history with the child alone without the parent or caretaker. This would make the child more comfortable to talk and would decrease the influence the caretaker may have on what the child says and the caretaker's reaction to the disclosure. Questions need to be mostly open ended and non-leading so that a detailed accurate history may be obtained and documented.

Medical information and details also need to be obtained from the caregiver. The medical provider needs to ask about the details of the disclosure and circumstances around it. These details may assist in the differential diagnosis of the presenting symptoms. Elements of the medical history also include asking about the past medical and surgical history, medications the child is taking, developmental history, and social history. Further information about the genitourinary and gastrointestinal history may also help in assessing children for other conditions that may mimic the presenting symptoms of abuse. The medical provider needs to ask about urinary symptoms, change in bowel habits, and genital bleeding or discharge.

One aspect when obtaining the history that the provider needs to be aware of is the age of consent in the jurisdiction, which is the age a person is considered to be competent to consent to sexual acts under the law. Children may provide a history that they consented for the sexual activity and that there was no coercion or force used. The medical provider, however, must be aware that the developmental disability may compromise the capacity of a child to consent for sexual activity even if the child has attained the legal age of consent. It is thus important not only to consider the age when evaluating cases of sexual assault but also the developmental abilities of the child and his/her understanding and ability to provide consent.

**Table 1. Normal genital anatomy to be examined
in cases of suspected sexual abuse**

Gender	Examination
Girls	The examination should include inspection and assessment for any signs of injury or trauma of the following areas: medial aspects of the thighs, labia majora and minora, clitoris, urethra, periurethral tissue, hymen, hymenal opening, fossa navicularis, posterior fourchette, perineum, and perianal tissues.
Boys	The exam should include inspection and assessment for any signs of injury or trauma of the following areas: medial aspects of the thighs, penis, scrotum, perineum, and perianal tissues

PHYSICAL EXAMINATION

Children who disclose sexual abuse or are suspected of being sexually abused require a complete comprehensive head-to-toe medical examination including an examination of the anogenital area. The physical examination findings or laboratory testing are rarely sufficient in making the diagnosis and it is the disclosure and history from the child that is of immense importance. However, the physical examination has several objectives making it a crucial part of the evaluation despite the low rate of positive findings (6, 10). The objectives include:

- Recognition of injuries and other medical needs that require immediate medical attention
- Comprehensive anogenital examination (see Table 1) and identification of abnormalities and interpreting findings or normal exams appropriately
- Identification of injuries outside of the anogenital region whether as a result of abuse or self-inflicted
- Detection and testing for sexually transmitted infections (see Table 2)
- Collection of forensic evidence
- Addressing patient and family concerns about physical health that may arise subsequent to abuse

Table 2. Testing for sexually transmitted infections and their implications in children evaluated for sexual abuse

STI	Testing	Implication
Chlamydia trachomatis*	Girls: Anal and vaginal cultures. NAATs can be used for detection in vaginal specimens or urine in girls. Boys: Anal cultures and a meatal specimen if urethral discharge is present.	Diagnostic for sexual abuse if not likely to be perinatally acquired and rare vertical transmission is excluded.
Neisseria gonorrhea*	Girls: Pharyngeal, vaginal and anal cultures. NAAT can be used for detection in vaginal specimens or urine from girls; however, culture remains the preferred method for testing urethral specimens or urine from boys and extragenital specimens (pharynx and rectum) from all children. Boys: Phayngeal, urethral, and anal cultures	Diagnostic for sexual abuse if not likely to be perinatally acquired and rare vertical transmission is excluded.
Trichomonas vaginalis*	Culture for *T. vaginalis* infection and wet mount of a vaginal swab	Highly suspicious for sexual abuse if not likely to be perinatally acquired and rare vertical transmission is excluded.
Human papillomavirus	Diagnosis is usually clinical, made by visual inspection. Biopsy is indicated only in specific cases	Suspicious and needs to be reported if evidence exists to suspect abuse, including history, physical examination, or other identified infections.
Syphilis	Serology for antibodies to *T. pallidum*	Diagnostic for sexual abuse if not likely to be perinatally acquired and rare vertical transmission is excluded.
HIV	When indicated, HIV antibody testing needs to be done during the original assessment, at 6 weeks, 3 months, and 6 months after the assault.	Diagnostic for sexual abuse if not likely to be perinatally acquired and rare vertical transmission is excluded.

NAAT: Nucleic acid amplification tests

* Reports of suspected sexual abuse need to be made in these cases to the appropriate authority

The medical evaluation in this high risk population is also important because it may identify other health care needs that need evaluation and medical care such as decreased visual acuity and dental caries (11). These medical needs may be higher in children with disabilities who may lack a medical home and have concurrent concerns of neglect.

The health care provider performing the examination must effectively communicate and explain the nature and the purpose of the examination to the child and to the parent or guardian as well. The child may choose for the parent to be present during the exam to relief anxiety and give a sense of security. The time of the examination is also a good opportunity to educate the child on body safety and why it is acceptable for the examiner to examine the anogenital area. Every effort should be made to preserve privacy including the use of drapes and gowns. As these examinations involve the evaluation of the anogenital area, the presence of a chaperone is recommended, and medical policy needs to be established and communicated to the family (12).

Parents and in some cases children may be highly anxious prior to the exam, and explaining that the medical evaluation is noninvasive and not painful may alleviate that stress. In addition, the health care provider needs to explain to the parents that the most important evidence in these cases is the child's disclosure of abuse and that physical findings are absent in most cases. It is also the role of the medical provider to further explain to the family and members of the multidisciplinary team why the examination is normal in most cases.

There have been a number of research studies that concluded that most child victims of sexual abuse and even those who disclose repetitive penile-genital contact that involved some degree of perceived penetration had no definitive evidence of penetration on examination of the hymen (13-15). Even when exams of pregnant teenagers were reviewed, most did not have observable evidence of penetration on examination of the genital area (16).

There are many reasons why the physical examination may not show any signs of trauma and these reasons should be taken into context when the medical provider explains the diagnosis in the medical report. Depending on the child's statement, the child may have disclosed forms of sexual abuse, such as being photographed or watching pornography, that do not involve contact and are not expected to leave any findings on physical examination. The sexual abuse may have involved only touching or fondling and would not result in injury or exam findings. In children who disclose penetration, the medical provider should note that penetration perceived by the child may only be penetration in-between the labia and not into the vagina, which is not expected to cause any medical findings.

In addition, most children do not disclose immediately and the disclosure may be delayed for days, weeks or even months after the sexual abuse took place. This period of time depending on the severity of the initial injury and location would have given enough time for the genital injuries to heal completely. Some genital injuries have been shown to heal as quick as a few days (17, 18). The hymenal and anal tissues also have the ability to stretch without injury, which is also a factor when explaining the absence of findings in children who disclosed penetration. Both the hymen and the anus may stretch without being injured. It is the medical provider's role to explain these reasons to the family and also to other members of the multidisciplinary team who may share misconceptions about the nature of the exam and expected medical findings.

One of the important roles of the medical evaluation is testing for STIs. However, each case should be evaluated individually for the need for testing and the rate of the STIs in the community where the child resides should be considered (19). Factors that should lead to testing children for STIs include the child being abused by a stranger or by a perpetrator known to be infected or at high risk for STIs. In addition, if the child has symptoms or signs of a STI such as genital discharge, or has experienced penetration or has evidence of healed penetrative injury to the genitals, anus, or oropharynx, the child should be tested. The physician also needs to test if a sibling, or person in the house hold has an STI and in cases where the parent or the child is concerned and requests the testing (6, 19, 20). For the commonly tested STIs, please refer to Table 2.

In most cases, only one medical examination of the anogenital areas by an experienced medical provider is needed and documented. However, follow-up medical evaluation may be indicated in certain cases, especially when the findings on the initial examination are unclear or questionable or when there is a need for further STI testing that was not identified or treated during the initial examination. Follow up may also assist in confirmation of the initial examination findings, when the initial examination was performed by an examiner who had conducted fewer than 100 of such evaluations, and for documentation of healing or resolution of acute findings present on the initial examination (8).

COMMERCIAL SEXUAL EXPLOITATION OF CHILDREN WITH DISABILITIES

Similar to sexual abuse, child commercial sexual exploitation (CSEC) and sex trafficking are global health problems requiring a multidisciplinary approach (21). Children in general are vulnerable to sexual exploitation; however, those with learning disabilities or a history of sexual abuse, physical abuse, or neglect are at a higher risk. In addition, other factors such as runaway youths and those with substance abuse problems, history of juvenile justice or child protective services involvement and those from dysfunctional families increase the risk for exploitation.

Although there is currently no validated clinical tool to identify CSEC, there are certain indicators that may help identify victims. When children give a history of someone asking them to have sex in exchange for money or other items such as food or shelter, if they were asked to have sex with someone else of if sexual pictures were taken of them and posted on the internet, sexual exploitation arises as a main concern and should be addressed and reported.

Identifying patients that are victims of sexual exploitation may be hard though as these victims often do not self-identify as such and depending on the level of their intellectual disability, may lack an understanding of exploitation and its dangers (22). A screening tool has been proposed to better identify these children and differentiate them from other sexual abuse victims in the adolescent population (23). The American Academy of Pediatrics suggests that pediatricians should become more aware of potential victims of human trafficking and gives guidance on how to provide for the medical needs of these victims (21). The medical professional's role is vital since most victims of human trafficking seek medical care at a certain point. In addition, the medical professional can serve as a link to initiate the multidisciplinary collaboration for evaluation these children.

CONCLUSION

Child sexual abuse is a public health problem affecting children with disabilities at higher rates compared to children with no disabilities. The evaluation needs to be completed by a multidisciplinary team specialized in evaluating victims of sexual abuse. The medical evaluation is an integral part of this evaluation. Specifically, the medical evaluation and assessment follows a similar approach with various modifications in the communication and examination techniques to address the child's special needs. Most children who are victims of sexual abuse have a normal exam, making the child's disclosure the strongest evidence that abuse has occurred. The medical provider needs to be trained on the appropriate evaluation, management and interpretation of findings or lack of thereof in children who were sexually abused. The medical provider also needs to be aware of resources in the community that ensure the child's safety and wellbeing and prevents further abuse from taking place. Future efforts need to focus on the training of health care providers and professionals on how to detect, evaluate, and respond to sexual abuse of children in general and more specifically for this increasingly vulnerable group.

REFERENCES

[1]   American Academy of Pediatrics Committee on Child Abuse and Neglect and Committee on Children with Disabilities. Assessment of maltreatment of children with disabilities. Pediatrics 2001; 108(2): 508-12.

[2]   Kempe CH. Sexual abuse--another hidden pediatric problem: The 1977 C Anderson Aldrich lecture. Pediatrics 1978; 62(3): 382-9.

[3]   Friedrich WN, Fisher J, Broughton D, Houston M, Shafran CR. Normative sexual behavior in children: A contemporary sample. Pediatrics 1998; 101(4): e9.

[4]   Kellogg ND. Sexual behaviors in children: Evaluation and management. Am Fam Physician 2010; 82(10): 1233-8.

[5]   Friedrich WN, Fisher JL, Dittner CA, Acton R, Berliner L, Butler J, et al. Child Sexual Behavior Inventory: Normative, psychiatric, and sexual abuse comparisons. Child Maltreat 2001; 6(1): 37-49.

[6]   Kellogg N, American Academy of Pediatrics Committee on Child Abuse and Neglect. The evaluation of sexual abuse in children. Pediatrics 2005; 116(2): 506-12.

[7]   Christian CW. Timing of the medical examination. J Child Sex Abuse 2011; 20(5): 505-20.

[8]   Adams JA, Kellogg ND, Farst KJ, Harper NS, Palusci VJ, Frasier LD, et al. Updated guidelines for the medical assessment and care of children who may have been sexually abused. J Pediatr Adolesc Gynecol 2016; 29(2): 81-7.

[9]   Finkel MA, Alexander RA. Conducting the medical history. J Child Sex Abuse 2011; 20(5): 486-504.

[10]   Fortin K, Jenny C. Sexual abuse. Pediatr Rev 2012; 33(1): 19-32.

[11]   Girardet R, Giacobbe L, Bolton K, Lahoti S, McNeese M. Unmet health care needs among children evaluated for sexual assault. Arch Pediatr Adolesc Med 2006; 160(1): 70-3.

[12]   Committee on Pediatric Ambulatory Medicine. Use of chaperones during the physical examination of the pediatric patient. Pediatrics 2011; 127(5): 991-3.

[13]   Adams JA, Harper K, Knudson S, Revilla J. Examination findings in legally confirmed child sexual abuse: It's normal to be normal. Pediatrics 1994; 94(3): 310-7.

[14]   Anderst J, Kellogg N, Jung I. Reports of repetitive penile-genital penetration often have no definitive evidence of penetration. Pediatrics 2009; 124(3): e403-9.

[15]   Berenson AB, Chacko MR, Wiemann CM, Mishaw CO, Friedrich WN, Grady JJ. A case-control study of anatomic changes resulting from sexual abuse. Am J Obstet Gynecol 2000; 182(4): 820-31; discussion: 831-4.

[16]   Kellogg ND, Menard SW, Santos A. Genital anatomy in pregnant adolescents: "Normal" does not mean "nothing happened." Pediatrics 2004; 113(1 Pt 1): e67-9.

[17]   McCann J, Miyamoto S, Boyle C, Rogers K. Healing of nonhymenal genital injuries in prepubertal and adolescent girls: A descriptive study. Pediatrics 2007; 120(5): 1000-11.

[18]   McCann J, Miyamoto S, Boyle C, Rogers K. Healing of hymenal injuries in prepubertal and adolescent girls: A descriptive study. Pediatrics 2007; 119(5): e1094-106.

[19]   Jenny C, Crawford-Jakubiak JE, Committee on Child Abuse and Neglect, American Academy of Pediatrics. The evaluation of children in the primary care setting when sexual abuse is suspected. Pediatrics 2013; 132: e558–67.

[20]   Workowski KA, Bolan GA, Centers for Disease Control and Prevention (CDC). Sexually transmitted diseases treatment guidelines, 2015. MMWR Recomm Rep 2015; 59(RR-03): 1–137.

[21]   Greenbaum J, Crawford-Jakubiak JE, Committee on Child Abuse and Neglect, American Academy of Pediatrics. Child sex trafficking and commercial sexual exploitation: Health care needs of victims. Pediatrics 2015; 135(3): 566-74.

[22]   Reid JA. Sex trafficking of girls with intellectual disabilities: An exploratory mixed methods study. Sex Abuse 2016. Published online Feb 17, 2016.

[23]   Greenbaum VJ, Dodd M, McCracken C. A short screening tool to identify victims of child sex trafficking in the health care setting. Pediatr Emerg Care 2015; 12: 856-9.

In: Child Abuse: Children with Disabilities
Editors: V. J Palusci, D. Nazer et al.

ISBN: 978-1-53612-035-6
© 2017 Nova Science Publishers, Inc.

Chapter 10

SEXUAL BEHAVIORS IN CHILDREN AND ADOLESCENTS WITH DEVELOPMENTAL DISABILITIES: ASSESSMENT AND TREATMENT

Alyse Mandel*, MS, LCSW and Ellen Datner, PsyD
Bellevue Hospital Frances L. Loeb Child Protection and
Development Center, New York City Health and Hospitals, New York,
New York, US

Humans are sexual beings. Like all aspects of development, sexual development begins in infancy and continues throughout the human lifecycle. Children develop across many domains: emotional, social and physical, and at different rates and developmental stages. The topic of sexual development is often overlooked as an expected area of development. This could be due to societal beliefs and/or parental, cultural or religious differences. The normative progression of sexual development may not apply within a clear framework if a child has a developmental disability or delay. This topic has not been frequently studied historically, but more clinicians and researchers are now looking at how young people with disabilities experience sexual feelings or behaviors, whether at a normative rate, as a result of trauma or abuse, or the possibility of another explanation. Unfortunately, children with intellectual disabilities and developmental delays experience sexual abuse at a higher rate than peers who are not developmentally delayed. These children are especially at risk for abuse due to cognitive, social and emotional deficits. As with typically developing peers, problematic sexual behavior (PSB) can occur in children with developmental delays as a result of sexual abuse, but there may also be other factors at play. In this review, we will first present a brief overview of normative and PSB in youth and then explore some of the reasons PSBs are prevalent in developmentally delayed

* Correspondence: Alyse Mandel, MS, LCSW, Bellevue Hospital, Child Protection and Development Center, 462 First Avenue, New York, NY 10016, United States. E-mail: Alyse.Mandel@bellevue.nychhc.org.

populations, focusing on children and adolescents diagnosed with higher functioning autism spectrum disorder (ASD) formerly known as Asperger's disorder (AD). We will also discuss various methods to assess sexual behaviors and treatment options for this population.

INTRODUCTION

Research from several disciplines has contributed to our understanding of sexual identity, attitudes and behaviors. Sexual development is influenced by a variety of factors including biological, social and environmental contexts which can result in a diversity of sexual behaviors at different developmental stages (1). Sexuality is a multifaceted part of human development that evolves in the context of interactions with one's environment (2). "Sexuality is influenced by the interaction of biological, psychological, social, economic, political, cultural, legal, historical, religious and spiritual factors" (3). It can be expressed in numerous ways such as through thoughts or fantasies, attitudes, behaviors, identity, relationships, beliefs and values, for example. However, each individual may not experience or express all these aspects of sexuality (3).

Sexual development falls across all developmental stages from birth through adolescence into adulthood (1). Youth experience different sexual feelings and engage in a variety of sexual behaviors depending on their developmental age. Children and adolescents' understanding of sexuality is influenced by their exposure to sexual material as well as their ability to understand the experience (4). They are influenced by their parents, media, technology and peers. Problems arise when sexual behavior becomes aggressive, persistent and/or falls outside society's norms. The Association for the Treatment of Sexual Abusers' (ATSA) Task Force on Children with Sexual Behavior Problems (5) defined PSB in children 12 years old or younger who initiate these behaviors as "behaviors involving sexual body parts (i.e., genitals, anus, buttock or breasts) that are developmentally inappropriate or potentially harmful to themselves or others" (5). In terms of causation, throughout the literature there appears to be a significant amount of research on the correlation between sexual abuse and sexual behaviors. However, few studies address this association among children with disabilities (6). Sexual behaviors can also result from other experiences and recent literature discusses these possibilities (2, 7, 8).

Despite sexuality being an integral part of child development and public concerns about atypical sexual behaviors and child maltreatment, there is a paucity of research on the complexities of both normative and PSB. Even fewer studies address these behaviors in young populations with intellectual and developmental disabilities. A lack of knowledge regarding childhood sexual behavior can have potential negative consequences for children and their families in the home, school and social environments as well as in health care and child welfare and legal systems. The aim of several current studies is not only to improve our understanding of sexual behaviors in youth but also to contribute to the development of guidelines that can assist professionals in the assessment and treatment of these behaviors (8).

The "Diagnostic and statistical manual of mental disorders, fifth edition (DSM-5)" has made autistic spectrum disorder (ASD) the umbrella term for three previously separate diagnoses: Asperger's disorder (AD), childhood disintegrative disorder, and pervasive developmental disorder, not otherwise specified (9). For the purpose of this review, we will use Asperger's disorder as a way to distinguish high functioning from low functioning autism, although the DSM-5 no longer recognizes this label.

NORMATIVE CHILDHOOD SEXUAL BEHAVIOR

In the beginning of the 20th Century, Freud introduced concepts that included sexuality as part of child development (10). At that time, ideas about childhood sexuality were primarily theoretical (11). Increased awareness of sexual abuse in the second half of the century, and more recent awareness of children engaging in sexually aggressive behaviors, have led to attempts to define typical sexual development in youth and sparked an increase in studies on the sexual behaviors of children. However, more research is needed, and a clear understanding of normative child sexual development including children's sexual knowledge, interests, experiences (10) and sexual behaviors is still lacking (8, 12).

Much of the existing research on childhood sexual behaviors is focused on PSB in children who have been sexually abused. Accurately differentiating typical sexual behavior in children from those resulting from maltreatment or other factors is of great importance. Such knowledge could aid in the proper assessment and identification of the presenting behavior (13) and inform developmentally-tailored treatment interventions (5, 13). For example, in cases of childhood sexual abuse (CSA), misdiagnosis of sexual behaviors can lead to negative and harmful outcomes for the child, family and/or accused perpetrator (13).

Different research methods have been used to obtain baseline information regarding typical childhood sexual behaviors (14) and the designs of the available studies appear to impact the measured prevalence rates of these behaviors (8). The majority of studies have gathered information from parents' and teachers' observations of their children's and students' sexual behaviors. Common measures used with caregiver and teacher informants to gather information on child sexual behavior include the sexual behavior items on the Child Behavior Check List (CBCL) (15) and the Child Sexual Behavior Inventory (CSBI) (16). The CSBI has been utilized in several studies on typical and atypical sexual behaviors and allows for comparison of studies (8). Additional studies have utilized adults' retrospective reports about their childhood sexual experiences and data gathered from populations of children seeking treatment for sexual behavior difficulties. Although more research is needed, what has been gathered so far has demonstrated some consistencies about childhood sexual behavior (17-19). For example, young children commonly engage in sexual behaviors such as genital touching, viewing others' genitals, showing genitals to others, attempting to touch a woman's breasts, playing "doctor" and masturbation (14, 18, 20).

A wide range of sexual behaviors have been observed in typically developing child populations at varying frequencies. However, potential mediators of normative behaviors as well as problem behaviors is less known (21). Children learn about themselves, their bodies and their roles through their environment (2). Young children's curiosity about their body, including their genitalia, and those of others is a developmentally expected occurrence (18, 20). Sexual knowledge and behavior in children is influenced by a variety of factors including, but not limited to, the child's age and developmental level, family environment, exposure to sexual material, culture and societal norms (5, 10, 18). In addition, the expression and interpretation of sexual behaviors in children can also vary across contexts (8). Therefore, defining what is "normal" childhood sexual behavior is an arduous task (4).

In addition to the complexities of defining normative sexual behavior in young children, defining norms for older children is even more complicated as this population is often socialized to hide their sexual activities. As youth mature, they tend to seek privacy and engaging in sexual behaviors in public may be viewed as taboo. Defining sexual behavior or interactions between children presents difficulties as well. Characteristics such as age, size and status used to determine if an encounter is typical or abusive may be difficult guides to assess child sexual play (10).

Very few studies exist on the impact of culture on childhood sexual behaviors and on behavioral differences between cultures. To address cultural influences, studies have compared rates of sexual behaviors in American and European populations. Consistencies were found in rates of less frequent sexual behaviors while more inconsistencies were discovered with more common sexual behaviors (8). One study (8) looked at American ethnic minority populations. Results showed that African American parents reported decreased solitary sexual behaviors compared to Caucasian parents. More research on diverse populations is greatly needed to further our understanding of the impact of culture on childhood sexual behaviors (8).

Children's knowledge and attitudes about sexuality and sexual behaviors are also influenced by the level of adult support and responses to their behaviors (10) and the beliefs of their families and communities (4). Western society tends to view children as "innocent," asexual beings who do not possess sexual thoughts or interests (10). Many adults and families hesitate to discuss or educate children about sexual development and behavior. In contrast, frequent images and themes of sexual behavior exist in our society. Children are often exposed to sexual images in the media and adults may delay discussing or explaining these images to children. They may also believe that children are not interested in or have the ability to understand mature sexual images (13). One researcher (10) suggested that the diversity of sexual attitudes and beliefs in society, and lack of guidance for parents to address sexuality with their children, leave youth to try to interpret and understand what is acceptable sexual behavior. Others (10) have suggested that the lack of comprehensive sex education programs that include not only responsible sexuality but also positive and pleasurable aspects of sexuality reflects a cultural belief that denies the data showing sexuality being a vital part of child development (10).

Sexual development includes physical changes, information learned about sexuality, and demonstrated behaviors (22). Sexual behaviors in children can cause concern for caregivers and professionals due to the association between sexual abuse and sexualized behaviors. However, it has been demonstrated that children of all ages engage in a variety of sexual behaviors. Understanding of normative sexual behavior can help to minimize alarm, to assess the potential source of the behavior and to manage the behavior (17). Given the important decisions, policies and interventions created for many children and families, it is also imperative for professionals, child protective services (CPS) and court systems to be knowledgeable about typical and PSBs in youth and those that may be indicative of maltreatment (5).

Despite increasing knowledge, more research is needed to determine typical sexual behaviors in children. Defining normative sexual behavior is not only important to the understanding of child development but also to the assessment and diagnosis of atypical childhood sexual behaviors (18). Lack of baseline data can lead to the minimization of problematic sexual behaviors or over-reaction to expected and developmentally appropriate behaviors. For example, normative sexual behaviors can be pathologized and/or misinterpreted as indicators of CSA or as unusual. Whereas, oversight of such behaviors can lead to a failure in the detection and intervention in cases of child abuse or psychopathology (19).

YOUNG CHILDREN

Gil (23) describes sexual curiosity and behavior as progressive over time. Children from birth to 4 years old commonly have limited peer contact. Their behavior focuses on self-exploration and stimulation and has a tendency to be disinhibited. They discover that touching certain body parts is pleasurable and may repeat this behavior. Sexual behaviors are mediated by caregivers' reactions and limit setting. If their reactions are punitive, the behavior may decrease or cease (e.g., touching self during a diaper change). Imitative play can be influenced by behaviors children are exposed to or have seen, for example, by role playing adult sexual activities. Toddlers and preschoolers experiment through play and may for example, stick objects into body orifices. However, if this behavior is repetitive and does not appear to cause pain to the child, further assessment of the behavior may be needed. According to Gil (23) school aged children interact more with their peers of both sexes, experience periods of inhibition and experiment with their interactions. They may also be exposed to new sexual behaviors by peers and experiment with these behaviors. Latency aged children continue to interact with school peers, may explore sexual interests and have periods of inhibition and disinhibition. Physical development and puberty at this stage impacts physical and emotional reactions, feelings and behaviors (23).

By their nature, typically developing young children are very curious and inquisitive (18). Early childhood is a time of discovery and exploration (13). There is a natural exploration of all body parts (2) and young children engage in genitally-oriented behavior (14). Sexual behaviors are observed starting in infancy (24). Infants engage in a variety of self-stimulating behaviors such as finger sucking, rocking and cuddling (1) and an explicit interest and play involving genitalia is most frequently observed in 2-6 year old children (17, 18, 21, 25). This overt interest declines as children age, become more involved outside the home and are subjected to societal norms (17, 18, 24). The preschool years are a time of rapid and sizable change (26). Curiosity about sexuality including sexual feelings, exploring body parts and stimulation is expected and has been commonly observed in youth (18). Some studies have shown that certain normative and PSBs have an inverse relationship with age (17, 28). Examples of proposed explanations for this relationship include the immaturity of younger children (17) and decreased opportunities for adults to observe older children engaging in sexual behaviors (18). Sexual behaviors that have been found to decrease as a child ages include exhibitionism (e.g., showing genitals), voyeurism (e.g., looking at others' naked bodies), behaviors related to personal boundaries (e.g., standing too close to others) and self-stimulating behaviors (e.g., genital touching); the most frequent behavior observed in young children. However, interest in the opposite sex, asking questions about sexuality, viewing nude pictures or drawing genitalia, for example, have been observed as more frequent in older children (28).

Parents and day-care providers have reported a variety of child sexual behaviors that are distinguished by their occurrence rates and specificity (8). Behaviors that are reported as occurring less frequently include behaviors that reflect adult sexual behaviors or that are more aggressive or intrusive (e.g., attempted intercourse, oral-genital contact, inserting objects into the vagina or rectum and masturbation with objects). Though such behaviors are shown to occur in approximately less than 3% of children in community samples, they are reported in all investigations using the CSBI (16, 19, 28).

Sexual behaviors are common in children, but the frequency of specific behaviors can vary (13). One European study (13) found that behaviors such as touching self and touching mother's breasts, for example, were widespread in children 0-11 years old. However, uncommon behaviors in this population included imitating sexual behavior with dolls, making sexual sounds and asking to watch explicit adult sexual behavior on television. These researchers also found that 1 in 4 of a group of 670 children showed their genitals to adults or peers. Some behaviors decreased in frequency with age (undressing others, touching mother's breasts, hugging strangers) while others were more frequent among older children. Older children tended to demonstrate interest in the opposite sex, play doctor, ask questions about sexuality, look at pictures of nude bodies, draw genitalia, talk about sexual acts, and ask to view sexually explicit television (13).

Larsson and Svedin (18) conducted a cross-sectional study comparing the frequency and range of sexual behaviors observed in the home environment and in day-care centers among 185 Swedish children aged 3-6 years. In addition, researchers asked caregivers and teachers about the children's general behaviors and their personal views of child sexual behavior. In this study, parents reported observing more sexual behaviors and day-care providers reported encountering more general behavior problems. A significant difference was found between the two setting where children tended to engage more in specific sexual behaviors (e.g., masturbation, showing own genitalia, trying to touch other children's genitals and talking about sex) in the home. A significant difference in sexual behaviors among boys and girls was found in the day-care setting only. Girls were observed by parents using sexual words, showing genitals to other children and role playing male roles significantly more (20-30%) at home than in day-care (4-5%). Boys at home were observed engaging more in four behaviors including rubbing genitals, masturbation with an object, touching genitals in public and talking about being female. However, these behaviors did not occur as frequently as others. On average, boys in the day-care centers engaged in more sexual behaviors. Children sought body contact with all adults but more so with their parents. The number of "advanced sex-play" behaviors was not significant in either setting. Larrson and Svedin's (18) research is consistent with other studies reporting more severe sexual behaviors as uncommon (14). Results of this and other studies indicate that non-maltreated children engage in a wide variety of sexual behaviors and highlights the difficulty of categorizing specific sexual behaviors that are indicative of sexual abuse in children (17, 24).

Sandnabba et al. (19) research looked at sexual behaviors in 364 Finnish 2-7 year olds attending day-care. The children were not assessed for developmental or psychiatric difficulties or histories of CSA. School staff served as observers/informants. The researchers looked at frequency of behaviors as well as age and gender differences. Information on the frequency of sexual behaviors in children can provide a framework for understanding sexual behaviors in children and distinguishing typical from atypical behaviors (10). Compared to earlier studies with normative samples and larger age ranges of subjects, the frequency of sexual behaviors in this population was lower. However, other studies have shown lower frequencies of sexual behaviors reported in day-

care settings compared to home settings (18). Proposed limitations of this study included but are not limited to the focus on preschool-aged subjects and the pre-school setting where there may be less opportunity to observe sexual behaviors and where behaviors may not be acceptable, the influence of the teachers' biases regarding behaviors and the direct nature of questions presented to informants. The authors highlighted that their study reflects an exploratory survey about students' childhood sexual behaviors and does not reflect the actual occurrence rates of these behaviors in the general population. Consistencies with other studies (14, 18, 20) were seen in the most frequently occurring sexual behaviors including, but not limited to, sexual interest and self-exploration, genital play, toilet behavior, engaging in behaviors with other children and voyeuristic behavior. Also consistent with other studies was the absence of behaviors not expected in this age group, including oral and genital penetration and intrusive and odd behaviors (19).

Davies et al. (14) interviewed a small, non-randomized but diverse group of 58 English preschool staff who reported commonly observing children's interests in genitalia through touching or showing genitalia, looking at peers' genitalia and touching women's breasts. Behaviors that infrequently occurred in this young population included insertion of an object into body orifices, oral contact with a peer's or doll's genitals and asking others to touch their genitals. Teachers reported less concern about common behaviors unless specific factors related to the behavior (e.g., frequency) or the child (e.g., child's age, demeanor and comments made while engaged in the behavior) were taken into account. Open and direct questions presented to the teachers appeared to influence their responses. Direct questions yielded responses describing the more rarely observed behaviors. Half of the subjects reported observing some children drawing or modeling genitalia occasionally, as a one-time occurrence or in a phase. Drawings identified as sexual in nature have been viewed by some professionals as an indicator of CSA and it is important to note that this may be a typical childhood sexual behavior. Despite some methodological differences, this study's (14) results regarding the occurrence of common and rare sexual behaviors are consistent with similar studies conducted in different cultures.

OLDER CHILDREN

Friedrich et al. (28) conducted a community-based survey of 880 preadolescent children to assess the frequency of sexual behaviors in a normative population and their association to age, gender, family variables and socioeconomic status. Mothers were questioned about their 2-12 year old children's sexual behaviors as well as demographic information. Youth with histories of CSA were excluded. Subjects reported a wide range of observed behaviors that varied in frequency and that peaked between the ages of 3-5 and decreased in frequency as the children matured. Aggressive and adult-like behaviors were rare. Older children were observed to engage in less sexual behaviors. Sexuality was related to general behavior problems and family nudity but not to socioeconomic status (SES).

In a later study, Friedrich et al. (17) studied the incidents of sexual behaviors in a somewhat diverse group of 1,114 children aged 2-12 years. Attempts were made to study children who did not have a history of CSA in order to identify other variables associated with childhood sexual behaviors. Questionnaires were used to gather data from the children's primary female caregivers. Examples of information gathered included demographic information, hours spent in day-care, occurrence of children's sexual behaviors, children's internalizing and externalizing problem behaviors, peer relationships, family sexuality, mother's views of childhood sexual behavior and children's exposure to family violence, illness and death. Results were consistent with previous studies and indicated that children display a wide range of sexual behaviors at varying frequencies. Most common behaviors found were self-stimulating behaviors, exhibitionism, and behaviors related to personal boundaries. Intrusive sexual behaviors were the least frequent in this population. As the children aged, the frequency of behaviors observed declined. Twenty percent of mothers of male and female children aged 2-5 years endorsed observing a wide range of sexual behaviors. Frequency of sexual behaviors peaked at age 5 years and continuously decreased until age 12. However, an increase in behaviors in 10 year old girls and 12 year old boys was observed and appeared to be related to a reported increased interest in the opposite sex. These results are consistent with Kendall-Tackett et al. (25) study that found sexual behaviors to be common in preschool children, decreasing with age and then reemerging in adolescence.

In the above study (17), researchers found that mothers with a higher level of education and who viewed childhood sexual behavior as normal, reported more sexual behaviors in their children. The study's authors hypothesized that these mothers may have more open attitudes about sexuality and more opportunities to observe their children's behavior. A direct relationship between family sexuality and children's sexual behaviors was also found and may be due to more openness around sexuality or more ease of reporting behaviors. Ethnicity was correlated to income but not to differences in sexual behaviors. Significant relationships were also found between observed sexual behaviors and hours spent in day-care. Reasons for this association are unclear but may reflect youths' exposure to other children with different levels of sexuality. Family violence and total life stress were associated with sexual behavior as well. These experiences have also been associated with other behavioral problems. The authors postulated that family stress may lead to inconsistent parenting, and that family violence often includes poor interpersonal boundaries and intrusiveness and could have impacted the children's behavior. Sexual behavior was also related to the mothers' reports of their children's overall behavioral difficulties. Sexual behaviors as well as other childhood behaviors are viewed on a continuum and can overlap at the extremes of the continuum. Limitations of this study included the possibility that some of the children may have had a history of abuse which therefore could increase the incidence of sexual behaviors. In addition, fewer behaviors observed in older children may reflect decreased opportunities for parents to observe their children engaging in such behaviors (17).

Pithers et al. (28) proposed that there are both common and rare behaviors associated with specific age groups. In their study, Sandnabba et al. (19) found that age had more of an impact on the extent of boys' behaviors especially as they matured. Their behaviors became more expressive while girls' sexual behaviors became more social with age. Girls engaged in more stereotypic gender role behaviors and boys were more explorative and engaged in information-seeking behaviors. In addition, these researchers found no gender differences in a group of behaviors that included for example, talking negatively about children of the opposite sex games that had romantic or sexual characteristics and that tended to increase with age. However, older girls demonstrated less involvement in behaviors related to development and expressed interest in the characteristics of the opposite sex.

Based on the results of several studies, a summary of typical sexual behaviors is presented in Table 1.

Table 1. Typical childhood sexual behaviors

Preschool children	Young children	School-aged children
-Exploring, touching, rubbing (with hand or object) and/or exposing genitals -Removing clothes -Peeking at others undressing or naked -Taking about "poop" and "pee" with same age peers	-Public or private masturbation -Mimicking adult social behaviors (e.g., kissing) -Playing "doctor" -Stating "naughty" words that they may or may not know the significance of	-Asking for more privacy -Privately masturbating -Engaging in sexual play (e.g., "truth or dare," "girlfriend/boyfriend") -Viewing nude pictures -Viewing sexual material through media -Experiencing sexual attraction towards peers

* Adapted from NCTSN (4) and NCSBY (26).

Data on observations of childhood sexual behavior may not be a true indicator of the prevalence and frequency of such behaviors given factors such as privacy or secrecy. Such factors may prevent observations of children engaging in sexual behaviors (14). Retrospective studies have been used to address the limitations of informant reports. In these studies, adults are asked about their early experiences engaging in sexual behavior. These studies have used different methodologies to define sexual behavior. Despite differences, the research indicates that broadly defined sexual experiences between children are common. Forty-two to 94 percent of young adults across studies reported engaging in sexual behavior with their peers. Frequency of experiences in the younger ages decreased, however. This may reflect the participants' ability to recall such early experiences (8).

SEXUAL PLAY

Compared to the small number of studies on typical sexual behavior in children, there is even less research on childhood sexual play. Sexual play is common in childhood (30), but becomes more covert as children mature. Overt sexual behaviors appear to decline with age in part due to the influence of social norms or expectations for such behaviors (17, 19). Children engage in play to re-experience past events as well as practice future (adult) roles and behaviors (10). Play activities can include sexual play with peers (18). Children between the ages of 3-7 years practice and explore gender roles and become aware of genital differences between males and females. Play activities may include "house" and "doctor" (10).

In a review of various retrospective studies using adults' recollections of their child sexual play, Elcovitch et al. (8) noted that various sexual experiences between children are common and that 42-94% of subjects across these studies reported engaging in sexual play. Based on a retrospective study with adult subjects, Lamb and Coakley (11) identified categories of typical childhood sexual play. A group of United States (US) female college students were asked to recall their childhood sexual play experiences. Researchers found that 85% of their population remembered engaging in a sexual game during their childhood and 76% engaged in this activity with their primary friends. Activities described by the subjects were categorized and included "playing doctor" (examining body parts, genitals), which was the most frequently reported game; exposing body parts to peers; exploring physical contact that included arousal; kissing games; exploring adult roles through fantasy sexual play and others (e.g., mimicking sexual activity with dolls). The average age the subjects reported engaging in sexual play was 7.5 years. The adults (majority being parents) in the subjects' lives reportedly found out about these activities in half of the cases. Limitations of this study included the subjects' ability to accurately recall their past experiences, their choice of experiences to discuss, underreporting, and generalizability of subjects' experiences to other populations. Games reported as played by this population were experienced as a source of sexual excitement. Subjects were more likely to have been persuaded or manipulated into the play by boys. The researchers suggested that the play may have reflected enactments of socially defined gender roles. The researchers also found that bullying and manipulation were a part of "normal" sexual play activities. Girls were more likely to feel coerced or manipulated into an activity that made them feel uncomfortable. It was suggested that girls may be less likely to stop or report abuse if coercive experiences are interpreted as play and if they initially and willingly participated in the play. Recommendations for assertiveness training for children who may be confronted by another child to engage in sexual play were also discussed (11).

In a later retrospective study, Larsson and Svedin (30) found that more than 80% of a group Swedish students in their late teens reported engaging in solitary and mutual sexual experiences with a peer prior to the age of 13. Sexual experimentation and exploration appeared to be most prominent in the years before puberty. While solitary, exploratory behaviors increased prior to puberty, exploratory play with a peer decreased after age 10. The majority of mutual play occurred with a peer of a similar age, while 5% reported engaging in sexual play with a sibling. This is consistent with another study (10) where 9% of college age subjects reported engaging in sexual behavior with a sibling. Larsson and Svedin (30) also found that male and female subjects reported positive reactions to their sexual experiences, however, girls experienced more feelings of guilt. Boys engaged in slightly more play with peers and girls engaged in more same sex mutual play. The majority of subjects described their sexual activities as typical. Thirteen percent reported being tricked, bribed, threatened or physically forced into sexual activity. Girls reported more experiences that involved coercion and 10% of girls and 2% of boys reported engaging in sexual behaviors with someone 5 years older. In most cases, the older person was a relative (non-sibling) or a friend under 19 years old. This group also reported more mutual experiences in general and more experiences involving coercion. A small percentage (8.2%) reported coercing others into sexual activity. Limitations of this study include the subjects' ability to remember details of their experiences and interpretation of their experiences. The study authors suggested future research should further address the impact of socialization on childhood sexual behaviors as well as differences between subjective and objective experiences of mutual and coercive sexual activities (30).

The ATSA report (5) differentiates problematic from typical childhood sexual play and curiosity. Normative sexual play is described as unprompted and sporadic. When the behavior involves other children, it is mutual and non-coercive and does not cause emotional distress. It also does not include adult sexual behaviors such as intercourse and oral sex. Typical child sexual development includes curiosity about sexual behavior and body parts and interest in sexual stimulation (5). How these behaviors are expressed is influenced by a child's developmental stage and culture (10, 28). Tolerance of behaviors in one culture may be prohibited in another (5). Children's relationships with caregivers and attachment experiences, which include positive physical contact, can influence future sexual and emotional relationships. In early childhood, children learn about gender roles and expectations through socialization experiences. Parents' restrictions on sexual behaviors can lead children to hide their behaviors and/or seek information from other sources such as peers and the media. Preadolescents may experience sexual attraction and sexual fantasies and as they get older may participate in dating and group activities with peers. Such activities provide them with social experiences to explore intimate relationships (1).

ADOLESCENTS

Adolescents are faced with changes associated with puberty including biological changes and an increase in sexual interests. These changes reflect sexual maturing. Social influences can have an impact on adolescent sexual involvement and behavior. Rates of engaging in heterosexual intercourse increase as adolescents age. In 1999, 48% of females and 52% of males in grades 9-12 reported engaging in sexual intercourse (31).

Age of first sexual intercourse experience varies across cultures. For example, one study (32) found African Americans first sexual experience occurs on average at age 15.5 while Mexican Americans have sex for the first time on average at 17 years old. Boys in these groups tend to have sex at younger ages than girls. Differences between these groups may reflect differences in the adolescents' family structure, church attendance and socioeconomic opportunities such as employment rates and parent education level. Another study (1) found that 5 to 10% of adolescent boys and 6% of adolescent girls report having a sexual experience with someone, usually another adolescent, of the same gender. A portion of these adolescents engage in very few of these experiences out of curiosity (1). One of the psychosocial tasks of adolescence is defining one's identity and role in society in an environment that provides contradictory or inconsistent information. Gender identity is an important part of one's overall identity. In addition, adolescents are faced with learning how to navigate relationships including emotional and physical intimacy. According to the Kaiser Family Foundation (1), youth aged 10-15 most frequently identified media (movies, television, magazines, etc.) as their source of information about sex and intimacy, while fewer identified their parents, peers, sex education programs and professionals.

Brown and Cantor (33) proposed that media has a dominant influence on adolescents and has become a significant part of modern western society. Latency and teen-aged youth use different forms of media up to several hours a day. Media has become more interactive and multisensory and is interpreted by youth in multiple ways. Youth can gather a lot of information about sexuality through the media though less is known about the effects of media exposure on youth. Exposure to media is also mediated by factors such as the child's age, sex, ethnicity and reasons for viewing the material (13). Brown and Witherspoon (34) reported a significant increase in sexual incidents portrayed in television since the mid-1970s. Sexual behavior on television is primarily verbal but physical portrayals occur in movies. Cable television and videos are means for youth to view adult sexual behavior at home. Music which historically focuses on love and sex has increasingly demonstrated sexual images. According to Brown and Witherspoon (34), half of adolescents learn about pregnancy and birth control through the media and half of females report learning about sex through magazines. Research has also demonstrated that children have learned the meaning of words such as prostitution and homosexuality from television and that television and music portray premarital sex as acceptable. Media exposure can influence youths' sexual knowledge and development. However, less is known about the influence of media exposure compared to incidents of young populations viewing sexual behavior through the media (13).

PROBLEMATIC SEXUAL BEHAVIOR (PSB)

Atypical and developmentally inappropriate sexual behaviors in children below the age of 13 have been gaining attention in the child welfare and mental health fields (5). Increased interest in these behaviors began with earlier research demonstrating a significant association between PSB and CSA (24, 25). Children presenting with PSBs are a heterogeneous group, engage in a variety of these behaviors and may require varied treatment approaches (29, 35). Both girls and boys exhibit sexual behavior problems (36). Children with PSB range in age and socioeconomic levels and come from a variety of cultural, social and familial environments and structures. Some have a history of traumatic experiences, maltreatment or mental health difficulties, while others do not. Children with PSB can involve other children, siblings or peers in their behavior and their behaviors are not related to their sexual orientation (37).

Research and clinical experience have demonstrated that children and adolescents engage in a variety of typical and developmentally expected sexual behaviors. Despite the common occurrence of these behaviors, some sexual behaviors in youth are atypical and potentially problematic (25). When a child's behavior or awareness of sexual behavior is not commensurate with his/her age and developmental level, there is cause for concern (13). Studies have looked at a variety of factors that are related, contribute to, and maintain problematic sexual behavior in children. These include biological, familial, economic and cultural factors (21). Research has also attempted to categorize subtypes of children with PSB but these categories greatly overlap (29) and suggest that PSBs differ in severity and intensity (5). PSBs have often been viewed on a continuum and the most aggressive behaviors are deemed the most pathological on the spectrum. In a retrospective study, Hall et al. (38) attempted to develop a typology of sexual behavior problems. They obtained data from the clinical records of a group of 3-7 year old children with a history of CSA. Characteristics related to the child and family functioning were included. The five types of sexual behavior problems derived from the study differed in terms of the behaviors as well as child and family functioning and treatment outcomes. Characteristics that differentiated the types of PSB most included aspects of the child's sexual abuse experience, opportunities for social modeling and practice with problematic behavior, and features of the family that impacted the occurrence of the behaviors. These factors also influenced treatment compliance and outcome. Implications for treatment interventions were discussed and highlighted the importance of tailoring treatment to the needs of the child and family (38).

Kendall-Tackett et al. (25) and others have identified several problematic sexual behaviors such as insertion of objects into the anal-genital regions of the body, excessive and/or public masturbation, asking adults or other children to engage in sexual stimulation, drawing genitalia, and knowledge of adult sexual behavior beyond the developmental level of the child. The types of PSBs that involve more than one child can differ as well, and the level of mutuality and potential for harm can vary. The most alarming PSBs involve children with significant differences in age and developmental functioning, aggressive or coercive acts that cause or have the potential to cause harm and advanced sexual behaviors (5).

The meta-analyses conducted by Kendall-Tackett et al. (25) identified sexual behavior problems in 34% of 351 sexually abused children up to the age of 12. Sexual behavior problems as well as symptoms of PTSD were the only sequelae that occurred significantly more in a population of sexual abused children compared to non-abused children from a clinical setting. Assessment of children presenting with sexual behavior problems should consider several psychosocial risks including CSA as contributing to the behavior (25). More research on the variety of PSBs and associated treatment outcomes is needed (8).

Problematic sexual behaviors can have a variety of origins (39) and can occur independently and concurrently with other behavior problems. Children with the most problematic sexual behaviors tend to have co-morbid mental health, familial and social difficulties (5). Efforts to understand and treat PSB is complicated by the various definitions of the behavior used in research studies (40). Chaffin et al. (5) suggested that younger children with PSB may be more diverse than adolescents with PSB and adult sex offenders, who are predominantly male. Given their immature developmental and cognitive abilities, including a lack of verbal skills, preschool children are prone to engage in sexualized behavior when faced with stressful and confusing situations (26). There are considerable amounts of young boys and girls with PSB (41), and they do not appear to have a unique group of characteristics that distinguish them from other groups of children. The number of children referred for CPS, juvenile justice systems or treatment for PSBs has recently increased. The cause of this increase is unknown and could be the result of increasing PSBs in children, increased awareness and identification of PSBs and/or changing definitions (5).

The antecedents to PSBs are still unclear. Early research implicated CSA as the primary source of PSB in children (24). However, more recent research has demonstrated that many children with PSBs do not have a history of CSA (41) and several factors have been identified as potential causes of PSBs. Studies (5) have identified family, social, economic and developmental factors, child maltreatment, poor parenting practices, media exposure to sexually explicit material, living in a sexualized environment and exposure to family violence as precipitants to sexual behavior difficulties. PSBs have also been shown to result from exposure to adult sexual material or behavior in and outside of the home, inclusion in sexual activities with an older child or adult and/or lack of boundaries, guidance and nurturance in the home (23). Additional precipitating factors include family sexuality patterns, non-sexual behavior problems and physical abuse (36). Pithers et al. (29) described PSBs as one piece of a configuration of disruptive behaviors, and Langstrom et al. (42) suggested that heredity may influence the presence of PSB. Childhood neurological and psychiatric disorders that include impulse control difficulties or obsessive–compulsive personality traits may contribute to an increased tendency for a child to engage in PSBs. Studies on such etiological factors and their development into adult maladaptive or offending sexual behaviors have received less attention in the literature (42).

Research has consistently identified several risk factors for the development of problematic sexual behaviors in preadolescence. These include both severe sexual and physical abuse, families highly distressed by factors such as poverty, perpetration of sexual abuse in the extended family, incarceration for criminal behavior, domestic violence, poor parent-child attachment and familial obstacles to recovery from maltreatment (27). Hall, Mathews and Pearce (38) also identified four predictors of problematic sexual behaviors in children with a history of sexual abuse, including sexual arousal or sadism during the child's own abuse, history of physical and/or emotional abuse, and who the child blames for the abuse.

PSB is not diagnosed as a medical or psychological disorder. Behaviors can present in a variety of combinations and are perceived as beyond society's view of acceptable behavior (5). Based on an analysis of several evaluations of sexual behaviors in developmentally appropriate children below the age of 12 years, Johnson (43) found groups of behaviors falling on a continuum. These groups comprised children with healthy sexual behaviors to sexually reactive children, children who mutually engage in adult-like sexual behaviors and children who sexually abuse other children. Proposed criteria to differentiate typical and problematic sexual behaviors between children include, but are not limited to, differences in the children's age, developmental level, size and status; type of sexual behavior; dynamics and affective quality of the sexual activity or play; frequency, intensity and impulsivity of the behavior; and the use of threats, coercion and dominance (5). Gil and Cavanaugh-Johnson (23) define "sexualized children" as children who engage in problematic sexual behaviors through language, behavior, and excessive thoughts. These children include those who force, bribe, coerce or trick other children to engage in sexual behaviors. Davies et al. (14) identified characteristics of sexual behavior in youth that pose concern including frequency and the child's demeanor or statements while engaged in the behavior. The purpose of PSBs may or may not be used to achieve sexual gratification or stimulation and may be associated with a variety of other factors such as anxiety, attention-seeking and self-soothing behaviors (5). Sexual behavior can become problematic when it is repetitive, interferes with a child's cognitive or social functioning, involves coercion, force or intimidation, occurs under emotional distress, occurs between children of significantly different ages and/or developmental levels, continues to occur in secret despite adult intervention and has the potential to be harmful (36).

ASSOCIATION WITH SEXUAL ABUSE

Atypical sexual behavior can be a red flag for child maltreatment (13). Given the significant incidence of CSA and increased attention in the media to CSA, it is no surprise caregivers and childcare providers become concerned when they observe children engage in sexual behaviors (22). Unfortunately, children around the globe are negatively affected by sexual abuse, and many exhibit PSB. In addition, a significant percentage of sexual abuse offenders are adolescents (44). CPS agencies suggest that a large percentage of sexual abuse is performed by youth below the age of 20 (27). In a sample of 66 children, Gray et al. (27) found that subjects with PSBs had a significant history of child maltreatment (sexual, physical and emotional abuse, and neglect) were abused by an average of 2.5 perpetrators and the perpetrator was under the age of 18 in 40% of the cases.

Sexual behaviors are more often reported by parents with children who have experienced CSA. Therefore, sexual behavior in children can raise concerns of possible abuse (14). However, sexual behaviors in all categories have been reported by parents who had no concerns of abuse (39), and research has demonstrated that although PSB difficulties can be one consequence of CSA, they can occur absent of an abuse history (7, 41). Therefore, the association between CSA and sexual behavior problems is not seen in all children with problematic sexual behaviors, and most children who are sexually abused do not demonstrate PSB. Those who are abused however, tend to exhibit more frequent and intrusive sexual behaviors (8).

Historically, research on the impact of CSA has focused on adults. However, this has changed in the last 2-3 decades. Studies on CSA in young populations have focused on specific types of child victimization and outcomes and used different methodologies, leading to more child-friendly interventions. This literature also allows for the consideration of a developmental framework, the influence of mediating factors and potential outcomes of CSA (25). Several studies have documented a relationship between CSA and sexual behavior problems (19, 24, 25, 44, 45). Many of these studies have looked primarily at clinical populations with a history of CSA and compared them with non-clinical, non-abused populations. Therefore, the focus is on problematic sexual behaviors in a population of sexually abused individuals. Rates of sexualized behavior in populations of sexually abused children were found to be higher compared to children who are not abused and children diagnosed with a psychiatric disorder (29).

Recent concerns about sexual abuse between children and between children and adolescents have identified a need to increase our understanding of normative sexual play. Distinguishing typical play from abusive behaviors is often complicated for caregivers, professionals and the court system. A better understanding of normative play may help in the assessment and intervention of problematic behaviors among children and adolescents. There is evidence (11) that a substantial number of CSA involves children or adolescents abusing other children. Abuse has been seen among siblings and cousins as well. In a pilot study (11), whether force or threats were used, the disclosure of abuse was less likely when it occurred with another child or adolescent. Authors hypothesized that children may not disclose the abuse because they may be unclear as to whether the behavior is abusive and may see themselves a responsible for choosing to engage in something that began as play but became exploitative (11).

A consequence of sexual abuse is traumatic sexualization, which can lead to a variety of psychological sequelae including, but not limited to, sexual aggression and preoccupation, and confusion of sex with love. Studies using parent and self-report psychological assessments and behavioral observations have differentiated sexually abused children, non-abused children and non-abused children with psychiatric diagnoses. Most of the research uses clinical samples. However, several studies comparing clinical populations, including neglected and physically abused children and children with a psychiatric history demonstrate differences in rates of sexualized behaviors. Assessment measures used appear to influence the observation of sexual behaviors (29). More research is needed to further clarify rates of PSB in child population (46).

Meta-analyses have demonstrated that CSA can lead to a variety of traumatizing outcomes. Sexualization and symptoms of PTSD are frequent but not universal outcomes of CSA. The range of outcomes for children who have been sexually abused including lack of symptoms makes assessment and diagnosis difficult. Lack of a single pattern of responses calls for a comprehensive assessment of CSA and has implications for forensic assessments. Symptoms alone or the lack thereof cannot confirm or disconfirm abuse. In addition, few research studies address what leads to symptoms, if present, subsequent to CSA (23). Data on the occurrence rates of sexual behavior in children is important to the diagnosis, treatment and investigation of child abuse cases (25).

Childhood sexual behaviors present and change in frequency at different ages (28). Gil (23) reported that inserting objects in the anal-genital areas of the body occurs with greater frequency in populations of sexually abused children. Kendall-Tackett et al. (25) showed that sexualized behaviors and PTSD are the most reliably associated outcomes of

CSA. However, a majority of these studies focused on the most problematic behaviors in clinical populations of sexually abused individuals as compared to non-clinical, non-abused samples (12) Although research has shown an increased frequency of sexual behaviors in populations of children with a history of sexual abuse, the abuse histories of subjects were not proven, results of the studies are mixed and the type and methods of research limits generalizability.

Research methods used to identify subjects who were sexually abused also complicates conclusions about the relationship between sexual abuse and sexual behavior problems. Using the CSBI, Drach et al. (39) studied a group of 247 children referred for CSA assessment by a multidisciplinary team in a forensic setting. Results did not indicate a significant association between sexual behavior problems and a diagnosis of CSA or a significant association between a diagnosis of CSA and behavior problems as assessed by the CBCL. Sexual behaviors were variable within and between each group of subjects. Variability has been shown in abused and nonabused populations. There is little consensus in the literature as to what defines healthy, typical sexual behaviors in youth. However, behaviors that imitate adult sexual activity are observed more in populations of sexually abused children (10, 18, 20, 24). This increase in behaviors may not persist over time compared to non-abused children, and a variety of hypotheses have been made to try and explain PSBs in this population (27).

OTHER POTENTIAL CAUSES FOR PROBLEMATIC SEXUAL BEHAVIOR

Given our current understanding and the research findings and limitations regarding the correlation between CSA and PSBs, it is important to consider multiple contextual variables and other child maltreatment experiences when evaluating sexual behaviors in children; assessment and future research should consider variables other than CSA as potential antecedents (18, 21). The National Research Council (12) suggested that to better understand the antecedents and outcomes of child maltreatment and specifically the relationship between sexualized behaviors and child maltreatment, consideration should be given to several characteristics of the maltreatment including but not limited to severity, age of onset, resulting injury, chronicity, substantiation and exposure to maltreatment. Merrick et al. (12) looked at characteristics of maltreatment (timing and type) other than CSA that contribute to sexualized behaviors. A large sample of primary caregivers was interviewed about their 8 year-old children's behaviors. Participants were obtained from the LONGSCAN Consortium. The children in the study had a history of maltreatment other than CSA or were at risk for maltreatment. Results indicated that early and late reports of physical abuse and late reports of emotional abuse increased the probability of the child engaging in sexualized behaviors. Whereas early reports of emotional abuse were associated with decreased probability of sexualized behaviors, a history of physical abuse was predictive of sexualized behaviors and predicted more sexualized behavior for boys (e.g., exposing private parts, sexual intrusiveness) compared to girls (e.g., boundary difficulties). Although effect sizes were small, they demonstrated that experiences other than CSA can influence the probability of a child engaging in PSB.

The authors of the above study (12) suggested several hypotheses for the association between PSB and maltreatment other than CSA. For example, maltreatment such as physical abuse can create anxiety and difficulties regulating emotions for children. Subsequently, children may engage in sexual behaviors to manage these emotions and/or seek intimacy to cope with traumatic experiences. Difficulties with regulating emotions and behavior can result in externalizing behavior problems. Sexual behavior is an externalizing behavior and may respond to effective self-regulation skills (21). However, maladaptive coping, including aggressive sexual behaviors (12) and contributing factors may lead to negative outcomes such as juvenile delinquency (29). In addition, maltreatment is associated with family characteristics that may increase a child's exposure to sexual material and poor socialization skills (12). Rates of developmental and mental health difficulties in children who have a history of maltreatment and exposure to risk factors range from 50-80%. These statistics highlight the importance of effective coping skills to buffer the negative effects of maltreatment (12).

Additional studies have explored antecedents other than CSA to PSB. For example, Friedrich et al. (24) found that a child's age, family sexuality (e.g., nudity) and hours spent in day-care contributed to sexual behaviors in children. In contrast, more recent studies found no correlation between hours spent in day-care and rates of sexual or other behaviors (18). In another study, Silovsky and Niec (41) found that rates of physical abuse and witnessing family violence to be higher than CSA in a population of preschool children with problematic sexual behaviors. In addition, research by Friedrich and Trane (21) demonstrated that physical abuse and domestic violence have been associated with sexual and other behavior problems in children. As mentioned above, Langstrom et al. (42) looked at the influence of genetic and environmental factors influencing child sexual behavior problems. They focused on masturbatory behaviors in a group of Swedish 7-9 year old same-sex twins. Data was collected from over 1,000 parents/caregivers using items on the CBCL that address sexual problems. Results indicated that the presence of problematic masturbatory behavior could be influenced by genetically determined "personality traits" (e.g., impulse control) and/or a genetically determined vulnerability to engage in problematic sexual behavior subsequent to environmental stress. They suggest that stressful life events as well as genetic factors should be considered in the evaluation of pre-pubertal children presenting with atypical masturbatory behavior. It is also theorized that children with PSBs have difficulty with emotional and behavioral regulation (5), externalizing behavior problems (40), and poor social skills (24).

A history of CSA is a risk factor for offending behavior; however, the majority of CSA victims do not subsequently offend. Furthermore, compared to experiences of CSA and neglect, a larger majority of physically abused kids have been shown to engaged in sexual offending (44). Scant research has been conducted on the sexual behaviors of young children and the influence of family variables and other child behaviors. More research has drawn general conclusions about specific child sexual behaviors and when they occur (17). Defining normative sexual behavior is not only important to the understanding of child development but also to the assessment and diagnosis of atypical childhood sexual behaviors. Lack of baseline data can lead to the minimization of problematic sexual behaviors or over-reaction to expected developmental behaviors. For example, normative sexual behaviors can be pathologized and/or misinterpreted as indicators of CSA or unusual behavior, whereas, oversight of such behaviors can lead to a failure in the detection and intervention in cases of CSA or psychopathology.

CHILDREN WITH ASD AND PSBS

Autism spectrum disorder (ASD) is a disorder of development that affects psychological and behavioral functioning. Both ASD and Asperger's disorder (AD) fall on a spectrum of severity but are characterized by deficits in reading social cues and social communication, by limited interests and perseverative or repetitive behaviors. AD differs from other disorders, however, in its relatively normal language and cognitive abilities (9, 47). Similar to typically developing peers, children with AD experience different sexual development stages. A common fallacy is that children with AD or other developmental disorders either do not experience sexual feelings or are extremely delayed. This can create problems for children with AD because they are not being adequately educated on sexual development and behaviors, such as appropriate touching of their own bodies as well as others. Children with disabilities need the same sex education and guidance as their typically developing peers in order to develop a sexual identity and have a framework for what is sexually appropriate and what is not. Without this information, coupled with an inability to understand social norms, social reciprocity, and likelihood of engagement in repetitive or self-stimulating behaviors, children with ASDs may be at risk for victimization, re-victimization or for victimizing others (35).

Sullivan and Caterino (48) suggested that individuals with ASD experience a large number of sexual behaviors which can be perceived as problematic due to societal norms.

Social norms are difficult for individuals with ASD to recognize. These social deficits are fundamental characteristics of the disorder, complicating forming appropriate relationships. Specific impairments include: difficulty respecting personal boundaries, differentiating public vs. private behaviors, obsessional interests which may not correlate with the developmental stage of peers and which may include sexualized behavior, challenges in accurately reading or interpreting social cues, lack of empathy or not considering the viewpoint of another and difficulties handling anxiety. Youth with ASD may also receive negative reinforcement from peers or caregivers for sexualized behaviors. For adolescents, premature sexual development or puberty can lead to changes in hormones which can affect or change behavior. If norms do not apply, specifically the core impairments of AD listed above, PSBs can emerge (48). Frequently reported inappropriate sexualized behaviors in individuals with ASD include, touching self, touching others, masturbation (excessive or in public), and sexual talk.

EFFECTS OF DISABILITY AND OTHER CO-MORBID FACTORS

Children and adolescents with ASD may present with comorbid psychiatric, medical and behavioral difficulties such as attention deficit hyperactivity disorder (ADHD) and oppositional defiant disorder (ODD). Comorbid conditions can increase the likelihood that youth with ASD engage in sexualized behaviors. (41, 47). For example, a study comparing individuals with ASD and those with obsessive compulsive disorder (OCD) found that people with both of these diagnoses reported more sexual obsessions than people with OCD without ASD (47). These two disabilities have overlapping features-- ritualistic behavior and obsessional qualities--which may be influencing the unwanted behaviors. Consider the following case example:

> A 10 year-old child with a complicated birth history has been diagnosed with multiple neurological and behavioral conditions, including AD and ADHD. This child has struggled with social, behavioral and attentional issues including impulsivity and poor decision making. It has been difficult to tease out the primary diagnosis due to the array of issues presented which have also complicated overall assessment and treatment planning. For several years, this child has exhibited problematic and perseverative behaviors but the primary treatment goal has focused on decreasing PSBs. As the child has gotten older, there is an increased desire to be with peers, but his behavioral issues, repetitive thoughts and difficulty accurately reading social cues have interfered with achieving success.

For individuals with ASD, anxiety is a primary affective experience and is commonly due to the desire to control their environment (49). Their anxiety can be manifested in self-stimulating behaviors and other behavioral issues. Individuals with AD struggle with social, attentional and behavioral issues including impulsivity, inattention, executive functioning difficulties and poor decision making (49). The 10 year-old child referred to above has had some success in decreasing several behavioral difficulties, but less success in permanently decreasing or eradicating the sexualized behavior. There may be several reasons for this, including the consequences given for the sexualized behavior having the opposite intended effect. Instead of decreasing the sexualized behaviors, negative consequences could be providing reinforcement in terms of giving attention. For many parents, not providing consistent consequences but providing an abundance of attention (although negative) may inadvertently encourage behavior. Educating parents about appropriate sexualized behavior, behavior management, accepting their child's limitations, understanding the reasons why the sexualized behaviors are manifested and the neurological component are necessary.

Ray and Marks (49) discussed the possibility of PSB becoming a "pattern of behavior." Children with AD cognitively understand right from wrong, but lack insight into their own behavior, misinterpret societal rules, and view what others may think in a secondary light. They can also perceive other children's lack of verbal refusal (e.g., saying 'no') or compliance as agreement to take part in behaviors. One 7 year-old client of average cognitive ability diagnosed with AD, for example, demonstrated her knowledge of rules regarding appropriate and inappropriate sexual behaviors but this knowledge did not deter her from engaging in PSB. In fact, lying and purposefully finding opportune moments where she can be alone with another child have manifested. A major concern for this child's future is that her sexual preoccupation and various other contributing factors become increasingly severe and problematic despite treatment efforts.

ADOLESCENTS WITH ASD AND SEXUALIZED BEHAVIORS

The challenges faced by children with autism continue into adolescence but can be further complicated by puberty and the desire for intimate relationships. Navigating adolescent relationships is challenging for all teenagers, but adolescents with ASD display more inappropriate sexualized behaviors due to significant problems with social skills, identifying their own feelings, experiencing empathy and a failure to accurately understand another person's intended message (47, 50, 51). The difficulty they have expressing their feelings should not be mistaken for not having feelings (47). Although adolescents with ASD experience sexual urges like their typically developing peers, problems arise because they have difficulty processing nonverbal interactions, such as body language, facial expressions and tone of voice, and they do not understand the social norms necessary to figure out the nuances of intimate relationships.

Adolescents with ASD or other developmental disabilities therefore are at increased risk for exhibiting inappropriate sexual behaviors as well as for being physically, emotionally and sexually abused. Chan and John (47) discussed several factors that may contribute to these risks. Depending on the severity of the ASD or other developmental disability, adolescents may need adult assistance or supervision with daily living skills. This assistance may include helping with physical needs (e.g., toileting, dressing). This population is also less likely to receive sex education from their parents or school personnel. Parents may not have the skills needed to provide their adolescents information about changes in physical development and/or appropriate and inappropriate touching or inappropriate sexualized behaviors. This lack of information can increase the adolescent's vulnerability and risks of being taken advantage of or victimized by others. Given that many adolescents with ASD experience social awkwardness and difficulty recognizing proper social cues, some parents may be fearful of providing their children information that they think could be misunderstood by their child or others as permission to engage in these behaviors. This can lead adolescents with AD to feel frustrated and angry as they try to seek out relationships and intimacy, and their behaviors may be misinterpreted as PSBs (46, 52).

Typical adolescents develop a sense of self and sexuality from many sources, including day to day interaction with peers. This can be difficult for a teenager with ASD who, as mentioned earlier, may not understand subtle social innuendos or have the opportunity to experience intimate relations. They may also not learn as well through observation of others and misinterpret what they see and/or hear. This can lead youth with ASD to copy behaviors that may be out of context or inappropriate for a given situation. For example, a 12 year-old female diagnosed with ASD observed her older sister kissing her boyfriend which she misinterpreted as permission to kiss others. Her subsequent kissing behaviors led her family to believe she could have been sexually abused. It is not uncommon for inappropriate sexual behaviors to be misconstrued as signs of sexual abuse (53). Peers also may not serve as the best role models for this population because they can purposefully provide inappropriate information in order to cause embarrassment or humiliation. For these reasons and others, it is essential for parents to provide information about sexuality and puberty.

The literature (46, 50, 51) has discussed the frequency of sexualized behaviors and masturbation amongst adolescents with AD/ASD. It is normal for all teenagers to have sexual urges and masturbate. Those without developmental difficulties, however, have enough insight and impulse control to do this in private, as appropriate (54). According to Henault (51), public masturbation is the most frequently reported form of inappropriate sexual behavior for male adolescents with ASD. Many people with ASD are impulsive and hyperactive, and may use masturbation as a self-soothing behavior when they have a sexual urge, are feeling anxious, or are in a stressful situation. These feelings can especially be brought on in a new environment, with new routines or when there is uncertainty about when future events will occur. Like other ASD behaviors, masturbation can become compulsive and/or a distraction and can lead to exposure of genitals. Connor (46) defined inappropriate masturbation as "that which is constant, is maintained regularly but associated with feelings of shame, or is carried out in front of people."

It is necessary for youth with ASD to understand that masturbation is a normal and expected behavior, but that boundaries are needed. Depending on the reactions of others to this behavior, adolescents may not understand these boundaries or feel they are doing something 'bad', which can create feelings of guilt. Concrete examples and supportive interventions need to be provided to help individuals distinguish between conducting this behavior in private vs. public places. It may also be beneficial to review multiple topics, including public exposure or masturbation, at an earlier age before behaviors become problematic (46, 51).

ISSUES FOR ASSESSMENT

For the assessment of childhood sexual behaviors, it is important to consider a variety of factors that could have precipitated or influenced the behavior. For example, does the behavior ordinarily occur among children of the same developmental stage or culture? Is the behavior repetitive? How preoccupied is the child with the behavior or sex? And can the behavior be corrected with adult intervention? When more than one child is involved in the behavior, assessment should consider for example, the difference in the children's ages and developmental stages, elements of force, coercion or intimidation, emotional distress in one or more of the children, potential for injury from the behavior and the possible negative impact on a child's social development from engaging in the behavior (55). Behavioral assessment of sexual behaviors should also include a chronology of behaviors and corresponding events using multiple informants (5).

Stress can have an impact on a child's behavior including exacerbating already existing behaviors. When a child is engaging in repetitive, stimulating sexual behaviors, it is important to assess if the behavior can be easily redirected, if the child performs the behavior in public and if the child's behavior is negatively affecting his/her overall functioning. Assessment of any sudden changes in behavior should also be considered. When gathering information about a child who engages in sexual behaviors, it is essential to assess if there is any history of child maltreatment, exposure to adult sexual material, such as pornography, and exposure to adult sexual activity. Assessment of sexual behaviors in children can yield different outcomes. For example, assessment results could lead to a referral to a child advocacy center to rule out child abuse, a report to CPS, and/or a referral for treatment (13).

Adult's knowledge, beliefs and personal experiences can influence their interpretation of observed sexual behaviors in children (14). Professionals should especially be aware of their personal biases and values when assessing child sexual behaviors and follow accepted guidelines. Assessment of sexual behaviors informs subsequent recommendations and interventions and accuracy of the assessment can potentially lead to a positive or negative outcome for the child. Lack of available information on typical and atypical sexual behaviors in youth can lead to the possibility of personal standards influencing assessment practices. Few studies have addressed professionals' interpretations of typical child sexual behaviors. Given the potential influence of their work and professional roles on their perceptions, Heiman et al. (10) chose to compare the perspectives of professionals working with sexually abused children with professionals and medical students working and training in the area of human sexuality. These researchers found that sexual behaviors involving oral, anal or vaginal penetration were consistently viewed as abnormal in children under 12 years old. A lack of consensus among subjects was found when self-directed behaviors were assessed. Interactive sexual play was assessed as more atypical than self-directed sexual behavior, even among similar behaviors. Consistent with other research, female subjects perceived sexual behaviors as more atypical than male subjects. The authors hypothesized that socialization and gender role responsibilities may have an influence on the interpretation of sexual behaviors. Professional role had a significant impact on interpretation of behaviors. Professionals working directly with sexually abused children assessed certain sexual behavior as more "abnormal." However, results did not indicate that the CSA experts overpathologized behaviors. Agreement was found among subjects regarding their assessment of a young child inserting her fingers into an anatomically detailed doll's vagina as typical. This finding is inconsistent with previous concerns about the misdiagnosis of abuse when dolls are used in child abuse investigations, and supports the observation that young children's exploration of dolls' body parts is typical. Significant disagreement was found on 6 of 20 scenarios presented between subjects with the most diverse professional backgrounds. The majority of these items represented interactive, adult-like, sexual behaviors and were similar to behaviors assessed in previous (e.g., 19) studies as low frequency behaviors. CSA experts and medical students demonstrated the most disagreement. Compared to medical students and CSA trainees, CSA experts tended to view behaviors as more "normal" and differentiated types of behaviors vs. assessing individual behaviors as "normal" or "abnormal." Trainees and facilitators of human sexuality groups demonstrated directional (towards abnormal or normal) bias (10). Sexual behaviors are one part of a child's overall functioning (43) and there is not one way to determine typical sexual behavior. However, lack of knowledge regarding typical and atypical sexual behaviors in youth may create a risk for professionals using personal standards to assess these children (56). In the investigation of suspected child sexual abuse, knowledge of age-appropriate sexual behaviors is imperative for the professionals assessing if abuse occurred (10).

As discussed in the ATSA report (5), a good assessment should attempt to identify the situation(s) in which the sexualized behaviors are occurring. An assessment should look at environmental, contextual and genetic factors and whether the sexualized behaviors are self-focused or directed at other children. Clinicians should try to determine if the behaviors are occurring when a child is feeling stressed or anxious, is responding to environmental triggers, or during moments of opportunity, such as during play dates or sleepovers. The frequency and duration of the behaviors as well as the presence of other behavioral issues should also be determined. Multiple sources can be used to gather this information. Sources may include parents, teachers, therapists and possibly other children in order to obtain a more accurate and complete picture (5).

In addition to assessment of sexual behaviors, children's general behavioral and psychological functioning, co-morbid conditions and history of traumatic experiences should be assessed. PSB can be a primary or secondary concern. Children with PSB may have co-morbid disruptive behavior difficulties, anxiety and depression, developmental and cognitive difficulties and a history of maltreatment and/or exposure to violence (5).

For research and clinical purposes, two standardized instruments have been used by professionals to assess sexualized behaviors. The Child Sexual Behavior Checklist (CSBCL–II) (5, 56) lists 150 behaviors related to sex and sexuality in children, and the Child Sexual Behavior Inventory (CSBI) (5, 16) measures the frequency of common and atypical behaviors and sexual knowledge. In 2002, Friedrich (57) developed the third edition, CSBI–III, which added four additional items that assess aggressive sexual behaviors. The outcome of these measures in conjunction with information obtained through other channels previously described can help guide professionals toward the most effective and best treatment options for each individual case.

If there is concern that a child has been sexually abused and the sexualized behaviors are seemingly secondary to the potential trauma, it is important to first conduct a forensic interview to help determine if in fact the abuse occurred. Forensic interviews are used as an initial assessment to rule out sexual abuse as the cause of inappropriate sexualized behaviors and protocols are put into place to conduct these interviews. There are special considerations that need to be taken into account when interviewing children or adolescents with ASD or any population with developmental disabilities (58, 59).

Difficulties with communication, length of the interview, likelihood of a single interview, and introduction to a new environment are some of the obstacles professionals may encounter when attempting to conduct a valid and reliable interview with these populations (49).

Prior to the first interview appointment, the forensic team should gather comprehensive information on the extent of the youth's developmental disability, including any psychiatric, psychological and educational evaluations and individualized education plans (IEP). An example of additional information to gather prior to the forensic interview includes, information regarding the child's emotional and behavior reactions to new situations. This data can be useful when preparing for the interview and support the forensic team's efforts to address the child's individual needs. During the initial stage of the forensic evaluation process, building rapport with the child and conducting an informal developmental assessment is especially important as the child's level of comfort and functioning can influence possible accommodations needed to conduct a reliable interview (58).

With all forensic interviews, the goal is to obtain the most valid and accurate information. This is typically achieved through open-ended questions in order to decrease suggestibility. For children or adolescents with developmental disabilities, there are several factors that may complicate the interview process For example, language difficulties, impaired memory, and problems with free recall may make using open-ended questions with this population difficult. However, youth with developmental disabilities can provide accurate and reliable information if they are interviewed properly (59, 60). The developmental and mental age of the child must be strongly considered, not just the chronological age. Questions should be asked at a slow pace, using simple language and correct pronouns. In addition, more open-ended questions should be introduced first, followed by cued invitations and more direct yet non-leading questions (61). Nonverbal interview aids should be available, such as crayons, dollhouses, visual aids or drawings to aid verbal disclosures. Other possible interview accommodations could include shortening the length of each session, eliminating noise or distractions, and/or utilizing an extended forensic interview model which allows for multiple sessions over time (59, 61)

After the forensic evaluation is completed, a comprehensive functional assessment can take place to help determine if the sexualized behaviors are the primary issue or secondary, and whether non-sexual behaviors could be impacting the sexualized behaviors. Sexual development in children with ASD or developmental delays is complicated by the increased likelihood of sexual abuse, comorbidities and various other factors related to their developmental delays such as anxiety and a decreased ability to read social cues and conform to social norms. There are a number of assessment tools and methods available to practitioners to help determine the drivers of sexualized behaviors in this population as well as various treatment options. The outcome of a comprehensive evaluation and/or functional assessment should help guide the clinician in formulating a treatment plan or to make appropriate referrals.

In contrast to forensic investigations that seek to determine if a behavior occurred or to rule out CSA, clinical evaluations of children with PSBs can aid in the development of interventions and treatment plans and provide recommendations to child welfare and juvenile justice agencies who are engaged in case planning and decision making (e.g., placement decisions). ATSA (5) recommends that assessments should be conducted by licensed mental health professionals with expertise in a variety of areas related to child development, childhood mental health, and behavioral difficulties and who are familiar with the current research in these areas. It is also suggested that these professionals have knowledge of factors related to children with PSB such as contextual factors impacting children's behaviors, and the influence of culture on parenting and child sexual behaviors. In addition, assessments should be tailored to individual cases and include an assessment of the environments (e.g., family and school environments) in which the behaviors occurred. Individual characteristics of a child may be less potent than the child's environment in influencing behavior. Changes in the environment are frequently necessary to change an individual child's behavior. Environmental factors both in and outside a child's home recommended to be assessed include, but are not limited to, the quality of the parent-child relationship and parenting skills, presence of positive role models, cultural influences, areas of resilience, history of traumatic experiences and child maltreatment, and exposure to sexual and/or violent material from adults, peers or through the media (5).

ISSUES FOR TREATMENT

PSBs can be resolved for most children with outpatient treatment and supervision. More severe and aggressive sexual behavior that may co-occur with a psychiatric or other behavioral disorder and that has not responded to other interventions may require a higher level of care (e.g., inpatient treatment). Children who are supervised and receive appropriate interventions for sexual behavior problems can live with other children. However, children who engage in ongoing intrusive and aggressive sexual behaviors and do not respond to close monitoring or treatment should be separated from other children until the behavior is resolved (36). For children in placement, assessment and intervention should occur in the current and future placements, including during reunification with the family of origin (5).

For children with AD, a change in environment may exacerbate or decrease sexualized behaviors. Prior to formulating a treatment plan, it may be helpful to determine if there are any triggers or whether environmental changes can be made in order to decrease sexual behaviors. This may include removing objects that are associated with the behavior or changing attire on the child, for example, by adding a belt (62). Placing children in a setting that is very structured may decrease feelings of anxiety and the need to control their surroundings. This type of predictable environment, coupled with consistent supervision, may also lead to a decrease in sexualized behaviors.

Given the multiple antecedents to and expressions of sexual behavior difficulties in youth, a variety of interventions may be needed (63). ATSA (5) describes PSBs as diverse and that vary in severity and potential for harm to other children. There is no specific set of characteristics that identifies youth with PSB or rules that dictate decisions regarding, for example, placement. Legal adjudication issues should be made on a case by case basis. In addition, interventions should be revisited regularly given the possible changes that can occur with the individual child and their environments. Treatment should include modifications to the environments surrounding the child to help eliminate factors that can trigger or maintain the PSBs and identification of resources that can help address the problem behaviors (5).

Much concern has been expressed regarding children who have sexual behavior difficulties and their potential for future sex offending behavior. Current research indicates that when proper treatment is provided, the risk for re-offending is low and no greater than with other clinical populations. The risk for future offences may equal the risk for victimization. Children with PSBs generally respond well to cognitive behavioral and psychoeducational interventions that involve their caregivers. Few cases of children with PSBs require more intensive and restrictive interventions. Children with PSB are quite different from adult sex offenders and are not seen as their child counterparts. Interventions for adults are not applicable to children with PSBs. In addition, actions that attempt to protect society by isolating and criminalizing children with PSB may only lead to more difficulties and shame for these children (5).

Treating children or adolescents with sexualized behaviors can be challenging. Specific treatment modifications need to be considered for youth with ASD, AD and other developmental disabilities due to their limited insight, impulsivity, concrete understanding of concepts, possible cognitive limitations, linguistic issues and difficulty generalizing acquired knowledge to real life scenarios. There are several treatment options depending on whether the sexualized behaviors are considered internalizing or externalizing behaviors. The focus of the interventions should be determined on a case to case basis after a careful analysis is completed and the primary problematic behavior is identified. Treatments such as trauma focused-cognitive behavioral therapy (TF-CBT), that target trauma symptoms (i.e., posttraumatic stress disorder) and may be indicated for children or adolescents with internalizing behaviors. However, if a child presents with externalizing or disruptive behaviors, the primary focus of this chapter, other behavioral interventions may be more effective (64).

Concrete behavioral strategies that use behavior charts and reward systems with immediate consequences can be effective in shaping target behaviors in children and adolescents with ASD. When formulating a chart, it is useful to isolate the primary problematic behavior and focus on decreasing the frequency of its occurrence prior to moving on to other issues. Other possible interventions for any child with behavioral difficulties, but specifically for individuals with ASD, include role playing, "social stories" and video modeling to help assist with social skills development, emotion regulation, linking feelings of anxiety to social situations, and helping the child understand the impact of their behavior on other people's feelings (47, 65, 67). Often children and adolescents with ASD present with behaviors that are more impulsive than compulsive, so strategies such as cognitive restructuring or understanding the abuse cycle may not be as effective with this population. Consistent use of effective interventions is an important element to ensure permanent eradication of an undesirable behavior. Short-term success and intermittent reduction in sexualized behaviors can often occur during periods of consistent supervision in a predictable environment. Therefore, interventions need to continue even if the sexualized behaviors decrease, or they will not likely have a lasting effect (68).

Several researchers (65, 67) have discussed the use of "social stories" to help children and adolescents manage problematic behaviors. The stories provide information youth may need to achieve success in a social situation. Using a step-wise approach, the stories address specific issues or situations by teaching the child or adolescent the appropriate expected behavior. The stories are individually tailored to the child's needs and developmental abilities. For individuals diagnosed with AD and language difficulties, the use of a social story can combine verbal directions with pictures or prompts. Self-monitoring strategies may also assist in decreasing sexualized behaviors, and techniques are dependent on the age or developmental level of the child. A self-regulation chart, such as an emotions thermometer, measuring levels of excitability, may be used to help a child with developmental disabilities recognize when he/she is overstimulated and how to respond accordingly. For example, a child may be directed to use self-calming strategies or take a break from the source of excitement. Other strategies may use visual aids or prompts, such as cards with red and green lights and stop signs. These can be placed around the home to indicate where certain behaviors are or are not acceptable. Pictures can also be worn around the child's neck as reminders or to help them generalize appropriate behaviors to other settings. Another behavioral intervention includes providing a replacement behavior that can help comfort or redirect a child from the undesired sexual behavior. For example, when working with a 10 year-old male who would frequently grab his genitals in public, a squeeze ball was introduced in order to redirect his attention.

Regardless of whether treatment is focused on young children or adolescents or which treatment option is employed, parental or primary caregiver support and consistency needs to be maintained to achieve any success (69). Communication between the clinician and the parent is important in order to ensure continuity and consistency of information given and techniques used, and to assist a parent in determining appropriate language used with their child and that corresponds with the age and abilities of their child. There are several methodologies that can be used to accomplish this including, dyadic treatment, parent collateral sessions and/or family therapy. Caregivers need to be educated about normal sexual development in order to recognize inappropriate sexual behaviors if they arise, and to be able to respond promptly and appropriately. They should provide their child information on appropriate and inappropriate touch, boundaries and privacy rules, model appropriate attire and affection with others, and encourage and demonstrate positive and appropriate peer interactions (5).

Professionals also need to consider a variety of factors that may impact families' reactions and receptivity to interventions that address sexuality and sexual behaviors. These include, but are not limited to, racial identity, ethnicity, religion, SES, cultural beliefs and norms, and social environments within which the child interacts. It is important to assess the family's beliefs, values and practices in terms of sexual knowledge and behavior. These include the family's implicit and explicit rules about sexual behavior, relationships and intimacy and comfort with addressing these issues. Openness, respect and understanding of a family's culture may strengthen the working relationship and make the family more receptive to the professional's interventions. Professionals should also be aware of their personal knowledge, beliefs and values about sexuality and sexual behavior that coincide or conflict with their family clients and that could have the potential to negatively impact the provision of services and the professional relationship. Information provided about sexuality and sexual behaviors should be consistent with the family's beliefs (4).

When incidents of sexual behavior or CSA and subsequent concerns about a child's safety warrant discussions with families whose practices (e.g., cultural or religious) do not include an openness about sexuality or sexual behavior, it is important for professionals to respect the family's values, explain the reasons for their interventions and work with the family to identify options, not only for discussing the presenting concerns, but also for recommendations and interventions. This requires flexibility on the part of the professional. Treatment interventions should consider the child's social and cultural context and developmental abilities, the family beliefs and values, and the parents' acceptance of information provided to their children during the treatment (4).

THE IMPACT OF CAREGIVERS

The development of a child's or adolescent's sexual knowledge is influenced by the information they receive from a variety of sources including their family, culture, school, peers, community, the media and the individual developmental abilities they possess to understand and interpret this information. This information can be implicit, explicit and conflicting. As children mature, they develop knowledge and attitudes that are also influenced by the presence or absence of support and reactions from adults (e.g., caregivers and teachers). Studies have shown that parents can help to reduce youth engagement in some risky sexual behaviors and mediate sexual information obtained through the media through close supervision and effective communication with their child (4).

Several theories explain the impact of context or environment on the child's emerging sexual development (2). Socialization has an early influence on an individual's development. Children are taught rules, norms and values about their culture, relationships, and behavior. These norms and values are learned through observation and imitation, the responses of others to their behaviors and direct instruction. This socialization process includes acquiring rules about sexuality. Gil (23) states that parent reactions to children's sexual behavior can mediate the child's sexual development. Parents who are inflexible and punish typical sexual behaviors may produce feelings of guilt and shame in their children and possibly lead them to hide subsequent behaviors or concerns about sexuality. In contrast, parents who do not limit exposure to sexual content may trigger their children to act out sexually. Children may learn that certain sexual behaviors are prohibited while others only occur in a private setting (21). Parents' decisions to provide information to their children can be influenced by the child's age and developmental level, concerns about safety and cultural factors, for example. Information about sexuality can be provided formally or informally to children (4). Sex education requirements across school systems vary and may be different from the information received in the children's home. Despite the shock and disbelief caregivers often experience when they observe their children engage in sexual behavior, the assumption that their children possess a sophisticated or mature understanding of sexuality and/or their sexual behaviors is often inaccurate and can add to the caregivers' concerns.

Larsson and Svedin (18) found that 67% of the parents and 41% of the teachers in their study never spoke to their children and students about sexual behaviors but their attitudes about sexuality were found to be quite open. Discussions more commonly occurred when the children initiated the conversation. More than half of the teachers spoke to parents about children's sexual behaviors while the majority (92%) of parents did not speak with the teachers. One fifth of all of the adults did not have names for the children's genitals. More adults named boys genitalia using accurate labels than girls, who more likely were given inaccurate or colloquial names for their genitals. The majority of the adults believed that it is normal for children to be curious about sexuality, engage in sexual play, and experience sexual feelings, but less frequently believed that children engage in sexual behavior.

Home environments tend to be less structured and provide opportunities for children to not only see family members undress, but to show curiosity about nudity, have conversations with their caregivers about body functions, and display sexual behaviors. The school environment tends to be a more structured and monitored group setting. Early in life, children are socialized to keep sexual behaviors private (10). School settings may place demands on children to conform with social norms and provide less opportunities for children to engage in sexual behavior. However, in the above study, teachers were viewed as slightly more liberal than parents regarding child sexual behavior (18).

Parents often have the unexpected experience of encountering their child exploring their bodies or engaging in sexual play. Many parents may feel uncomfortable or uncertain in these often spontaneous events and can react in a number of ways. They may react with shock, anger, anxiety and/or embarrassment and have concerns about their child's safety and development (22). The increase in information and attention on sexual abuse may also produce confusion for parents addressing issues of sexuality with their children. Parent's responses or management of sexualized and non-sexualized behaviors can influence a child's sexual development (13). Adult expectations for gender specific behaviors or "gender role stereotypes" can also influence a child's socialization and behaviors (19). It is important to normalize sexual behaviors in children for parents (13) and to address the distress they may experience when witnessing their children engage in sexual behaviors.

Educating children about sex and sexuality is often a difficult task for parents. It is suggested that they provide accurate and developmentally appropriate information to their children in order to enhance safety, healthy habits and self-confidence with their bodies (4). It is suggested that parents talk with their children about sexuality and development, privacy, and safety. Parents awareness and guidance can help address information the child is exposed to outside home, clarify questions, and define what is acceptable. In addition, supervising the child's media use can help to protect, prevent, and address exposure to inappropriate sexual material (13).

Children learn rules of physical interactions through the reactions of others to their behavior. Boundaries for such behavior can promote privacy for self and others and identity protection in future sexual interactions. The reactions of adults and peers to young children who break such boundaries can produce feelings of shame for the child that can be long lasting and internalized. Parents are often surprised and anxious when they encounter their child engaging in sexual behavior. Their alarm may result in a variety of questions and concerns. They may fear that their child has been exposed to adult sexual material or been abused. They may also question if their child's behavior is developmentally inappropriate or typical. Parents' reactions can vary and are influenced by their familial and cultural backgrounds and belief systems. When appropriate, validating the child's behavior as typical can often ease parents' fears of sexual abuse and influence their reactions and management of the behavior. They often need support and education regarding developmentally expected child behaviors. Intervention includes the family and it is important to assess the parents' backgrounds and beliefs about sexual development and behavior as well as their past experiences including trauma history and current stressors (13).

Parenting a child with sexualized behaviors and DDs can be very stressful, have negative implications for the family unit, and lead to feelings of isolation from friends or family. It may be helpful for parents to join a support group for families with children exhibiting similar problematic behaviors. With additional support, families have an opportunity to understand and accept the deficits surrounding their child's diagnosis and how DDs may contribute to sexualized behaviors. Depending on the origin of the sexualized behaviors, the parents' understanding that their child may be unable as compared to unwilling to stop these behaviors could help them possibly empathize with the child's inability to stop. The possibility of a neurological component in individuals with multiple diagnoses (e.g., ADHD, AS, OCD) may affect the client's ability to control their sexual impulses. Understanding the implication of a neurological origin may help reduce the parent's self-blame and reinforce the need for supervision, highlight the necessity for behavioral interventions and the formation of a safety plan, and guide treatment decisions (70, 71).

SEX EDUCATION

In order to help decrease PSBs and risks for sexual abuse as well as support positive feelings of sexuality and the formation of healthy relationships, individuals with DDs and ASD should be involved in an age and developmentally-appropriate sex education program and/or receive information about sexuality and sexual development from an early age through adolescence. Possible topics to be addressed include information about their bodies and how they work, basic hygiene, personal safety, inappropriate and appropriate touching and saying 'no' followed by individualized instructions that are brief, concrete, concise and repetitive (53, 72, 73). The amount of information offered, and to what extent, will depend on the individual child or adolescent's cognitive and linguistic abilities. Within any program, youth should be taught how to identify a potentially abusive situation, increasing the likelihood they can avoid one. This is especially important in populations diagnosed with a DD where individuals may be more likely to trust others and be easily manipulated. Lumley and Miltenberger (69) discussed the importance of assessing an individual's knowledge following the completion of a specific sex education program using role-play and in situ assessment. This would allow clinicians to see how much information is retained and if newly learned skills have been generalized to real life scenarios.

Although there has been attention on the importance of providing sex education to individuals with developmental delays and AS, there has been less discussion in the literature about formal sex education curricula. The few programs reviewed focus on sex education for individuals with ASD or AD are centered on social and communication issues, but elements of these programs can and should be modified to each individual depending on their cognitive, developmental, linguistic, social and emotional abilities. The overall goal of these programs is to provide information, protect against victimization, increase self-esteem and promote age-appropriate sexual habits. Three established programs specifically mentioned in the literature are TEACCH, which focuses on 4 levels of curriculum depending on the child's cognitive ability, the Devoreaux Centers, which attempt to use parents as teachers as much as possible to communicate a wide array of topics, and the Benhaven program, for more severely impaired individuals focusing on self-care and appropriate behavior (48, 73). For adolescents with AS, Stokes and Kaur (54) discussed the need for a 'specialized' sex education program with an emphasis on social interactions integrated into the program.

CONCLUSION

The topic of sexual development is often overlooked as an expected area of development, especially among children with disabilities. However, more clinicians and researchers are now looking at how young people with disabilities experience sexual feelings or behaviors normatively, as a function of their disability and/or comorbidities, as a result of trauma or abuse, or as the result of other risk factors. Unfortunately, children with intellectual disabilities and developmental delays experience sexual abuse at a higher rate than peers who are not developmentally delayed due to cognitive, social and emotional deficits. As with typically developing peers, problematic sexual behaviors can occur in children with developmental delays as a result of sexual abuse, but there are often other factors at play. In this chapter, we first presented a brief overview of normative and problematic sexual behaviors and then explored some of the reasons they are more prevalent in developmentally delayed populations, focusing on children and adolescents diagnosed with higher functioning Autism Spectrum Disorder. We then discussed various methods to assess sexualized behavior and treatment options for this population with a focus on working with their families in their cultural context and providing appropriate sex education.

Based on current research and our clinical experience in a hospital-based children's advocacy center that specializes in the evaluation of child maltreatment of children with disabilities, we believe that there is a core set of skills and competencies which can be developed to optimally assess and treat children with disabilities who may have been abused. However, many professionals currently doing this work have expertise in either the evaluation and treatment of child maltreatment or with children with disabilities, but not both. These children require an integrated approach with additional professional time, services and expertise, as well as sex education and preparation tailored to their specific abilities and needs. This is particularly true when they have entered the child protection system which, unfortunately, often does not have the resources available for these often complex evaluations. With additional training and research into typical sexual development and how cultural context and maltreatment affects sexual behavior in children with disabilities, we believe we can improve lives and mitigate harm among this very special, but very vulnerable, population.

Chaffin (74) provided commentary regarding misconceptions placed on children and adolescents who display PSB and recent scientific data which may alter policies involving treatment, practice, and perceptions of these behaviors. Knowledge and effectiveness of utilizing evidence-based treatment for children with PSBs has grown over the last decade and has shown a positive outcome with less likelihood of sexual behaviors reoccurring. He points out that "re-education" of professionals and policy makers is necessary to prevent every adolescent and child with a history of PSB from being labeled a perpetrator. An incorrect label could change the direction of the most effective treatment options (74).

Children and adolescents with developmental delays exhibiting PSB's can be especially difficult to interview and assess, therefore, compromising the formulation of an effective treatment plan and placing the child at risk for incorrect and damaging labels. Future research needs to go beyond developmentally-appropriate individuals and focus efforts on evidence-based practice that is developmentally sensitive and considers cognitive, emotional, and behavioral characteristics which are often overlooked in this vulnerable population. At an institutional level, future research could assist in determining efficacy of different treatment modalities specific to this population (68).

At an administration level, in order to provide effective, comprehensive and sensitive services to all child clients, there must be proper training for staff about normative sexual development, PSB's, and developmental disabilities. Lack of expertise amongst clinicians, inadequate knowledge regarding the developmentally delayed population, high turnover rate, and poor communication and collaboration between agencies and providers are on-going issues that need to be addressed. With additional training and research on normative and problematic sexual development as well as how cultural context and maltreatment affects sexual behavior in children with disabilities, we believe we can improve the lives and mitigate harm among this at-risk population.

REFERENCES

[1]   DeLamater J. Human sexual development. J Sex Res 2002;39:110-4.

[2]   Balter AS, Van Rhijn TM, Davies AWJ. The development of sexuality in childhood in early learning settings: An exploration of early childhood educators' perceptions. Can J Hum Sex 2016;25(1):30-40.

[3]   World Health Organization. Report of a technical consultation on sexual health, 28–31 January 2002, Geneva: WHO, 2006.

[4]   National Child Traumatic Stress Network (NCTSN). Cultural and family differences in children's sexual education and knowledge. Culture and Trauma Brief 2008;3:1. URL: http://www.NCTSN.org.

[5]   Chaffin M, Berliner, L, Block, R, Cavanaugh Johnson, T, Friedrich, W Garza Louis, D. Report of the ATSA Task Force on Children with Sexual Behavior Problems. Child Maltreat 2008;13:2:199-218.

[6]   Mandell D, Walrath C, Manteuffe B, Sgro G, Pinto-Martin J. The prevalence and correlates of abuse among children with autism served in comprehensive community-based mental health settings. Child Abuse Negl 2005;29:1359-72.

[7]   Bonner BL, Walker CE, Berliner L. Children with sexual behavior problems: assessment and treatment – final report. Washington DC: US Department of Health and Human Services, National Clearinghouse on Child Abuse and Neglect, 1999.

[8]   Elkovitch N, Latzman RD, Hansen DJ, Flood MF. Understanding child sexual behavior problems: A developmental psychopathology framework. Clin Psychol Rev 2009;29:586-98.

[9]   American Psychiatric Association. Diagnostic criteria for autism spectrum disorder. Washington, DC: APA, 2013. URL: http://www.dsm5.org.

[10]   Heiman ML, Leiblum S, Cohen ES, Malendez PM. A comparative survey of beliefs about "normal" childhood sexual behaviors. Child Abuse Negl 1998;22:289-304.

[11]   Lamb S, Coakley M. "Normal" childhood sexual play and games: Differentiating play from abuse. Child Abuse Negl 1993;17:515-26.

[12]   Merrick MT, Litrownik AJ, Everson MD, Cox CE. Beyond sexual abuse: The impact of other maltreatment experiences on sexualized behavior. Child Maltreat 2008;13(2):122-32.

[13]   Hornor G. Sexual behavior in children: Normal or not? J Pediatr Health 2004;18(2):57-64.

[14] Davies, SL, Glaser, D, Kossoff, R. Children's sexual play and behavior in pre-school settings: Staff's perceptions, reports, and responses. Child Abuse Negl 2000;24(10):1329-43.

[15] Achenbach T, Edelbrook C. Manual for the child behavior checklist and revised child behavior profile. Burlington VT: University of Vermont, Department of Psychiatry, 1983.

[16] Friedrich WN. Child sexual behavior inventory: professional manual. Odessa, FL: Psychological Assessment Resources, 1997.

[17] Friedrich WN, Fisher J, Broughton D, Houston M, Shafran CR. Normative sexual behavior in children: A contemporary sample. Pediatrics 1998;101(4):E9.

[18] Larsson I, Svedin CG. Teacher's and parent's reports on 3 to 6 year old children's sexual behavior--A comparison. Child Abuse Negl 2002;26:247-66.

[19] Sandnabba NK, Santtila P, Wannas M, Krook K. Age and gender specific sexual behaviors in children. Child Abuse Negl 2003;27:579-605.

[20] Lindblad F, Gustafsson PA, Larsson, I, Lundin B. Preschooler's sexual behavior at day-care centers: An epidemiological study. Child Abuse Negl 1995;19:569-77.

[21] Friedrich WN, Trane ST. Sexual behavior problems across multiple settings. Child Abuse Negl 2002;26:243-5.

[22] National Child Traumatic Stress Network (NCTSN). Sexual development and behavior in children: Information for parents and caregivers 2009. URL: http://nctsn.org/nctsn_assets/pdfs/caring/sexualdevelopmentandbehavior.pdf.

[23] Gil E, Johnson TC. Sexualized children: Assessment and treatment of sexualized children and children who molest. Rockville, MD: Launch Press, 1993.

[24] Friedrich WN. Sexual victimization and sexual behavior in children: A review of recent literature. Child Abuse Negl 1993;17:59-66.

[25] Kendall-Tackett KA, Meyer Williams L, Finkelhor D. Impact of sexual abuse on children: A review and synthesis of recent empirical studies. Psychol Bull 1993;113:164-80.

[26] Hewitt SK. Assessing allegations of sexual abuse in preschool children: Understanding small voices. Thousand Oaks, CA: Sage, 1999.

[27] Gray A, Pithers WD, Busconi A, Houchens, P. Developmental and etiological characteristics of children with sexual behavior problems: Treatment implications. Child Abuse Negl 1999;23(6):601-21.

[28] Friedrich WN, Grambsch P, Broughton D, Kuiper J, Bielke RL. Normative sexual behavior in children. Pediatrics 1991;88:456-464.

[29] Pithers WD, Gray A, Busconi A, Houchens P. Children with sexual behavior problems: Identification of five distinct types and related treatment considerations. Child Maltreat 1998;3:384-406.

[30] Larsson I, Svedin CG. Sexual experiences in childhood: Young adult's recollections. Archives of Sexual Behavior 2002;31:3:263-273.

[31] Center for Disease Control (CDC). National survey of family growth. URL: http://www.cdc.gov/nchs/nsfg/key_statistics/s.htm#.

[32] Day RD. The transition to first intercourse among racially and culturally diverse youth. J Marriage Fam 1992;54:749-62.

[33] Brown JD, Cantor J. An agenda for research on youth and the media: Conference proceedings. J Adolesc Health 2000;27:2-7.

[34] Brown JD, Witherspoon EM. The mass media and American adolescent health: Supplemental article. J Adolesc Health 2002;31:154-70.

[35]   Greydanus DE, Pratt HD. Childhood and adolescent sexuality. In: Greydanus DE, Patel DR, Pratt HDS, Calles Jr JL, Nazeer A, Merrick J, eds. Behavioral pediatrics, 4th ed. New York: Nova Science, 2015:413-38.

[36]   National Center on the Sexual Behavior of Youth (NCSBY) Fact sheet: Adolescent sex offenders: Common misconceptions vs. Current evidence. Oklahoma, OK: University of Oklahoma, 2003.

[37]   Child Traumatic Stress Network (NCTSN). Understanding and coping with sexual behavior problems in children: Information for parents and caregivers, 2009. URL: http://nctsn.org/nctsn_assets/ pdfs/caring/sexualbehaviorproblems.pdf.

[38]   Hall DK, Mathews F, Pearce J. Sexual behavior problems in sexually abused children: A preliminary typology. Child Abuse Negl 2002;26:289-312.

[39]   Drach KM, Wientzen J, Ricci LR. The diagnostic utility of sexual behavior problems in diagnosing sexual abuse in a forensic child abuse evaluation clinic. Child Abuse Negl 2001;25:489-503.

[40]   Allen B. Children with sexual behavior problems: Clinical characteristics and relationship to child maltreatment. Child Psychiatr Hum Dev 2016 Feb 29.

[41]   Silovsky JF, Niec L. Characteristics of young children with sexual behavior problems: A pilot study. Child Maltreat 2002;7:187-97.

[42]   Langstrom N, Grann M, Lichtenstein P. Genetic and environmental influences on problematic behavior in children: A study of same sex twins. Arch Sex Behav 2002;31:343-50.

[43]   Johnson TC. Understanding the sexual behavior of young children. Washington, DC: SIECUS Report, 1991:8-15.

[44]   Pratt HD, Patel DR, Greydanus DE, Dannison L, Walcott D, Sloane MA. Adolescent sex offenders. Int Pediatr 2001;16:1-8.

[45]   Palusci VJ, Cox EO, Cyrus TA, Heartwell SW, Vandervort FE, Pott ES. Medical assessment and legal outcome in child sexual abuse. Arch Pediatr Adol Med 1999;153(4):388-92.

[46]   Connor MJ. ASD and inappropriate (as perceived) sexualized behavior. OAASIS 2007. URL: http://www.mugsy.org/connor90. htm.

[47]   Chan J, John RM. Sexuality and sexual health in children and adolescents with autism. J Nurse Pract 2012; 8:306-15.

[48]   Sullivan A, Caterino L. Addressing the sexuality and sex education of individuals with autism spectrum disorders. Educ Treat Child 2008;31:381-94.

[49]   Ray F, Marks C, Bray-Garretson H. Challenges to treating adolescents with Asperger's syndrome who are sexually abusive. Sex Addict Comp 2004;11:265-85.

[50]   Realmuto GM, Ruble LA. Sexual behaviors in autism: Problems of definition and management. J Autism Dev Disord 1999;29:121-7.

[51]   Henault I. Asperger syndrome and sexuality. London: Kingsley, 2006.

[52]   Hellemans H, Deboutte D. Autism spectrum disorders and sexuality. Presentation to the World Autism Congress, Melbourne, 2002.

[53]   Greydanus DE, Omar HA. Sexuality issues and gynecologic care of adolescents with developmental disabilities. Pediatr Clin North Am 2008;55:1315-35.

[54]   Stokes MA, Kaur A. High functioning autism and sexuality. Autism 2005;9:266-89.

[55]   Hall DK, Mathews F, Pearce, J. Factors associated with sexual behavior problems in young sexually abused children. Child Abuse Negl 1998;22:10:1045-1063.

[56]   Johnson TC, Friend C. Assessing young children's sexual behaviors in the context of child sexual abuse evaluations. In: Ney T, ed. True and false allegations of child sexual abuse: Assessment and case management. Philadelphia, PA: Brunner/Mazel, 1995:49-72.

[57]   Friedrich WN. Psychological assessment of sexually abused children and their families. Thousand Oaks, CA: Sage, 2002.

[58]   Ballard MB, Austin S. Forensic interviewing: special considerations for children and adolescents with mental retardation and developmental disabilities. Educ Train Dev Disabil 1999;34:521-5.

[59]   Edelson-Goldberg M. Sexual abuse of children with autism: factors that increase risk and interfere with recognition of abuse. Disabil Stud Q 2010;30(1). URL: http://www.dsq-sds.org/article/view/1058/ 1228.htm.

[60]   Dent H. The effects of age and intelligence on eyewitnessing ability. In: Dent H, Flin R, eds. Children as witnesses. Chichester: John Wiley, 1992:1-13.

[61]   Cronch LE, Viljoen JL, Hansen DJ. Forensic interviewing in child sexual abuse cases: current techniques and future directions. Aggress Violent Behav 2006;11:195-207.

[62]   Pithers WD, Gray A, Busconi A, Houchens P. Caregivers of children with sexual behavior problems: Psychological and familial functioning. Child Abuse Negl 1998;22:129-41.

[63]   Tuzikow J. Responding to inappropriate sexual behaviors displayed by adolescents with autism spectrum disorders. URL: http://www.opwdd.ny.gov/node/118.

[64]   Allen J, Berliner L. Evidence-informed, individual treatment of a child with sexual behavior problems: a case study. Arch Sex Behav 2015;44:2323-2331.

[65]   Gray CA, Garand J. Social Stories: improving responses of students with autism with accurate social information. Focus Autistic Behav 1993;8:1-10.

[66]   Reynhout G, Carter M. Social stories for children with disabilities. J Autism Dev Disord 2006;36:445-69.

[67]   Ali S, Frederickson N. Investigating the evidence base of social stories. Educ Psychol Pract 2006;22:355-77.

[68]   McLay L, Carnett A, Tyler-Merrick G, Van der Meer L. A systematic review of interventions for inappropriate sexual behavior of children with adolescents with developmental disabilities. Rev J Autism Dev Disord 2015;2:357-73.

[69]   Lumley VA, Miltenberger RG. Sexual abuse prevention for persons with mental retardation. Am J Ment Retard 1997;101:459-72.

[70]   Children with sexual behavior problems. TDMHSAS best practice duidelines, 2007. URL: https://tn.gov/assets/entities/behavioralhealth/ attachments/.

[71]   O'Malley K, Rich S. Clinical implications of a link between fetal alcohol spectrum disorders (FASD) and autism or Asperger's disorder. A neurodevelopmental frame for helping understand and management. In: Fitzgerald M, ed. Recent advances in autism spectrum disorders, vol 1. Rijeka, Croatia: INTECH, 2013. URL: http://dx.doi.org/10.5772/54924.

[72]   Balazs T. Review of effective interventions for socially inappropriate masturbation in persons with cognitive disabilities. Sex Disabil 2006;24:151-68.

[73]   Koller Rebecca. Sexuality and adolescents with autism. Sex Disabil 2000;18:125-35.

[74]   Chaffin M. Our minds are made up-don't confuse us with the facts: commentary on policies concerning children with sexual behavior problems and juvenile sex offenders. Child Maltreat 2008;1:110-121.

In: Child Abuse: Children with Disabilities
Editors: V. J Palusci, D. Nazer et al.

ISBN: 978-1-53612-035-6
© 2017 Nova Science Publishers, Inc.

Chapter 11

RECOGNIZING AND RESPONDING TO SUSPECTED MALTREATMENT OF CHILDREN WITH MEDICAL COMPLEXITY: MEDICAL NEGLECT, MEDICAL CHILD ABUSE AND CHALLENGES FACING FAMILIES, MANDATED REPORTERS AND MEMBERS OF THE HEALTH CARE AND CASE PLANNING TEAMS

Alex Okun[*], *MD*
New Alternatives for Children, New York, New York, US

This chapter on recognizing and responding to suspected maltreatment of children with medical complexity is organized around several questions: 1) What is meant by the term, "children with medical complexity?" Does this term represent something distinct from "children with special health care needs," or "children who are medically fragile?" 2) What constitutes medical neglect of children with medical complexity? How can it be distinguished from expected and reasonable shortcomings in the care that can realistically be provided to a child? 3) How can health care providers recognize instances of "medical child abuse" in which the harm results from interventions that health care providers undertake in response to exaggerated or fabricated reports from parents or other family caregivers? 4) What are some of the challenges facing mandated reporters and members of the health care and case planning teams in recognizing and responding to suspected medical neglect or abuse of children with medical complexity?

---

[*] Correspondence: Alex Okun, MD, Medical Director, New Alternatives for Children, 37 West 26th Street, New York, NY 10010, United States. E-mail:aokun@nackidscan.org.

INTRODUCTION

This chapter reviews our knowledge about recognizing and responding to suspected maltreatment of children with medical complexity. There are many challenges facing mandated reporters and members of the health care and case planning teams in recognizing and responding to suspected medical neglect or abuse in this population, beginning with its definition. The term, "children with medical complexity" has been variously defined and refers to a subset of "children with special health care needs," many of whom are also considered to be "medically fragile." What constitutes medical neglect of children with medical complexity is also poorly defined as it can be difficult to distinguish from expected and reasonable shortcomings in the care that can realistically be provided to a child. This also directly impacts whether health care providers can recognize instances of "medical child abuse" in which the harm results from interventions that health care providers undertake in response to exaggerated or fabricated reports from parents or other family caregiver.

Fictional case histories of two children ("Angel" and "Robin") are presented to illustrate issues that arise when maltreatment is suspected in children with medical complexity. These three-part vignettes are complicated and lengthy, in keeping with the nature of biomedical, psychosocial and care coordination needs of children with medical complexity, but they highlight the many important issues for this especially vulnerable population.

THE CASE OF ANGEL, PART I OF III

Angel was a 34 month old born at 24 weeks' gestation, weighing 650 gm (1 lb., 7 oz.). The mother's early pregnancy was complicated by alcohol and cocaine use before she became aware that she was pregnant. Several years prior, her two oldest children, now adults, had been placed in foster care following police reports of domestic violence and allegations against the mother that she was engaging in commercial sex work. Angel's mother and father lived together with their healthy 3 year-old.

Angel required respiratory support for the first six months of life. Most of the intestines had to be surgically removed due to necrotizing enterocolitis (a severe inflammatory or infectious condition affecting the GI tract), resulting in a gastrostomy, jejunostomy and colostomy (in which the intestinal contents drain through holes, or ostomies, created in the abdominal wall) and dependence on parenteral (intravenous) nutrition.

Shortly after the first birthday, Angel was discharged from the neonatal intensive care unit with the diagnoses of short bowel syndrome (in which too little of the intestines remain to meet a person's overall nutritional needs), liver disease associated with parenteral nutrition, and chronic lung disease of prematurity (also known as broncho-pulmonary dysplasia). Prior to discharge, the mother demonstrated what were judged to be good skills meeting Angel's special needs. The home care regimen included supplemental oxygen, parenteral nutrition, trophic enteral feeds (a slow trickle of formula fed continuously into the stomach in order to promote intestinal growth), and nine medications, each given once to four times daily. State Medicaid authorized 40 hours per week of private duty nursing services to be provided in the home.

WHAT IS MEANT BY THE TERM "CHILDREN WITH MEDICAL COMPLEXITY"?

The literature on classification of "children with special health care needs" includes a vast body of work in the fields of policy, advocacy and research. A long list of terms, such as "children with chronic conditions," "children who are medically fragile" and "children with medical complexity," has been used to describe and classify children that are the focus of this chapter. Some of these terms are listed in Table 1.

Table 1. Terms used to refer to children with special health care needs, or the chronic conditions with which they live, over the past five decades

Time	Term
Pre 1970s	Crippled (or handicapped) children Chronic illness or disease Disabled children
1970's	Chronically ill children
1980's	Chronic conditions Technology-dependent (later, technology-assisted) children Children with chronic physical, developmental, behavioral or emotional conditions Children with special needs Children (or children and youth) with special health care needs Medically complex children
1990's	Children with significant disabilities Condition (proposed to replace the terms, "illness," "disease," "disorder," "disability," "impairment," "handicap") Children/persons with developmental disabilities/intellectual disabilities Complex medical needs

Table 1. (Continued)

Time	Term
2000's	Medically fragile children
	Functional limitations
	Children with medical complexity
	Complex chronic conditions
	Complex needs
	Complex health conditions
	Significant chronic conditions

Most early research on psychological and social outcomes of children with chronic health conditions was conducted on groups of children with identical or similar disorders (e.g., reports of depressive symptoms among adolescents with cystic fibrosis or of body image among children with inflammatory bowel disease). From the research of Stein (1, 2) and others (3) the needs of families and children living with chronic health conditions were shown to be quite similar across a broad range of diagnoses (e.g., service gaps in common among children with diabetes, hemophilia, severe asthma, or cerebral palsy and their families, or psychological and financial impact on caregivers and children living with these conditions) (1-3).

"Children with special health care needs" are defined as those who are at "increased risk for chronic physical, developmental, behavioral or emotional condition(s)" and "require health and related services of a type or amount beyond those required of children generally" (4). This conceptualization, referred to as a "non-categorical definition," led to transformation of the processes used to determine eligibility for Social Security/Disability benefits, based previously on whether the conditions of children applying for coverage could be found on lists of qualifying diagnoses.

Increased attention has been directed more recently to the needs of "children with medical complexity," those with the most complicated chronic conditions, and to those of their families. Inquiry has been directed towards ways to improve the care they receive, enhance the quality of their lives and reduce health care costs. Some of this research, conducted using administrative datasets drawn from large population groups, has given rise to new terms and conceptualizations such as, "significant chronic conditions," and subgroups of "chronic conditions" classified as "dominant," "moderate," "minor," "catastrophic" and "malignant" (5-7). Definitions of terms used most commonly in reference to children with special health care needs appear in Table 2.

Table 2. Definitions of a sample of terms used to refer to children with a variety of special health care needs and their conditions

Chronic health condition: "Any medical condition that can be reasonably expected to last at least 12 months (unless death intervenes) and to involve either several different organ systems or 1 organ system severely enough to require specialty pediatric care and probably some period of hospitalization in a tertiary care center" (9, p. 206).

Children with special health care needs: "Those who have or are at increased risk for a chronic physical, developmental, behavioral, or emotional condition and who also require health and related services of a type or amount beyond that required by children generally" (4, p. 138).

Technology-dependent: Refers to need for support by technology for basic life function (e.g., a feeding tube, tracheostomy, ventilator, dialysis unit).

Technology-assisted: Refers to support by technology that provides compensation for lost function but is not essential for survival (e.g., power wheelchair chair or assistive communication device).

Children who are medically fragile: High morbidity and mortality, require extensive nursing care in the home in order to prevent death or worsening disability, and depend on skilled supportive services, often technology-based, to support fundamental organ function (24).

Functional status differences, per the ICF Classification scheme (25):
- *impairment:* When specific body system or body part's functioning are impacted
- *activity limitation:* When a whole individual's function is impacted, resulting in difficulty doing basic tasks
- *participation restriction:* When an individual is unable to fully engage in life events

Children with medical complexity: Those who have chronic conditions, functional limitations, high health care use and "medical fragility and intensive care needs that are not easily met by existing health care models." This definition incorporates (12, pp. 529-530):
- "characteristic chronic and severe conditions;"
- "substantial family-identified service needs;"
- functional limitations; and
- high health care resource use, involving:
  - "intensive hospital and or community based service need;"
  - "reliance on technology, polypharmacy and or home or congregate care to maintain basic quality of life;"
  - risk of "frequent or prolonged hospitalizations;" and/or
  - "elevated need for care coordination"

While children with medical complexity make up less than 1% of the pediatric population, their health care needs have been estimated to consume up to one third of the costs of health care for children in the United States (8). They are considered to be at extremely high risk for complications and challenges in the domains of physical, developmental and psychosocial well-being. Families of children with medical complexity report spending substantial time each week on care coordination and direct home care (9). Most experience significant financial difficulties, find that a family member must leave their job in order to care for the child, and report challenges accessing non-medical services for their children (10).

A consensus definition for "children with medical complexity" is still evolving. Several tools have been developed and validated to identify individual children with special health care needs (11), but no valid and reliable instrument has been published to classify children as having medical complexity.

THE CASE OF ANGEL, PART II OF III

During the first year and a half at home, Angel was hospitalized over a dozen times and made many more emergency department visits for suspected bloodstream infections; skin breakdown around the ostomies; diarrhea and weight loss; catheter obstruction, fracture or dislodgement; and exacerbations of chronic lung disease. Members of the health care teams involved recognized that these episodes of illness compromised Angel's nutritional status and overall well-being were but were not surprised by their frequent occurrence, given the degree of medical complexity. They were primarily concerned that liver disease associated with long-term use of parenteral nutrition was worsening and would lead to liver failure.

Staff at the hospital also wondered whether Angel's poor weight gain and some of the complications involving the central venous catheter could have been averted had more skilled care been provided in the home. They were aware that the family experienced poverty and other psychosocial stressors but did not understand them in depth, as Angel's mother preferred not to discuss them. They were reassured by evidence of the mother's bond to Angel and her attendance at most outpatient appointments. Some described the status of Angel's care as situated chronically in a "grey zone," in which reports of medical neglect could have been justified on any of a number of occasions but were strongly indicated on none of them.

Emerging neurodevelopmental problems included expressive language delays, spastic diplegia (a common type of cerebral palsy, predominantly affecting the legs) and myopia (nearsightedness). Angel was prescribed corrective lenses to prevent the development of amblyopia (permanent vision impairment). After the second birthday, Angel was referred to a special preschool with capacity to serve children with complex medical needs, where a variety of therapies could be provided.

After a few months, staff at the school became concerned when they noticed that Angel was arriving at school in diapers and clothes that appeared not to have been changed recently, and without glasses. Some days, Angel arrived over an hour late. The school sent home supplies of diapers and donated clothes and asked that the mother bring the glasses to school, where they could be stored in the classroom for Angel to wear there. The school social worker attempted to ensure that Angel's mother could access federal, state and community based entitlements (such as SSI/Disability, WIC, food stamps and public assistance) and other supportive services, as had social workers at the hospital.

Two months later, Angel came to school one day without a sufficient supply of parenteral nutrition or formula. The following week, the central venous catheter dressing was discovered detached and soiled when Angel arrived. At a meeting held at the school, the mother was noted to have facial bruises and injury to the front teeth. She acknowledged suffering with depression and having had a physical altercation with Angel's father. She asked that the school keep this confidential, lest her family face eviction by a landlord to whom she owed back rent and who did not want law enforcement officials visiting the home.

The first in a series of reports to state child protective services was made by the school. Angel eventually stopped attending the school altogether. When local child protective service workers visiting the home noted Angel to be malodorous and dehydrated, Angel was admitted to the hospital for stabilization. From the hospital, Angel was discharged to foster care.

Angel's case meets all the criteria for medical complexity proposed by Cohen et al. (12). Several chronic and severe conditions existed, the most significant of which were consequences of short bowel syndrome: progressive liver disease, nutritional compromise and poor wound healing, among others. Substantial family-identified service needs included extreme poverty; threats to safety, housing and permanency; maternal depression and possible substance use disorder; and support from home care services that fell short of meeting Angel's needs. Angel had functional limitations, which though significant, were far less severe than they are for many children with medical complexity. A large proportion of children with medical complexity have severe neurological impairment resulting in intellectual disability, irritability, chronic pain, epilepsy, feeding difficulties, progressive lung disease and musculoskeletal disorders. Angel's care consumed extensive health care resources, the final criterion proposed by Cohen et al. (12).

Health care professionals and staff at the school were concerned that Angel's medical needs were not being met consistently. At many junctures in Angel's life at home, the failure to provide needed medical care could have been considered medical neglect.

WHAT CONSTITUTES MEDICAL NEGLECT OF CHILDREN WITH MEDICAL COMPLEXITY?

Medical maltreatment or neglect was first defined in the US in a revision of the Child Abuse Prevention and Treatment Act of 1974 (CAPTA) simply as, "failure to provide adequate medical care." It was considered reportable to state child protective service agencies when it was associated with "harm or significant risk of harm" to the child (13). Specific definitions and processes for responding to reports of medical neglect were left to the states to develop. Through 2011, eleven of the fifty states had done so, most choosing broad descriptions such as "failure to provide needed medical or mental health care" (14).

Children with medical complexity experience elevated risk of maltreatment and medical neglect, as do children with disabilities generally. This can occur in the form of omission of or inconsistent adherence with important regimens of medications, feeds, therapies or use of technologies; a level of supervision at home that is unreliable or inadequate to assure safety; lack of regular follow up with primary or subspecialty medical care; dental neglect; and excessive school absences.

When Angel was brought to school with soiled clothes and diapers, it posed no significant harm or threat to health, although it was recognized as a sign of stressors in the household or the mother's life. School staff appreciated that Angel's mother experienced numerous barriers to meeting Angel's care needs more consistently and felt that she tried as hard as she could to do so. The proposal to store Angel's glasses in the classroom was thought to be a good compromise solution to one unmet need.

When Angel arrived with inadequate supplies of parenteral nutrition or formula, or with the entrance site of the central venous catheter exposed and vulnerable to infection, staff at the school felt that there was significant risk of harm. As mandated reporters, they acted accordingly to notify child protective services of suspected medical neglect.

In the year before preschool enrollment, Angel and the mother had extensive contact with a number of health professionals and teams providing outpatient, emergency and inpatient care. These individuals and groups regarded the consequences of Angel's short bowel syndrome as substantial. They felt, as did staff at the school, that Angel's mother was trying as hard as she could to care for her child.

The remainder of this chapter is devoted to challenges faced by health care providers, families and social service workers when medical neglect of children with medical complexity is suspected. First, we will look at a special subtype of medical complexity in which numerous serious disorders are believed to exist in a child but the truth is more complicated.

THE CASE OF ROBIN, PART I OF III

Robin was a 5 year old who, as an infant, had been admitted frequently to "Children's Hospital" for suspected intestinal dysmotility (slowed intestinal peristalsis), weight loss, and accounts of irregular breathing observed in the home during sleep. The mother had reported episodes at home, none witnessed by emergency responders, when she had found Robin pale or blue, and either limp or posturing. Physicians were concerned that these might represent manifestations of epilepsy, metabolic or mitochondrial disease (dysfunctions at the level of the body's cells or systems of energy production) or a central disorder of the control of respiration (a functional deficit, originating in the brain, leading to inadequate breathing). Work-ups included extensive imaging studies and analyses of blood, urine and spinal fluid; numerous EEGs; invasive procedures involving the GI tract; and biopsies of skin, muscle and rectum.

At the time, Robin's mother was regarded by hospital staff as an educated and reliable reporter, usually to be found at the bedside. They empathized with her frustration at not having found an answer to Robin's instability at home. Despite negative studies, Robin was treated with antacids, pro-motility agents (drugs to promote peristalsis), anti-epileptic drugs and an array of special formulas. Eventually these were fed by nasogastric tube, followed by the creation of a gastrostomy to assure adequate nutrition.

The family moved out of state when Robin was 16 months old and returned when Robin was 5. The mother reported that in the interim, the diagnosis of intestinal dysmotility had been confirmed, and that severe constipation had developed. Robin had also been found to have a low-lying brainstem (known as Chiari malformation) and possible hydrocephalus (accumulation of excess spinal fluid in and around the brain). Two surgical procedures were performed urgently in which portions of bone were removed from the base of the skull to alleviate any impact this could be having respiration (which is driven by a center in the brainstem), and placement of a ventriculoperitoneal shunt (a catheter tunneled underneath the skin that allows excess cerebrospinal fluid to drain into the abdomen). The shunt had been revised or replaced emergently on several occasions in response to complaints of recurrent headache that were accompanied, on occasion, by breathing pauses observed at home.

At the time of return to Children's Hospital, Robin was being given two anti-epileptic medications, two antacids, continuous feeds of an elemental (non-allergenic) formula 20 hours per day through a gastrojejunostomy tube (a long, thin tube threaded through a gastrostomy, ending in the small intestine), two medications to alleviate constipation, and a low dose of corticosteroids for possible adrenal insufficiency (an endocrine disorder that, unrecognized, can lead to dehydration and shock). The mother reported that Robin had developed allergies to wheat, soy, eggs, cow's milk protein, acetaminophen, morphine, diphenhydramine, hydroxizine (both antihistamines), senna, docusate (both treatments for constipation) and several brands of adhesive tape and dressings.

The mother expressed frustration that the constipation remained refractory to medical treatment, because she felt that this worsened the dysmotility. She was worried that Robin would eventually require parenteral nutrition. She inquired about the creation of a colostomy to permit irrigation of the colon as another means to address the constipation. She asked that once the state-based insurance was active, Robin be prescribed a pulse oximeter so that in the event that Robin's breathing slowed during sleep (and the blood oxygen level dropped), an alarm would sound and awaken her. The team learned that she had moved out of state years before to escape a relationship with Robin's father that was characterized by violence and controlling behaviors, and that each time he learned of their new whereabouts, she and Robin would move to a different address.

HOW CAN HEALTH CARE PROVIDERS RECOGNIZE INSTANCES OF "MEDICAL CHILD ABUSE?"

Now 40 years since the classic case reports by Meadow (15), what was then labeled "Munchausen Syndrome by Proxy" has come to be re-conceptualized in ways that emphasize recognizing and acting on suspicions that the child is a victim of "medical child abuse" (16-18). The terms, "factitious disorder" and "caregiver fabricated illness" have been proposed in recent years to replace "Munchausen syndrome by proxy," but the original label remains in common use.

In cases of "medical child abuse," as explained by Roessler and Jenny in their 2009 book, *Medical Child Abuse: Beyond Munchausen Syndrome by Proxy*, the "instruments" or "vehicles" of the abuse are the health care providers (16). Based on reports of serious concerns that, unbeknownst to them, are invented or exaggerated by a parent or one or more family caregivers, they feel compelled to order invasive studies and treatments, often repeatedly. Why do providers find themselves colluding, unintentionally, in this abuse?

Routine medical care for children is based in the assumption that reports provided by parents or other family caregivers are honest and as accurate as possible. This is particularly important when the information provided has critical implications for the child's well-being. This assumption is part of an unspoken "contract" between provider and parent or other family caregiver, more of which will be explored in the next section of this chapter. As in other forms of child maltreatment, when medical child abuse is occurring, this contract has in effect been broken, something that is often hard to recognize.

Medical child abuse is among the most covert forms of child maltreatment. The concerns expressed by parents or family caregivers are typically believable and deeply concerning. In Robin's case, each of the neurosurgical interventions performed during the time away from Children's Hospital took place in an atmosphere of crisis following reports by the mother of portentous signs and symptoms that were not documented or observed by medical personnel.

Health care providers may be astonished when parents or other family caregivers who have been regarded as loyal, persistent, courageous, even heroic advocates for their very sick children are revealed to have been deceitful and, in effect, seduced providers into enacting the abuse in the form of medical procedures. At interdisciplinary team conferences convened to discuss the possibility that medical child abuse is taking place in the care of a particular patient, it is not uncommon for one member of the care team to object vehemently to the proposed explanation, being offended by the suggestion by other members of the team that the reports of deeply concerning signs and symptoms did not require intervention.

Medical providers are trained to be vigilant for potentially serious signs and symptoms and act expeditiously to assure that important diagnoses or complications are not missed. Invasive tests or procedures may be recommended, "just to be on the safe side." Physicians may also be worried about the consequences of a missed diagnosis and their liability in the event that the family brings legal action against them. The irony in these situations is that many decisions made in the care of children experiencing medical child abuse serve to perpetuate the abuse, rather than ensuring their safety.

The performance of procedures and studies continues to be rewarded in most settings today on a fee-for-service basis. No empiric study has been published into the extent to which this may influence physicians' decision making in the care of children with medical complexity and promote further invasive interventions.

When providers are asked to investigate worrisome complaints about a childlike Robin but feel it would be better to avoid intervening further, they may worry that saying "no" to the family will provoke confrontation or lead the family to transfer the child's care elsewhere (16). When the possibility of medical child abuse is being considered, providers are urged to follow many of the same steps, listed in Table 3, adapted from chapter headings in Roessler and Jenny's work (16), that are indicated in caring for other children who are suspected as having been maltreated. Hospitalization may be required. Restricting access the family or certain caregivers are permitted to have to the child can generate conflict. There is a role for covert video surveillance in the diagnostic investigation of some cases of suspected medical child abuse. Hospitals should have established policies and procedures in place whenever this is considered. Despite the most careful and fair implementation processes, covert video surveillance, if exposed, can lead to backlash on the family's part and even create additional risk to the child (19).

Table 3. Medical child abuse: Steps needed (16)

- Identify that the abuse has occurred
- Stop the abuse from occurring
- Provide for ongoing safety of the child
- Treat the physical consequences of the abuse
- Treat the psychological consequences of the abuse
- Try to maintain integrity of the family

THE CASE OF ROBIN, PART II OF III

At age 5, Robin appeared thin but otherwise well, with surgical scars and the shunt and tube described. Robin preferred not to leave the mother's side and did not speak to members of the team at Children's Hospital. After a series of requests for medical records from the medical center where Robin was treated out of state, the team found chart notes indicating that Robin was believed to have severe constipation, but likely not intestinal dysmotility. They saw that extensive assessments of brain anatomy and intracranial pressure had never been definitively abnormal, even though the neurosurgical procedures had in fact been performed. The mother had expressed concerns for multiple allergies and adrenal insufficiency, but testing had been performed and the disorders "ruled out." Because Robin's mother had continued to request that investigations and treatment be pursued for what she maintained were multiple disorders in spite of repeated reviews of study results and attempts at reassurance, she was suspected of "Munchausen Syndrome by Proxy." The providers at that medical center made a state child protective services report.

The care team at Children's Hospital was now faced with arriving at consensus as to whether some or all of the concerns for Robin's health had been invented by the mother, leading to invasive and burdensome interventions by medical providers, including members of their own team some 4 years previously. It sought to decide what actions to recommend now that would help Robin avoid a potentially unnecessary procedure like the requested colostomy or intensification of monitoring at home, and still promote the opportunity to re-establish a therapeutic relationship with Robin's mother.

WHAT ARE SOME OF THE CHALLENGES FACING MANDATED REPORTERS AND MEMBERS OF THE HEALTH CARE AND CASE PLANNING TEAMS IN RECOGNIZING AND RESPONDING TO SUSPECTED MEDICAL NEGLECT OR ABUSE OF CHILDREN WITH MEDICAL COMPLEXITY?

Investigating cases of suspected medical child abuse or medical neglect is threatening to families and challenging for all professionals involved. Health care professionals and other mandated reporters face significant moral, ethical and practical challenges throughout the process of child welfare involvement for children with medical complexity and their families. These challenges may arise long before a state child protective service report is called in, during an extended period, like the "grey zone" described by some of Angel's providers, when reports of medical neglect would be justified but there are other interventions that seem preferable to try first.

Amidst the many uncertainties that characterize decision-making in the care of children with medical complexity, health professionals and other mandated reporters may question whether their suspicions of neglect are justified. The ways that these doubts can lead to repeated, potentially harmful interventions by health care providers are described in the previous section of this chapter on medical child abuse.

Children with medical complexity and their families often have long-lasting, close relationships with members of the health care team that are characterized by mutual loyalty, honesty, commitment and respect. Health professionals may feel that making a child protective services report represents a betrayal of that relationship, particularly when there are feelings of affection for the parent or other family caregivers.

Removal from the family household is among the most painful consequences for any child and family involved in investigation of suspected maltreatment. Parents and other family caregivers may feel unjustly accused by the very care team on which they relied for their child's life-sustaining care; vulnerable by virtue of the limited capacity of some child protective service workers to appreciate the complexities of their child's needs and family stressors; helpless in court systems in which decisions can seem arbitrary and inconsistent; and susceptible to prejudice and discrimination by systems of medical care, child protective services, law enforcement and the courts.

Providers are aware of these foreseeable harms to the child and family. Based on past experience, they may anticipate that child protective service involvement is unlikely to lead to positive change or benefit to the child. They feel committed first to find ways to address unmet needs and improve care for the child and may defer or postpone making child protective service reports.

The time and effort required of health care providers to be involved in child protection work for children with medical complexity can be enormous, generally unreimbursed, and characterized by redundancy, uncertainty, and frustration. Many physicians are reluctant to give deposition or testify in court proceedings, given the challenges recalling precise details of remote events and facing hostile cross-examination. Child protective service workers and legal professionals often struggle to comprehend the concerns for medical neglect or medical child abuse in children with disorders of which they understand little. They carry large and challenging caseloads and experience pressure for casework to come to closure quickly. They typically work with children and families with needs that are far more common and easily understood than the nuances of suspected medical neglect of children with rare and complex conditions. They commonly experience difficulty reaching involved physicians, obtaining their full participation in the investigatory process, deciphering confusing accounts of diagnoses and treatments, and retaining physicians' ongoing involvement in case planning activities.

Families with stronger socioeconomic, social and family support systems are best equipped to handle the overwhelming needs of care at home for children with medical complexity. They are more likely than families living in poverty to have the resources to afford the needed time off from work; enlist the help of family and other members of their social network; overcome barriers to transportation and care for their other children that would otherwise impede availability to attend numerous outpatient appointments; and advocate effectively with health care organizations, suppliers, insurers, education systems and other agencies and programs charged with supporting care at home for their children with medical complexity.

Other families may not have such assets to call on in times of need. Disparities persist in access to care and quality of care provided to children living in poverty and those who are members of racial and ethnic minority groups. Children identified as African-American or multiracial made up 25% of those in foster care in 2014, a significant overrepresentation relative to the population distribution of the United States

(20). Aware of these inequities, providers must be mindful of any component of implicit bias that may be operant during the decision making process around initiating child protective service involvement.

Taken together, these experiences, disincentives and sensitivities may discourage some health care professionals from reporting suspected medical neglect of children with medical complexity. Independent of their legal obligation, physicians have ethical and professional commitments to report suspected medical neglect. These include minimizing the risk of harm, present and future, and doing all that is feasible to maximize the chances of best outcomes in the child's health, quality of life and, in some instances, survival.

Sensitive, respectful and responsible work with families requires that health care professionals take steps to interpret caregivers' actions in the context of culturally based health beliefs and practices. They need to take into account the impact that poverty, family chaos, limited health-related knowledge and distrust of the health care system can have on care that the family is able to provide (21). Beyond recognizing and treating the biomedical complexities of their patients, they have an obligation to address problems related to violence, substance use disorders, mental health problems and other life stressors that impair the capacity of families to care optimally for their children with medical complexity (22, 23).

In some settings, state and local child protective service systems have developed collaborations with groups of committed and qualified pediatric medical providers in children's hospitals or across communities, or with private, non-profit child welfare organizations that have expertise in work with children with a range of special health care needs and their families. At one such organization based in New York City, master's level social workers serve as case planners for children with special health care needs and families who are involved in foster care, prevention, aftercare programs and other initiatives. Restricted caseloads permit intensive, community-based work with each child's medical, educational and other service providers, and with the parent's, family caregivers' and other children's providers of medical and mental health and community based services. Casework is conducted in collaboration with agency-based team professionals who have expertise in pediatric complex care, pediatric nursing, child and adult psychiatry, psychotherapy, psycho-educational and developmental evaluation, educational advocacy, recreation and creative arts. Contracted payments for casework and reimbursement for the pediatric medical and mental health services provided fall far short of supporting such resource-intensive services. Long-term sustainability remains dependent on private and government grant provision and charitable support.

THE CASE OF ROBIN, PART III OF III

The team at Children's Hospital came to consensus not to grant Robin's mother's request to create a colostomy for irrigation. It offered to hospitalize Robin electively for the purposes of an extensive multispecialty work up involving possible sleep study, video EEG recording, motility studies, allergy testing, definitive relief of constipation and potential food challenges. Contact with the mother was subsequently lost. A state child protective service report was made, but the family could not be located at its address or by other means of contact on record.

THE CASE OF ANGEL, PART III OF III

Angel was placed in care with a foster parent who had retired from work as a nurse in a pediatric intensive care unit and had cared in her home for several children who were assisted by technology. Formula feedings were advanced. Angel gained weight well, the abdominal wounds healed, and parenteral nutrition was weaned over the course of the next six months. The liver disease resolved.

Angel's mother engaged in mental health services, renewed an order of protection against Angel's father and was assisted in securing affordable housing. She made consistent and reassuring visits with Angel, supervised at first, then progressing to overnight visits in her new home. She cared effectively and safely for Angel during these stays and met all other goals of the service plan. Angel was returned to her care after 16 months in foster care and continued to gain weight, even after skilled nursing services were curtailed. Angel was not readmitted to the hospital.

CONCLUSION

Children with medical complexity comprise a small proportion of the population of children in the United States yet require immense expenditures to provide ongoing, costly, specialized multidisciplinary care to ensure their survival and optimal health outcomes and quality of life. When they are suspected as being subject to medical neglect or medical child abuse, the level of involvement required of members of health care, educational and social service teams is extensive, complex, largely unreimbursed and fraught with challenges for the professionals involved. The development of innovative, collaborative interventions demands support, expertise, creativity and teamwork to an extent that exceeds what has generally been available in order to address successfully the profound medical and social complexities involved.

REFERENCES

[1]   Stein RE. To be or not to be...noncategorical. J Dev Behav Pediatr 1996;17:36-7.

[2]   Stein RE, Bauman LJ, Westbrook LE, Coupey SM, Ireys HT. Framework for identifying children who have chronic conditions: The case for a new definition. J Pediatr 1993;122:342-7.

[3]   Perrin EC, Newacheck P, Pless IB, et al. Issues involved in the definition and classification of chronic health conditions. Pediatrics 1993;91:787- 93.

[4]   McPherson M, Arango P, Fox H, Lauver C, McManus M et al. A new definition of children with special health care needs. Pediatrics 1998;102:137-40.

[5]   Neff JN, Sharp VL, Muldoon J, Graham J, Popalisky J, Gay JC. Identifying and classifying children with chronic conditions using administrative data with the clinical risk group classification system. Amb Pediatr 2002;2:71-9.

[6]   Feudtner CF, Feinstein JA, Zhong W, Hall M, Dai D. Pediatric complex chronic conditions classification system version 2: Updated for ICD-10 and complex medical technology dependence and transplantation. BMC Pediatr 2014;14:199-205.

[7]   Simon T, Cawthon ML, Stanford S, Popalisky J, Lyons D, Woodcox B, et al. Pediatric Medical complexity Algorith: A new method to stratify children by medical complexity. Pediatrics 2014;113:e1647-54.

[8]   Berry JG, Hall M, Neff J, et al. Children with medical complexity and Medicaid: Spending and cost savings. Health Aff (Millwood) 2014;33(12):2199-206.

[9]   Feudtner CF, Christakis DA, Connell FA. Pediatric deaths attributable to complex chronic conditions: A population-based study of Washington State, 1980-1997. Pediatrics 2000;106:205-9.

[10] Kuo DZ, Cohen E, Agarwar R, Berry JG, Casey PH. A national profile of caregiver challenges among more medically complex children with special health care needs. Arch Pediatr Adolesc Med 2011;165(11):1020- 6.

[11] Van der Lee JH, Mokkink LB, Grootenhuis MA, Heymans HS, Offringa M. Definitions and measurement of chronic health conditions in childhood: A systematic review. JAMA 2007;297(24):2741-51.

[12] Cohen E, Kuo DZ, Agrawal R, Berry JG, Bhagat SKM, et al. Children with medical complexity: An emerging population for clinical and research initiatives. Pediatrics 2011;127:529-38.

[13] American Academy of Pediatrics (AAP) Committee on Bioethics. Conflicts between religious or spiritual beliefs and pediatric care: Informed refusal, exemptions and public funding. Pediatrics 2013;132:962-5.

[14] Casey Family Programs State Welfare Policy Database. Medical Neglect specifically defined in statute. URL: http://www.childwelfarepolicy. org/maps/single?id=144.

[15] Meadow R. Munchausen Syndrome by Proxy: The hinterland of child abuse. Lancet 1977;310:343-5.

[16] Roesler TA, Jenny C. Medical child abuse: Beyond Munchausen syndrome by proxy. Elk Grove Village, IL: American Academy of Pediatrics, 2009.

[17] Flaherty EG, Macmillan HL, AAP Committee on Child Abuse and Neglect. Caregiver-fabricated illness in a child: A manifestation of child maltreatment. Pediatrics 2013;132(7):590-7.

[18] Bass C, Glaser D. Early recognition and management of fabricated or induced illness in children. Lancet 2014;383:1412-21.

[19] Fisher MA. Caring for abused children. Pediatr Rev 2011;32(7):e73-8.

[20] US Department of Health & Human Services, Administration for Children and Families, Administration on Children, Youth and Families, Children's Bureau. Child maltreatment 2014. Washington, DC: Author, 2016. URL: http://www.acf. hhs.gov/programs/cb/research-data-technology/statistics-research/child-maltreatment.

[21] Jenny C, AAP Committee on Child Abuse and Neglect. Recognizing and responding to medical neglect. Pediatrics 2007;120(6):1385-9.

[22] Palusci VJ, Haney ML. Strategies to prevent child maltreatment and integration into practice. APSAC Advisor 2010 (Winter):8-17.

[23] American Professional Society on the Abuse of Children. Practice Guidelines: Integrating prevention into the work of child maltreatment professionals. Columbus, OH: Author, 2010.

[24] Law M, Rosenbaum P. Service coordination for children and youth with complex needs. Hamilton, ON, Canada: CanChild Centre for Childhood Disability Research, McMaster University, 2004.

[25] World Health Organization. International classification of functioning, disability and health (ICF). URL:http://www.who.int/classifications/icf/en/

Chapter 12

LEGAL ISSUES IN CHILD WELFARE CASES INVOLVING CHILDREN WITH DISABILITIES

Frank E Vandervort, JD and Joshua B Kay, PhD, JD*
University of Michigan Law School, Ann Arbor, Michigan, US

This chapter examines the legal framework applicable when child maltreatment and disability intersect. It begins with a brief description of the constitutional foundation for parent-child-state relations. It provides an overview of relevant federal child welfare laws, which today shape each state's child protection system. It then considers the application of various federal laws governing work with children and families when a child has a disability. In doing so, we consider the Americans with Disabilities Act, the Individuals with Disabilities Education Act, and Section 504 of the Rehabilitation Act, and we touch upon Social Security benefits for children. This chapter does not examine child well-being legislation that establishes and funds programs such as Temporary Assistance to Needy Families (TANF), Supplemental Nutrition Assistance Program (SNAP), or publicly funded health care for children such as the State Children's Health Insurance Program.

INTRODUCTION

According to the Census Bureau in the United States (US), approximately 2.8 million school-aged children (ages 5–17 years) have a disability (1). These disabilities range from physical to cognitive, sensory to emotional. Having a disability may place a child at

---

* Correspondence: Professor Frank Vandervort, University of Michigan Law School, 701 S. State Street, Ann Arbor, Michigan 48109, United States. E-mail:vort@umich.edu.

higher risk for maltreatment. In turn, maltreatment may cause a child to have a disability, such as when a child suffers from an inflicted head injury. Inevitably, children with disabilities will come into contact with the child protective system. Nationally each year, the confirmed cases of child maltreatment approach 1,000,000, which involve some 3,000,000 children. Among these are hundreds of thousands of children with disabilities and maltreatment in the US who will be involved in disparate legal proceedings designed for one or the other, but not both.

UNITED STATES CONSTITUTIONAL FRAMEWORK

The Constitution of the United States does not explicitly mention parents, children or families. For nearly a century, though, the Supreme Court has interpreted the Constitution to protect the rights of parents to raise their children and the rights of children to benefit from familial attachment free from interference by governmental authorities. At the same time, the Court has recognized a compelling governmental interest in protecting children from maltreatment at the hands of their parents, guardians or custodian. The establishment of these rights is rooted in the xenophobia surrounding World War I (2).

Before the advent of World War I, most states in the country protected the right of parents to educate their children in the language of their choice. During that war, however, a number of states enacted legislation requiring that public school children be taught in English, and prohibited educational lessons taught in other languages. The State of Nebraska enacted one such law in April 1919, which "made it a misdemeanor to teach any subject in a foreign language, or any foreign language as a subject" (2).

A year after the statute was enacted, a county attorney entered the classroom in Hampton, Nebraska, where Robert Meyer was teaching in German. Meyer was charged with violating the statute prohibiting the use of any foreign language when teaching school children. He was convicted of the misdemeanor and given the minimum fine provided by the law, $25. He appealed his conviction on grounds that the law prohibiting him from teaching in German violated his right to liberty under the Fourteenth Amendment to the Constitution, which provides that "No state shall … deprive any person of life, liberty, or property without due process of law" (3). The Nebraska Supreme Court upheld his conviction, and he appealed to the US Supreme Court.

In 1923, the Court issued its opinion in the case. The Court acknowledged that it had "not attempted to define with exactness the liberty thus guaranteed" (3). However, the court noted, "Without doubt, it denotes . . . the right of the individual . . . to marry, establish a home and bring up children . . . and generally to enjoy those privileges long recognized at common law as essential to the orderly pursuit of happiness by free men"

(3). Thus, the court observed, "it is the natural duty of the parent to give his children education suitable to their station in life" (3). Because the parents of Mr. Meyer's students possessed this "natural duty," they had a right, protected by the liberty clause of the Fourteenth Amendment, to engage Mr. Meyer to fulfill this responsibility. Although the court recognized the State "may do much, go very far...in order to improve the quality of its citizens, physically, mentally and morally...the individual has certain fundamental rights which must be respected" (3).

Two years later, in *Pierce v. Society of Sisters* (1925), the Court held that the fundamental right established in *Meyer* extended to a parent's right to choose to educate his or her children in non-public, religious or military schools (4). In doing so, the Court observed that "The child is not the mere creature of the State; those who nurture him and direct his destiny have the right, coupled with the high duty, to recognize and prepare him for additional obligations" (4). Together, the *Meyer* and *Pierce* cases established the fundamental right of a parent to direct the upbringing of his or her child without undue interference from governmental authorities.

In both *Meyer* and *Pierce*, however, the Court made clear that State authorities are not entirely without power to regulate schools or, more broadly, parents' choices in directing their children's upbringing. The limitations on a parent's right to direct their children's upbringing were addressed in 1944. Massachusetts had enacted certain child labor laws, which prohibited children of certain ages from engaging in certain activities. Sarah Prince was charged with violating the law when she permitted her two children and a third child over whom she had legal guardianship to sell religious pamphlets for $.05 on the streets of Brockton, Massachusetts. She was convicted of violating the law and appealed.

The case *Prince v Massachusetts* raised two issues related to the Constitutional right to liberty: 1) the right of a parent to direct a child's religious development; and 2) the right of the children to observe and participate his or her family's religious activities. In *Prince*, the Court more squarely articulated the sometimes adverse positions of the parent and the state vis-à-vis the child. The Court acknowledged both the parent's interest in raising her or his child without governmental interference and the right of the State, as the ultimate guardian of the child, to act to protect the child's welfare. The Court noted, "It is cardinal with us that the custody, care, and nurture of the child reside first in the parents" (5). But the Court went on to state that "the family is not beyond regulation in the public interest...neither the rights of religion nor rights of parenthood are beyond limitation. Acting to guard the general interest in youth's well-being, the state...may restrict the parent's control" in a number of ways, including by mandating school attendance and prohibiting child labor (5). Thus, the Court ruled, "the state has a wide range of power for limiting parental freedom and authority in things affecting the child's welfare" (5).

What of the rights of children relative to the rights of the state and the parents in this mix? The rights of children in this triangle of rights are somewhat less defined. Courts have, however, recognized that, generally speaking, parents and children have reciprocal rights. Parents have the right to raise their children as they see fit and children have the right to benefit from the day-to-day nurturing provided by parents and to their benevolent decision-making (6). That is, parents have the right to care, custody and control in raising of their children and children have the right to benefit from that care and concern. However, "the power of the parent...may be subject to limitation under *Prince* if it appears that parental decisions will jeopardize the health or safety of the child, or have a potential for significant social burdens" (7).

In subsequent years, the Supreme Court has applied this basic doctrine balancing the rights of parents and the rights of state authorities to familial living arrangements (8), medical and mental health decision-making (6), and whether a grandparent has the right to visit a child over the objections of the custodial parent (9). The rule that pertains from the Court's cases, read together, is that a fit parent, one who has not been found to have maltreated his or her child, has the right in the first instance to raise his or her child as he or she sees fit. Parents' rights are weakest when they have been shown to have maltreated their child.

CHILD MALTREATMENT AND
THE UNITED STATES CONSTITUTION

The law begins with the presumption that a parent is fit and will, therefore, make parenting decisions that are in the best interests of her or his child. The Supreme Court has articulated the rationale for this presumption: "The law's concept of the family rests on the presumption that parents possess what a child lacks in maturity, experience and capacity for judgment required for making life's difficult decisions...[H]istorically, it has recognized that natural bonds of affection lead parents to act in the best interests of their children" (6). While the state may have a legitimate interest in separating a child from an abusive or neglectful (i.e., unfit) parent, the state has no legitimate interest in separating a child from a fit parent (10).

When one wishes to invoke the law in order to protect a child from parental neglect or abuse, that individual must assume the burden of demonstrating parental unfitness. In asserting the unfitness of a parent to parent his or her child, the law will not rest on presumptions, and the actual unfitness of the parent must be demonstrated (10). Thus, for example, where the State of Illinois enacted a law that presumed that all unmarried fathers were unfit to provide care and custody for their children upon the death of the child's mother and automatically took the children into the foster care system, the Court held the law to be an unconstitutional violation of the father's right to both equal protection of the law due process of law (10). Under the state's statutory scheme, a mother, a married father or a divorced father had the right to have a hearing at which state authorities were required to demonstrate the parent's unfitness before their children could be removed. The statute, however, allowed the state to remove children from their father if he had never married their mother on the theory that because most unwed fathers were unfit, the children of all these fathers could be removed. The Supreme Court struck down this law, requiring that state authorities demonstrate that the particular father at issue is unfit to care for his children.

Cases involving the fathers of children present some unique legal challenges. While a child's mother is known, and her rights established, at the time of birth, the identity of a child's father may be more difficult to ascertain, and determination of his rights more complicated. In *Lehr v. Robertson*, the Supreme Court was required to define the rights of a father who was not married to the child's mother and who had never established a relationship with his child (11). Because the father did not grasp the opportunity to parent his child, he did not have the same rights as a father who had grasped that opportunity. In short, a father must actually exercise his parental rights and attend to his parental responsibilities or he may be deprived of his rights more easily than a father who has asserted them.

While parents and children possess reciprocal rights in their relationship with one another and share an interest in the preservation of their family free from governmental interference (12), there is no absolute constitutional right to remain together as a family, and state authorities, acting on the orders of a court, may remove a child from an abusive or neglectful parent's custody (13). Once a state trial court finds that a parent is unfit, the State's "urgent interest" in protecting the child from harm prevails over the parent's right to care, custody and control of the child.

While child protective services caseworkers may act to protect a child from harm by seeking to remove him from abusive or neglectful parents, the state is under no obligation to do so. Thus, where children's protective services were involved with a family but failed to remove the child from the parent's custody, the child could not successfully sue the state authorities after his father beat him causing extensive brain damage (13).

While the state may demonstrate parental unfitness by a preponderance of the evidence standard (i.e., that child maltreatment more likely than not occurred), it may not permanently terminate a parent's rights unless it can show by clear and convincing evidence that abuse or neglect has occurred (12). The Supreme Court has explained the need for this higher burden of proof:

> The fundamental liberty interest of natural parents in the care, custody, and management of their child does not evaporate simply because they have not been model parents or have lost temporary custody of their child to the State. Even when blood relationships are strained, parents retain a vital interest in preventing the irretrievable destruction of their family life. If anything, persons faced with forced dissolution of their parental rights have a more critical need for procedural protections than do those resisting state intervention into ongoing family affairs. When the State moves to destroy weakened familial bonds, it must provide the parents with fundamentally fair procedures. (12)

Note that this standard applies only to non-Indian children. A higher standard, "beyond a reasonable doubt," applies to the termination of parental rights to an Indian child, as will be discussed more fully later in this chapter. While the Supreme Court has held that the Constitution does not require, as a matter of due process of law, that parents be appointed legal counsel in every case (15), most states, either in interpreting their constitutions (16) or by way of statutory enactment (17), provide for the appointment of a lawyer in every child protection proceeding at public expense if the parent is unable to afford one. Although appointment of legal counsel is not constitutionally required, the provision of a transcript of the trial court proceedings at public expense is mandatory if the parent is unable to afford to pay for the transcript to be produced (18). With this constitutional framework in mind, we will next consider the statutory schemes utilized by states to protect children from inadequate parenting.

THE FEDERAL STATUTORY FRAMEWORK OF CHILD WELFARE CASES

Every state has a statutory scheme for responding to alleged child maltreatment that occurs at the hands of a child's parents or legal custodians. (19) While these statutes differ in their particulars, they are substantially similar largely because of the federal government's involvement in funding child protection services since the mid-1970s. To understand how this came to be, it will be helpful to begin with a very brief history lesson.

The United States has always provided some mechanism by which the larger community can step in and assume the care of a child who is without parents or whose parents are unable or unwilling to provide an appropriate home. By the early 1800s, the doctrine of *parens patriae*—the notion that the sovereign was ultimately responsible for safeguarding the welfare of those who lacked legal capacity—was well-established in American law. Where children were placed when their parents were unable to provide and appropriate home has changed over time, from basically indenturing them to placing them in congregate care facilities, to foster family homes.

In the 1960s, in the wake of the publication of the Kempe et al. seminal paper "The battered child syndrome" in the Journal of the American Medical Association (20), states began to enact laws requiring physicians and other professionals to report cases of suspected child abuse to state authorities (21). Those laws were expanded over time to broaden both what was to be reported—e.g., child neglect and sexual abuse in addition to physical abuse—and categories of professionals who were mandated to report their concerns— initially only medical professionals were required to report, but that was expanded to social workers, teachers and others professionals who come into frequent contact with children. These laws resulted in substantial increases in the number of abused and neglected children coming to the attention of state child protection authorities.

By the mid-1970s, there were about a half-million children in the foster care system nationwide. It was not unusual for children entering the foster care system to remain in the system for years with no effort being made either to reunify them with their families of origin or to move them into alternative permanent homes. This phenomenon came to be known as foster care "limbo" and was accompanied by another phenomenon, foster care "drift," in which children would often move from home to home. Children remained in foster homes for so many years that the United States Supreme Court was called on in *Smith v. Organization of Foster Families for Equality and Reform* to determine whether long-term foster families had the same or similar constitutional rights as biological families. Eventually, these concerns were brought to the attention of Congress, which enacted legislation intended to bring about reform of the nation's child protection systems. Space limitations do not permit a detailed discussion of federal child welfare law.

CHILD ABUSE PREVENTION AND TREATMENT ACT

The United States is a federal system, which means that some matters of public policy are handled by the federal government while others are handled by the individual states. Legal issues relating to families are regulated by the states. The federal government may influence state policy by enacting legislation pursuant to its spending authority and placing conditions on the receipt of federal money. In the child protection arena, the federal government has established a stream of funding that allows the states to draw down large amounts of federal money if they design their state child protection systems to meet federal standards.

The first such statute that Congress enacted was the Child Abuse Prevention and Treatment Act (CAPTA). Signed into law in 1974, and repeatedly amended and reauthorized since, CAPTA provides support for state systems of preventing and responding to reported cases of child maltreatment. CAPTA also provides funding to support research into all aspects of child maltreatment—causes, prevention, and consequences—as well as program evaluation and technical assistances to states, Indian tribes and non-profit organizations (22).

ADOPTION ASSISTANCE AND CHILD WELFARE ACT OF 1980

Concerned about the number of children in foster care, the length of time they remained in what was intended to be a temporary system, and placement instability, in 1980, Congress passed and the President signed into law the Adoption Assistance and Child Welfare Act of 1980. This statute added two sections to the Social Security Act to provide funding to states to address child protection. Broadly speaking, this statute, which, like CAPTA, has been amended and reauthorized repeatedly since its initial enactment, has three purposes: 1) reducing the number of children entering foster care; 2) shortening stays in foster care; and 3) moving children to permanent homes, either through return to their family of origin, or, when return home is not possible, moving children into adoptive homes. We will look at each of these goals in a bit more detail.

To reduce the number of children entering foster care, the law required that state child welfare authorities make "reasonable efforts" to prevent children from entering the system by developing programs to provide in-home services to children and their families aimed at maintaining the family. To accomplish this, Congress added Title IV-B to the Social Security Act, which funnels federal money to states to prevent the removal of maltreated children from their homes. In response, states developed intensive family preservation programs which seek to address the family's needs and problems in functioning in order that children may remain safely in their homes.

Next, the statute addressed those cases in which the child cannot be safely maintained in the home and must be removed. To accomplish this, Congress created Title IV-E of the Social Security Act. The law incentivizes states to make "reasonable efforts" to return children to their families. To accomplish this goal, state child protection authorities are required to develop individualized case plans aimed at addressing the needs of individual family members such as drug or mental health treatment for parents and medical and mental health care for the children. The aim of the service plan is to resolve the problems in functioning that lead to the child's removal and facilitate the safe return of the child to the custody of his or her parents.

The third requirement of the statute is that states consider "the child's sense of time." rather than adult's sense of time. Generally, Congress determined that children need decisions about returning home or being freed for adoption to be made much more quickly than was happening before the enactment of the stature. Thus, the law required that states hold permanency planning hearings (PPH) after a child had been in foster care for a designated period of time. Originally, the PPH was to be held 18 months after the child entered foster care. That requirement was subsequently shortened to one year.

Finally, the 1980 law provided a package of adoption incentives that were intended to move children from temporary foster care into permanent homes. These incentives include the state rather than the adoptive family paying for the costs of the adoption (e.g., court fees) and by providing both cash assistance and medical benefits for special needs children (e.g., children with disabilities and older children).

In the early 1980s, these statutes began to have their intended impact, the numbers of children entering foster care edged down slightly. But then two phenomena converged to increase the numbers of children entering care. First, a more conservative federal government began to cut public benefits available to families, increasing the risk of child maltreatment. Secondly, the combination of the crack cocaine epidemic and the advent of HIV/AIDS had devastating impacts on certain communities. The need for foster care increased.

A related problem also emerged. In the 1980 law, Congress never defined what it meant by "reasonable efforts," and many states, in part as a means of saving money, defined it to mean every conceivable effort had to be made before a child could be removed from the home. That is, states began to overuse intensive family preservation programs beyond their capacities, which resulted in a number of high profile child deaths and many lesser harms inflicted on children (23).

ADOPTION AND SAFE FAMILIES ACT

As a result, in 1997, Congress passed and President Clinton signed into law the Adoption and Safe Families Act (ASFA), which was intended to clarify the intent of Congress regarding the 1980 Act in general and the "reasonable efforts" requirement in particular. While it renewed the federal government's commitment to family preservation, it made clear that children's health and safety are to be the paramount concerns of the nation's child protection systems.

The ASFA maintained the basic framework of the 1980 Act but made a number of adjustments and clarifications. The new law tightened the timeline for permanency planning hearings from 18 months to one year. It also made clear that there is a set of cases involving very serious child maltreatment—e.g., death of a child, torture of a child—in which "reasonable efforts" shall not be made to preserve or reunify the family, and the state authorities are mandated to seek the termination of the parents' rights immediately.

Next, ASFA permitted each state to define for itself a category of "aggravated circumstances" cases in which state authorities may determine that "reasonable efforts" to either preserve or reunify a family are unnecessary, and thereby permit the child protection agency to pursue immediate termination of parental rights. While each state is free to define this group of cases for itself, the federal legislation suggests that appropriate circumstances for its use include abandonment, chronic abuse, and sexual abuse.

The final major change in the law under ASFA is that the state child welfare agency may seek, and the juvenile or family court may grant, termination of parental rights in any case without making "reasonable efforts" to preserve or reunify the family if the specific circumstances warrant such action. Illinois is one state that has codified this possibility. It statute provides that parental rights may be terminated "in those extreme cases in which the parent's incapacity to care for the child, combined with an extremely poor prognosis for treatment or rehabilitation, justifies expedited termination of parental rights" (24).

In the wake of ASFA's enactment a number of states have adopted definitions of "reasonable efforts" in order to guide state child welfare authorities and courts in making decisions about whether this requirement has been complied with. For instance, Missouri law provides as follows:

> "Reasonable efforts" means the exercise of reasonable diligence and care . . . to utilize all available services related to meeting the needs of the juvenile and the family. In determining reasonable efforts to be made and in making such reasonable efforts, the child's present and ongoing health and safety shall be the paramount consideration. In support of its determination of whether reasonable efforts have been made, the court shall enter findings, including a brief description of what preventive or reunification efforts were made and why further efforts could or could not have prevented or shortened the separation of the family. The [state child welfare authorities] shall have the burden of demonstrating reasonable efforts. (25)

ASFA also permitted the use of concurrent planning, which allows state child protection authorities to simultaneously seek to reunify the family and develop an alternative plan in the event that reunification services are not successful. By engaging in the duel planning process, children's stays in foster care can be shortened and they can achieve permanency more quickly. The law also expanded permanency options to include both permanent legal guardianship and a designation called "another planned permanent living arrangement," which is typically used in cases of older foster children who can neither be returned to their families of origin nor placed for adoption, and includes alternatives such as independent living or, perhaps, discharge into the adult foster care system for incapacitated adults.

MULTIETHNIC PLACEMENT ACT AND THE INTERETHNIC ADOPTION PROVISIONS

Historically, minority children, particularly African Americans, were excluded from receiving public child welfare services. In more recent years, there has been concern not of underserving minority children but of the overrepresentation of minority — again, specifically African American — children in the child protection system. As a result, there has been debate about the availability of services to meet the needs of these children. One ongoing controversy is the placement of African American children across racial lines for adoption. One response to this concern was for state authorities to engage in conscious race matching. As a result, some African American children's placement from institutional care into foster family homes or for adoption in a suitable home was delayed or denied. Some jurisdictions had explicit waiting periods before a child could be placed into or adopted across racial lines.

In 1994, Congress enacted the Multiethnic Placement Act, which sought to eliminate (or, at least, dramatically reduce) the use of race, color or national origin as a basis on which foster or adoptive placement could be determined. The law's language, however, was easily interpreted as permitting some racial matching, so two years later, Congress passed clarifying language in the Interethnic Adoption Provisions, which were intended to ban outright the use of race, color or national origin in placement decision-making except in the rarest of circumstances.

If the placement of a child into either a foster or adoptive home is delayed or denied on the basis of race, color or national origin, the law explicitly provides that the aggrieved person—the child or the foster/adoptive parent—may sue the state child welfare agency. This is a rare exception to the governmental immunity from lawsuits typically enjoyed by child welfare agencies.

THE FOSTER CARE INDEPENDENCE ACT

Each year, approximately 20,000 children age out of the foster care system. Many of these youth are ill-prepared to make a successful transition to young adulthood. Historically, most had not graduated from high school, many were ending up homeless, nearly half were themselves parents, and some 80% of them were unable to support themselves financially. To address the unique problems facing this sub-population of the foster care population, Congress enacted The Foster Care Independence Act in 1999, commonly known as the "Chafee Act," so named for its author, Senator John Chafee (1922-1999).

The Chafee Act provided a separate funding stream to states to allow them to develop programming for children who were in the foster care system on or after their 14th year birthday. In addition to providing Medicaid coverage for these youth until the age of 21 years, the Act required that foster parents of these youth be specially trained to meet their needs and that state agencies assist youth in developing independent living skills such as how to seek employment and how to manage a household budget. Agencies were also to provide assistance with completing high school and making the transition to job training or college. The law also provided additional adoption subsidies to encourage and support the adoption of these older children.

In 2008, the Congress amended Title IV-E to allow states to extend these youth in the foster care system until their 21st year birthday. It also mandated that state agencies develop a personalized, youth-directed plan for each youth in order to address the transition to adulthood, including educational, housing, health insurance, and other considerations.

INDIAN CHILD WELFARE ACT

In 1978, in an effort to respond to overzealous child welfare practices aimed at assimilating Indian children into the dominant culture through unnecessary removals, Congress enacted the Indian Child Welfare Act (ICWA). Unlike the other federal child welfare laws discussed in this chapter, which are funding statutes, the ICWA is substantive law. That is, unlike the funding statues, which the states may choose to follow or not (if they choose not to, of course, they will not be able to draw down some or all of the federal funding they would be able to draw down if they complied), the states are mandated to comply with the ICWA in every child protection case involving an

"Indian child." This distinction results because the Constitution of the United States explicitly reserves to the Congress the authority to make laws relating to the Indian tribes.

Two threshold issues are important to keep in mind regarding the application of the ICWA. First, the law defines an "Indian child" as "any unmarried person who is under age eighteen and is either (a) a member of an Indian tribe or (b) is eligible for membership in an Indian tribe and is the biological child of a member of an Indian tribe." The federal government has given formal recognition to 567 "tribal entities" across the country. Of note, it is possible for a child to be of Native American ancestry but not qualify as an "Indian child" within the meaning of the law, because each tribe defines for itself its tribal eligibility requirements. Some, but not all, tribes have a blood quantum requirement. Secondly, unlike child protection proceedings involving non-Indian children, in a proceeding involving an "Indian child" the child's tribe is a party to the proceeding. Thus, the tribe or the parents may, generally speaking, elect to move the case from the state court to a tribal court. Alternatively, the tribe may intervene as a party to and participate in a state child protection proceeding.

When an "Indian child" resides on a reservation, state courts may make only emergency orders that are necessary to ensure a child's immediate safety. In situations such as this, the law provides that the case must be transferred the tribal court. Most tribes that have tribal courts have separate child welfare codes. However, these codes are substantially similar to state child welfare codes. As with state child protection systems, the various federal laws allow tribes to access federal funding to support their child protection efforts so long as the tribal system meets the federal requirements.

The ICWA provides a unique set of procedures applicable to cases of Indian children that are explicitly intended to make it more difficult to remove an Indian child from his or her home. The law accomplishes this goal in several ways. First, it increases the amount of evidence (i.e., the standard of proof) which state authorities must present to a court before an Indian child may be removed from the home. While a non-Indian child may typically be removed from the home based upon a showing of probable cause that a child has been harmed, before an Indian child may be removed, the state authorities must present clear and convincing evidence. This is the same standard by which the parental rights of a non-Indian child's parent may be permanently terminated. To terminate the rights of an Indian child's parents requires proof beyond a reasonable doubt, the highest standard of proof known to the law, which is typically used to convict a defendant of a criminal offense.

The ICWA also requires that at both the removal stage and the termination of parental rights stage in a child protection proceeding state authorities prove that "active efforts" have been made to maintain or reunify the Indian family. The Bureau of Indian Affairs within the Department of the Interior in 2015 issued updated guidance for state authorities in applying the ICWA. (26) It said that, "Active efforts are intended primarily to maintain and reunite an Indian child with his or her family or tribal community and constitute more than reasonable efforts" as required by other federal funding legislation. The BIA provides examples of "active efforts," including:

- "Identifying appropriate services and helping the parents to overcome barriers, including actively assisting the parents in obtaining such services."
- "Taking into account the Indian child's tribe's prevailing social and cultural conditions and way of life, and requesting the assistance of representatives designated by the Indian child's tribe with substantial knowledge of the prevailing social and cultural standards."
- "Offering and employing all available and culturally appropriate family preservation strategies."
- "Completing a comprehensive assessment of the circumstances of the Indian child's family, with a focus on safe reunification as the most desirable goal."

Some question the viability of the ICWA given that consideration of race in matters of public decision-making is restricted, and ask how the ICWA squares with the Multiethnic Placement Act and the Interethnic Adoption Provisions. The basic answer is that tribes are sovereign nations, and enrollment in a tribe constitutes a political designation rather than a racial or ethnic classification.

In response to the enactment of the ICWA, several states—e.g., Iowa, Michigan, Minnesota—have enacted comparable statutes at the state level. These statutes may be more expansive or protective than the federal law, and therefore may apply to children and families that would not be covered under the federal ICWA.

APPLICATION OF DISABILITY LAW TO CHILD WELFARE CASES: THE AMERICANS WITH DISABILITIES ACT AND SIMILAR LAWS

The services provided in child welfare cases to prevent the removal of a child from a parent's custody or to reunify a family often are designed to address parenting problems identified by the child welfare agency. These problems with parenting may be the ones that prompted agency involvement in the first place or may be ongoing or new concerns that contribute to continued foster care placement. In contrast, less attention may be paid to the social service and educational needs of children involved in the child protection system. Child welfare agencies need to carefully ascertain what kinds of assistance children may require, and special attention must be paid to ensuring that the needs of children with disabilities are met.

It is well-established that any services provided to parents by child welfare and associated agencies must reasonably accommodate a parent's disability under Title II of the Americans with Disabilities Act (ADA) (26). If these services do not reasonably accommodate a parent's disability, they may not be considered "reasonable efforts" by the courts, jeopardizing the state's access to federal funding in that case and potentially interfering with later efforts by the agency to terminate the parent's rights. Similarly, but perhaps considered less frequently by child welfare agencies and the service providers with whom they work, the ADA also protects children with disabilities. Therefore, any services provided to a child with a disability must accommodate that disability such that the child has an opportunity to benefit from the service as much as a non-disabled child might.

The ADA is a federal civil rights law that is designed "to provide clear, strong, consistent, enforceable standards addressing discrimination against individuals with disabilities" (27). It is not the only law to do so. For example, Section 504 of the Rehabilitation Act of 1973 also addresses disability discrimination, but only in entities that receive federal funding (28). Many organizations and agencies providing services to children in the child welfare system receive federal funds, so Section 504 would apply to them much as the ADA does. So too would analogous state disability rights statutes where they exist. Because the application is quite similar between these statutes, and the ADA is the more encompassing federal law, this chapter focuses on how the ADA applies in these cases. Readers should simply be mindful that other disability rights laws are likely to apply as well.

APPLICATION OF THE ADA

The threshold for whether the ADA applies to a child in a given child welfare case is whether the child has a disability. Disability is defined as "(A) a physical or mental impairment that substantially limits one or more major life activities of [the] individual; (B) a record of such an impairment; or (C) being regarded as having such an impairment" (29). Whether a person is disabled is to "be construed in favor of broad coverage" (30). The statute provides a non-exhaustive list of many "major life activities," both physical and cognitive, that may be limited and therefore fall under the Act (31). These include learning, reading, concentrating, thinking, and communicating, all tasks that are germane in educational and other contexts, such as psychotherapy and health care, in which children may engage. Impairments in these and other areas of functioning may interfere with a child's ability to benefit from services provided by child welfare and other agencies if reasonable accommodations are not made.

Unless the agency will stipulate to the fact that a child is disabled or has portrayed the child as disabled in its court pleadings or other documents or verbal statements, evidence of disability will be needed to trigger ADA protections. This evidence may include information from medical and mental health evaluation reports or other records, Social Security determinations, or educational evaluations and records. Although child welfare agencies frequently describe disabling impairments in parents, it is less common for them to note how the child functions in different domains. Therefore, practitioners should not rely on the agency to "tip them off" to a child's disability, and thorough evaluation of the child is a critical component of ensuring that any disabilities are identified and accommodated.

Sometimes, however, the agency does report that the child has a disability or describes the child's functional status in a way that implies that it regards the child as disabled. In these cases, the ADA applies. Under the ADA, disability may be inferred if a person is treated by a public entity as having an impairment that substantially limits a major life activity (32). In essence, this treatment by the agency amounts to the child being regarded as having an impairment, thereby triggering ADA protections.

In order to be eligible for ADA protection, the child must be a "qualified individual with a disability," which is defined as a person who, "with or without reasonable modifications," "meets the essential eligibility requirements for the receipt of services or the participation in programs or activities provided by a public entity" (33). There is no doubt that children with disabilities who are involved in child welfare proceedings are eligible to receive services from the agency and are therefore qualified individuals under the ADA. Finally, child welfare agencies are clearly public entities, including private agencies that enter into contracts with the state or county child welfare agency to do work that would otherwise fall to the public agency. Therefore, they are required to follow the requirements of the ADA. It is important to note that the ADA applies to child protection agencies regardless of whether the case is court-involved. Child welfare agencies take only a small fraction of cases to court, mostly when children must be removed from the custody of their parents. Many cases are handled by the agency directly with the families involved and never go to court, and in all of these matters, the agency must comply with the ADA. Therefore, the agency must accommodate the disabilities of the parents and children with whom they work, from ensuring accessibility to agency and other facilities to providing any educational materials in an accessible format and using training approaches tailored to the needs of the individual.

DEVELOPING REASONABLE ACCOMMODATIONS

When reasonable accommodations are required in order to meet the needs of a child with a disability who is receiving services, it is important to think carefully about exactly what kinds of accommodations might be in order. That determination may rely on having a thorough assessment, which may need to be a multidisciplinary assessment, of the child's needs. That assessment should take a "functional" view of disability. The functional view emphasizes the child's actual, functional abilities across whatever domains are relevant (34). Therefore, a functional evaluation may reveal how the child learns best or applies what he or she learns, or how the child navigates the word physically, or the child's behaviors in various circumstances, and the like. In addition, the functional perspective emphasizes the interaction of the individual and his or her environment, recognizing that the environment itself, including not only physical barriers but also policies, attitudes, and teaching styles, can be disabling or contribute to diminished functioning (35). A functional approach provides the most guidance in planning interventions, including how best to accommodate the disability.

In contrast, a "categorical" view of disability emphasizes the criteria for various categories of disability, such as a type of mental illness, intellectual disability, or a specific physical disability, much like a medical diagnosis. (34) The categorical approach reveals little about the person's actual functioning and thus provides scant information for the purpose of service planning and reasonable accommodations. Unfortunately, many professionals are tempted to approach disabilities categorically, because it is easier to diagnose and label than it is to do a deeper, more meaningful assessment. Over-reliance on the categorical approach contributes to service provision that is not tailored to the actual needs of the individual.

Given the complexities of disability coupled with the trauma history that is inherent to most child protection cases, the gold standard for an assessment that is likely to result in excellent service planning tailored to the child's needs is multidisciplinary, trauma-informed assessment completed by a team that has expertise in working with children with disabilities. These types of evaluation can yield rich data that effectively guide interventions across the medical, mental health, and educational spectra. When considering reasonable accommodations, there are no set approaches, and it is best to consult with the child if he or she is old enough, his or her parents, providers who may have worked with the child in the school, medical, and mental health contexts, and expert evaluators in order to determine what accommodations may be needed.

SPECIAL EDUCATION LAW

It is critical to consider the educational needs for every child in the child welfare system, and children with disabilities may encounter extra challenges in school. They also are supposed to receive specific protections. Children with disabilities are legally entitled to receive a "free, appropriate public education" (FAPE), and the special education system is intended to provide them with just that (36). The Individuals with Disabilities Education Act (IDEA) is the main federal law that governs the provision of special education services, though the ADA and Section 504 of the Rehabilitation Act of 1973 can be useful as well. A special education program is deemed appropriate if it was created through an Individualized Education Program (IEP) process and is reasonably calculated to confer educational benefit (37). Through special education, children with disabilities can receive specialized instruction, adapted transportation to and from school, various therapies, and a wide range of supplementary aids and services, including assistive technology devices, to the extent that any of these services are needed in order for the child to receive a FAPE (38).

Generally, education rights flow through the *parents* of children, not the children themselves. If a child with a disability remains with his or her parent during the pendency of a child welfare case, the parent can seek special education services for the child. Assistance from the child welfare agency in doing so may be necessary and appropriate, but the caseworker cannot sign an IEP. If a child is in foster care, a parent can still seek special education services, as can a foster parent (39). In addition, the court may designate an educational surrogate for the purposes of special education planning if a child is a court ward (40).

A written referral indicating that a student may need special education services begins the process. School personnel may write these referrals, as can parents, guardians, or foster parents. The referral triggers an evaluation to determine the child's eligibility. Special education evaluations must be designed to assess both the student's eligibility and the student's educational needs in order to inform what services should be put into place (41). IDEA has numerous eligibility categories, such as cognitive impairment, specific learning disability, speech and language impairment, etc., but it is important to note that the category does not determine or limit what services the child might receive (42). Rather, the category simply makes the child eligible for all necessary services to benefit from his or her education. Therefore, advocates and caregivers should consider the eligibility category merely as a means of entry into the special education system. Once a parent or other caregiver consents to an evaluation, the school district has sixty calendar days or less to complete it (43).

Once an evaluation is completed, an Individualized Education Planning Team (IEPT) is convened to determine the student's eligibility for special education services based on the evaluation. As noted above, if a student is eligible for special education services, an Individualized Education Program (IEP) must be developed by the IEPT (44). The IEP must be reassessed at least yearly, and either the school or parent can request that an IEP meeting be held sooner if needed. The child must be educated in the least restrictive environment that is appropriate to meet his or her needs (45). The IEP should indicate the settings in which services will occur, exactly what services will be provided, how long and how often services will be provided, the student's current level of functioning, how progress will be measured, and any supplementary aids or services that are necessary for the student to receive a FAPE. The goals for what the student is expected to achieve in the following year should be clear, objective, and measurable. Special education students must be included in state educational testing, albeit with accommodations, or in alternate assessments if they cannot participate in state educational testing even with accommodations (46).

For children in foster care, all of this may be more difficult to accomplish, especially if the child has changed schools. If the parent is uninvolved, there may be a dearth of background knowledge about the child and his or her educational programming, even if the school has up to date records. Agency personnel and the child's lawyer should endeavor to bridge any gaps, which may include arranging for school personnel from the child's previous school to attend an IEP meeting and consult with the new school in an ongoing manner. Another option may be to advocate for a thorough re-evaluation.

Finally, caregivers and advocates should be aware that while IDEA is the primary legal scheme under which special education services are provided, some children with disabilities do not qualify under IDEA's eligibility categories. In such cases, the Americans with Disabilities Act or Section 504 of the Rehabilitation may still mandate that the school accommodate the child's disability. It is important to consult with a student advocacy center or with the state's Protection and Advocacy office for representation or advice about how to access special education services or other accommodations as appropriate. See www.ndrn.org for a list of state Protection and Advocacy offices.

SOCIAL SECURITY

Children with disabilities may be eligible for Supplemental Security Income (SSI) payments from the Social Security Administration. For SSI purposes, a child is considered disabled if he or she is under 18 years of age and "has a medically determinable physical or mental impairment, which results in marked and severe functional limitations, and which can be expected to result in death or which has lasted or can be expected to last for a continuous period of not less than 12 months" (47). If the child is in foster care, SSI payments will go to the child welfare agency to offset the cost of the child's care. Despite the fact that such payments might not appear to benefit the child directly, it is important to apply for SSI benefits if the child might be eligible. The child's disability may require ongoing financial support beyond the time that the child is in foster care, and either the child's family of origin or the child's adoptive family could benefit substantially from SSI payments, materially improving the child's standard of living. If a child is in foster care, the child welfare agency should apply for SSI benefits on the child's behalf.

To determine whether the child is disabled and therefore eligible for SSI benefits, Social Security requires detailed information about the child's condition and how it affects his or her functioning in daily life, including at home, in school, and in other contexts. Reports or other data from doctors, therapists, teachers, etc., also provide information for the eligibility determination. Unfortunately, it may be difficult to gather adequate medical and school records for children in foster care, especially if they have changed schools or providers and records have not transferred successfully, but it is important to try to do so. Also, the income and resources of the child's household will be considered in the SSI eligibility determination—if income and resources are more than the allowed amount, the child will not be eligible for SSI payments. However, this requirement should not affect children living in foster care.

CONCLUSION

It is inevitable that some children with disabilities will come to the attention of child protection authorities or that maltreated children will become disabled. This chapter has addressed the legal framework for addressing the needs of children when these two phenomena intersect. It has summarized the constitutional framework governing relationships between parents, child, and the state and provided an overview of important federal child protection and disability law. It is essential that child welfare agency caseworkers, lawyers, and other professionals consider a child's disability in the course of a child protection case and seek expert consultation as necessary so as to ensure that children's needs are met.

REFERENCES

[1]   US Department of Commerce, Economic and Statistics Administration, U.S. Census Bureau. School—aged children with disabilities in the U.S. Metropolitan Statistical Areas: 2010. Washington, DC: US Census Bureau, 2011.

[2]   Cappozzola R. Uncle Same wants you: World War I and the making of the modern American citizen. London: Oxford University Press, 2008.

[3]   Meyer v. Nebraska, 262 U.S. 390 (1923).

[4]   Pierce v Society of Sisters, 268 U.S. 510 (1925).

[5]   Prince v. Massachusetts, 321 U.S. 158 (1944).

[6]   Parham v. J.R., 442 U.S. 584 (1979).

[7]   Wisconsin v Yoder, 406 U.S. 205 (1972).

[8]   Moore v. City of East Cleveland, Ohio, 431 U.S. 494 (1977).

[9]   Troxel v. Granville, 530 U.S. 57 (2000).

[10] Stanley v. Illinois, 405 U.S. 645 (1972).

[11] Lehr v. Robertson, 463 U.S. 248 (1983).

[12] Santosky v. Kramer, 455 U.S. 745 (1982).

[13] Doe v Oettle, 293 N.W. 2d 760 (Mich. 1980).

[14] DeShaney v. Winnebago County Department of Social Services, 489 U.S. 189 (1989).

[15] Lassiter v. Department of Social Services, 452 U.S. 18 (1981).

[16] Reist v Bay Circuit Judge, 241 N.W.2d 55 (Mich. 1976).

[17] Boyer BA. Justice, access to the courts, and the right to free counsel for indigent parents: The continuing scourge of Lassiter v. Department of Social Service of Durham. Loyola U Chicago Law J 2005;36:363-81.

[18] M.L.B. v. S.L.J., 519 U.S. 102 (1996).

[19] Mnookin RH, Weisberg, DK. Child, family, and state: Problems and materials on children and the law. New York: Aspen, 2009.

[20] Kempe CH, Silverman FN, Steele BF, Droegemueller W, Silver HK. The battered child syndrome. JAMA 1962;181:17-24.

[21] Vandervort FE. Mandated reporting of child maltreatment: Developments in the wake of recent scandals. APSAC Advisor 2012;24(4):3-9.

[22] Child Welfare Information Gateway, About CAPTA: A legislative history, 2011. URL:https://www.childwelfare.gov/pubPDFs/about.pdf.

[23] Gelles RJ. The book of David. How preserving families can cost children's lives. New York: Basic Books, 1996.

[24] 705 Ill Comp Stat Ann § 405/1-2(1)(c).

[25] Mo Ann rev Stat § 211.183(2).

[26] Kay JB. Representing parents with disabilities. In: Guggenheim M, Sankaran VS (eds). Representing parents in child welfare cases. Chicago, IL: American Bar Association Books, 2015:253-68.

[27] 42 U.S.C. § 12101(b)(2).

[28] 29 U.S.C. § 794.

[29] 42 U.S.C. § 12102(1).

[30] 42 U.S.C. § 12102(4)(A).

[31] 42 U.S.C. § 12102(2)(A)

[32] 28 C.F.R. § 35.104; 42 U.S.C. § 12102(3)(A).

[33]   42 U.S.C. § 12131(2).

[34]   Tymchuk AJ. The importance of matching educational interventions to parent needs in child maltreatment: Issues, methods, and recommendations. In: Lutzker JR, ed. Handbook of child abuse research and treatment. New York: Plenum Press, 1998:421-48.

[35]   Watkins C. Beyond status: The Americans with Disabilities Act and the parental rights of people labeled developmentally disabled or mentally retarded. Cal Law Rev 1999;83:1415-75.

[36]   20 U.S.C. § 1401(9).

[37]   Board of Education v. Rowley, 458 U.S. 176, 206 (1982).

[38]   See generally 20 U.S.C. § 1401 *et seq.*

[39]   20 U.S.C. § 1401(23)(A). State law may differ as to whether a foster parent can sign an IEP.

[40]   20 U.S.C. § 1401(23)(D).

[41]   20 U.S.C. § 1414(b).

[42]   34 C.F.R. § 300.304(c)(6).

[43]   34 C.F.R. § 300.301(c). State law or regulation may provide a shorter timeframe, which then overrides the federal rule.

[44]   20 U.S.C. § 1412(a)(4).

[45]   20 U.S.C. § 1412(5).

[46]   20 U.S.C. § 1412(16).

[47]   42 U.S.C.§ 1382c(a)(3)(C)(i).

In: Child Abuse: Children with Disabilities
Editors: V. J Palusci, D. Nazer et al.

ISBN: 978-1-53612-035-6
© 2017 Nova Science Publishers, Inc.

Chapter 13

PREVENTING MALTREATMENT IN CHILDREN WITH DISABILITIES

Vincent J Palusci, *MD, MS, FAAP*

New York University School of Medicine and the Frances L Loeb Child Protection
and Development Center, Bellevue Hospital,
New York, New York, US

Those caring for children with disabilities have many reasons for wanting to prevent child abuse and neglect, not the least of which are to reduce pain and suffering and future health problems. These goals are particularly relevant for the weak and vulnerable in our population. However, the details of why, how, when, and where health care professionals can promote prevention may seem murky or ill-defined, especially as maltreatment and violence against children remains undercounted and underaddressed by many segments of society and by many of the systems designed to improve child welfare. This chapter provides both the rationale and strategies for prevention as well as some concrete ideas about how to professionals can integrate it into the day-to-day care of children with disabilities.

INTRODUCTION

Preventing child abuse and neglect spares children physical and psychological pain and suffering and improves their long-term health outcomes. Dubowitz (1) noted that

---

* Corresponding author: Vincent J Palusci, MD, MS, Professor of Pediatrics, New York University School of Medicine, Bellevue Hospital Center, 462 First Avenue, New York, NY 10016, United States. E-mail: Vincent.palusci@nyumc.org.

prevention "is intuitively and morally preferable to intervening after the fact," and recent work from our understanding of the long-term physical and mental health effects from adverse childhood experiences calls us to action. Earlier intervention is more effective in preventing abuse and neglect, saves money for society, and improves peoples' overall health and well-being, perhaps the most important goals for civil society to accomplish.

The United States Advisory Board on Child Abuse and Neglect (2) reported that child maltreatment (CM) is an emergency requiring leadership through professional societies and research. Prevention is explicitly not the responsibility of any one agency, profession, or program, but is best framed as the responsibility of all to create a society less conducive to child maltreatment. In this paradigm, individual skill development, community and provider education, coalition building, organizational change, and policy innovations are all part of the prevention solution. Professionals who provide clinical or supportive services to victims of maltreatment or families facing serious challenges have a role and an obligation to be aware of and support the prevention efforts in their community and to be able to appropriately refer the families they see to these resources.

The American Academy of Pediatrics has made recommendations specifically for pediatricians as well (3). There is increasing evidence to demonstrate the elements of successful interventions, the populations and programs of most benefit, and the implementation research to demonstrate that we have met our goals. This chapter reviews current strategies in child abuse prevention and guides professionals in the integration of prevention activities into their daily work with children with disabilities (CWD).

THE CASE FOR PREVENTION

Research has identified the physical and mental conditions increasingly being associated with adverse childhood experiences, such as physical abuse, sexual abuse, and neglect. Neurologic imaging and traumatology studies have delineated the physiologic and structural changes that occur after chronic stress and abuse (4). Chronic stress and abuse are associated with specific disease processes and poor mental health outcomes in adults, and adverse childhood experiences (ACEs) have been associated with increased rates of teen pregnancy, promiscuity, depression, hallucinations, substance abuse, liver disease, chronic obstructive pulmonary disease, coronary artery disease, and identifiable permanent changes in brain structure and stress hormone function (5-8). Children with disabilities have been noted to have more ACEs than do children without disability, thereby increasing their risk even more (9). Emotional conditions associated with abuse and neglect, including depression, posttraumatic stress disorder, and conduct disorders, compound any direct physical injuries inflicted on individual children. As children mature, increased risk of low academic achievement, drug use, teen pregnancy, juvenile delinquency, and adult criminology add further burden. Although treatment after the fact can improve mental and physical health and prolong life and productivity, the direct and indirect costs of child maltreatment for both children and adults in lost health, pain, and suffering themselves warrant our taking action to prevent child abuse and neglect (10).

WHAT IS PREVENTION?

Child maltreatment prevention is endorsed by all those who are familiar with the problems associated with child maltreatment, and efforts aimed at preventing abuse are promoted by agencies, governmental officials, and individual practitioners. Unfortunately, beyond a blanket endorsement of the concept, there are many different ideas about what prevention actually means and what activities are considered effective. Definitions vary, yet three categories of prevention are generally described (11):

1. Primary: Efforts aimed at the general population for the purpose of keeping abuse from happening.
2. Secondary: Efforts aimed at a particular group with increased risk to keep abuse from happening.
3. Tertiary: Efforts aimed at preventing abuse from happening again to those who have already been victimized. This level includes treatment to reduce harm from the original abuse.

The US Centers for Disease Control and Prevention (12) have emphasized that abuse operates in a societal context and requires an entire spectrum of necessary prevention strategies over time, thinking of prevention in terms of **when** it occurs (before or after abuse), **who** is the focus (everyone, those at greatest risk, or those who have already experienced abuse), and **what** point to intervene (individual, relationship, community, or society level). A simplistic conceptual model is offered in Figure 1. These efforts are based on Bronfenbrenner's ecological model, which promotes intervening at the individual, relationship, community, and societal levels (13,14). Approaches implied from these new labels emphasize a shift away from risk reduction as the predominant prevention approach and toward promotion of positive social change. Some argue that prior definitions limited prevention strategies by focusing primarily on potential individual targets of abuse and how to intervene rather than the environmental and societal context that supports and even condones abusive acts. Definitions of prevention based on timing which apply to all populations are:

1. Primary: taking action *before* CM has occurred to prevent it from happening.
2. Secondary: intervening *right after* CM has occurred.
3. Tertiary: taking the long view and working *overtime* to change conditions in the environment that promote or support CM.

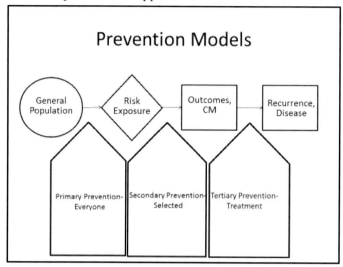

Figure 1. Prevention levels and intervention points in child maltreatment (CM).

CHILD MALTREATMENT PREVENTION STRATEGIES

Daro (15) has noted three important goals of CM prevention: (a) to reduce the incidence of abuse and neglect; (b) to minimize the chance that children who are maltreated will be re-victimized; and (c) to break the cycle of maltreatment by providing victims the help they need to improve how they parent children in the next generation. Systematic comparative effectiveness research is in its early infancy in this area, and the long-term effectiveness of most programs is still being researched (16). Most strategies, such as home visiting, are not uniformly effective in reducing all forms of CM but do appear to improve parenting or one or more risk factors. Some family programs are successful in reducing physical abuse but not neglect, for example, and sexual abuse educational programs have created controversy despite some promising improvements in child mental health measures. Additional health and welfare outcomes, such as improved physical growth and development for infants, have also been noted, sometimes without concurrent measurable reductions in CM.

Table 1. Examples of strategies by prevention level

Level	Strategy	Example(s)
Primary	Prepregnancy/Perinatal	"Safe haven" laws (38)
	Newborn AHT education	Don't Shake the Baby (40), Period of Purple Crying (41)
	Homevisiting	Nurse Family Partnership (22), Healthy Families America (27)
	Medical services	Practicing Safety (46), No Hit Zone (42)
	Sexual abuse education	Personal Space & Privacy (68), Policies (50)
	Public health	Media campaigns (12)
	Social capital building	Triple P (48), subsidized child care (56)
Secondary	Family Wellness	Family preservation (32), Family Connections (58), parenting programs (34)
	Parent training	Parent-Child Interaction Therapy (60), Family Nurturing Program (35)
	Pediatric services	Anticipatory guidance (44), SEEK (43)
	Adolescent parents	Teen mother's groups (45)
	Substance abuse	Substance abuse treatment (51)
Tertiary	Mandated reporting	Universal mandated reporting laws (57)
	Mental Health Treatment	Counseling after psychologic maltreatment (66), Groups for children (52)
	Fatality review	Child death review programs (49)

Few studies have look specifically at children of intellectually or developmentally disabled parents. Many parents with intellectual disabilities lose custody of their children due to real or perceived parenting inadequacies, but it is not clear how parents who keep their children differ from parents who don't. In one study (17) comparing 30 mothers with an intellectual disability (ID) who still had custody of all their children to 17 mothers whose children were placed in care, mothers who still had custody of their children were more involved in their community, were more satisfied with the services they received, had higher incomes and younger children than mothers who had lost their children. No significant differences were found concerning the behavior of their children, the mothers' health, adaptive behaviors, or the number of persons in their social network. They authors concluded that services should be offered to both mothers and children with IDs and should be adapted as the children grow.

Many available strategies tailor their programs to one or more levels of prevention while addressing different risk factors for intervention in different populations (see Table 1). This is appropriate given our understanding that child maltreatment occurs because of many factors acting simultaneously on the parent, child, family/relationship, community, and society levels (18). Some focus on children, others on parents, while still others address parent-child dyads or the environment in which parents raise children. Patno (19) has appropriately reminded us that "there is not, and never will be, one program that prevents all abuse and neglect" given its multifactorial causes. Thus, we will need multiple strategies which vary by method and approach to effectively address different forms of CM in different populations. While high standards must be set, there remains room for creativity and the use of feedback from diverse community settings to respond to shape strategies to meet their unique needs and situations. Some strategies may be hampered in their opportunity to be truly comprehensive, to reach broader audiences, and to use creative methods because of lack of funds, a problem that has been identified by many prevention program leaders. Demands for quality need to be combined with demands for adequate funding for prevention so that truly valuable programs can exist. Different forms of CM in distinctive communities and cultures will require unique types of prevention strategies.

Klevens and Whitaker (20) systematically reviewed the literature for 1980-2004 utilizing existing databases and found 188 primary prevention interventions that addressed a broad range of risk factors. However, few had been rigorously evaluated, and only a handful demonstrated impact on child maltreatment or its risk factors. From a public health perspective, they recommended that interventions that target prevalent and neglected risk factors such as poverty, partner violence, teenage pregnancy, and social norms tolerating violence toward children need to be developed and evaluated, and more attention should be given to low cost interventions delivered to the public by society, or that require minimal effort from recipients.

The US Children's Bureau (21) has suggested that all prevention services need to embrace a commitment to a set of practice principles that have been found effective across diverse disciplines and service delivery systems. They have published a list of best practice standards that represent elements that lie at the core of effective interventions. To the extent that direct service providers and prevention policy advocates hope to maximize the return on their investments, supporting service strategies that embrace the following principles will be essential:

- A strong theory of change that identifies specific outcomes and clear pathways for addressing core outcomes, including specific strategies and curriculum content

- A recommended duration and dosage or clear guidelines for determining when to discontinue or extend services that is systematically applied to all those enrolled in services
- A clear, well-defined target population with identified eligibility criteria and strategy for reaching and engaging this target population
- A strategy for guiding staff in balancing the task of delivering program content while being responsive to a family's cultural beliefs and immediate circumstances
- A method to train staff on delivering the model with a supervisory system to support direct service staff and guide their ongoing practice
- Reasonable caseloads that are maintained and allow direct service staff to accomplish core program objectives
- The systematic collection of information on participant characteristics, staff characteristics, and participant service experiences to ensure services are being implemented with fidelity to the model, program intent, and structure

One should keep in mind other important principles as we discuss a number of strategies which have been used in an attempt to prevent or reduce child maltreatment. These include considering the conceptual model represented by the strategy, whether a risk factor or intermediate outcome is being addressed, whether there are co-morbidities or other factors which modify or moderate the effects, how things are being measured and paid for, whether a strategy is implemented with fidelity, and how it is disseminated and scaled to larger populations. It is also important to consider whether analysis has been done looking at efficacy, effectiveness or cost-effectiveness.

HOME VISITING

Home visiting programs aim to prevent child abuse and neglect by influencing parenting factors linked to maltreatment. These are: (a) inadequate knowledge of child development, (b) belief in abusive parenting, (c) lack of empathy, (d) insensitive, unresponsive parenting, (e) parent stress and lack of social support, and (f) the inability to provide a safe and stimulating home environment. By changing these factors, home visiting programs also seek to improve child development and health outcomes associated with CM. There have been reductions noted of 40% in child maltreatment in certain models (22,23). In a comprehensive review, Gomby (24) found home visitation programs were most effective when they targeted families with many risk factors and used highly trained professionals who carefully followed a research-based model of intervention. Long-term follow-up with low-income single mothers who received home visitation services suggests that these programs are also effective in reducing child abuse and neglect in families where domestic violence is *not* present, decreasing the number of subsequent pregnancies, arrest rates, and the amount of time receiving public assistance (25). Home visiting by nurses has been consistently more effective at reducing preterm and low-weight birth, increasing well child care medical visits and reducing deaths and hospitalizations for injuries and ingestions (16,26). The findings have been replicated in a population of medically at-risk infants, where home visiting using paraprofessionals was associated with lower use of corporal punishment, greater safety maintenance in the home, and fewer reported child injuries (27).

Programs such as Healthy Families America (HFA) have used paraprofessionals to provide services. In a randomized trial of HFA in New York, mothers in the program committed only one-quarter as many acts of serious abuse and neglect as did control mothers in the first two years (28). An evaluation of Healthy Families Florida found that the program using paraprofessionals had a positive impact on preventing child maltreatment, showing that children in families who completed treatment or had long-term, intensive intervention experienced significantly less child maltreatment than did comparison groups who had received little or no service. This effect was accomplished in spite of the fact that, in general, participants had significantly higher risk for child maltreatment than the overall population. According to Williams, Stern and Associates (29), participants in HFA in Florida found 20% less child maltreatment in families in their target service areas. In addition, families who completed the program fared much better than their comparison group counterparts and were more likely to read to their children at early ages. Also, HFA positively affected self-sufficiency defined as *employment*. The program met or exceeded its goals for preventing maltreatment after program completion, provision of immunizations and well-baby checkups, increasing time between pregnancies, and participant satisfaction with services.

The Nurse-Family Partnership (NFP) is an evidence-based nurse home visitation program that improves the health, well-being, and self-sufficiency of low-income, first-time parents and their children. NFP models have been evaluated longitudinally across sites using randomized trials (36) and have been replicated in more than 250 counties. One analysis showed that for every $1 spent on the NFP, there were $4 in savings for taxpayers (30). Other specific programs have been reviewed, but overall, it is difficult to show improvements in key outcomes such as child abuse and neglect because the programs have wide variability in the job description of the home visitor, program implementation, and costs (31).

FAMILY WELLNESS AND PARENTING PROGRAMS

Family wellness programs include a variety of parent and family interventions and have been demonstrated to have some positive effects. These programs range from short-term counseling to parenting classes, sometimes with home visiting and sometimes with intensive "wrap-around" services for families at high risk for maltreatment. Many of these have been grouped together, making assessment problematic, but meta-analyses show promising reductions in child maltreatment (32). Intensive family preservation programs with high levels of participant involvement, an empowerment/strengths-based approach, and social support were more effective. In one series of 1,601 inner-city clients with moderate risk, programs designed to meet families' basic concrete needs and to provide mentoring were more effective than parenting and child development programming, and center–based services were more effective than home-based ones (33). "At-risk" parents who do not receive parent coaching or education have higher rates of child maltreatment, parent arrest, and child hospitalization for violence (30).

Parenting programs, delivered by heath visitors, have been found to improve child mental health and behavior and reduce social dysfunction among parents in one randomized controlled trial (34). Parent training models often differ, however, which often precludes direct comparisons. Parent training can include reviewing child development, teaching and practicing specific skills, identifying and addressing maladaptive behaviors, and supporting parents in managing their own emotions and responding to stress. Effect sizes overall have been found to be moderate, with outcomes affected by how the training was delivered and under what conditions. Finally, family socioeconomic status, relationship with the trainer, inclusion of fathers, the need for additional child therapy, inclusion of a home visitor, proper length, delivery mode, and delivery setting must also be addressed to maximize potential outcomes (34).

A CDC meta-analysis of parent training programs (35) looked at program components and delivery methods that had the greatest effect on child behavior and parent skills. It concluded that teaching parents emotional communication skills and positive child interaction skills, while requiring practice with their children during each session, was the most effective in helping them to acquire effective parenting skills and behaviors. Teaching parents about the correct use of time out, responding consistently to their child, interacting positively with their child, and requiring practice were all associated with decreases in children's externalizing behaviors (35). In another model, Palusci et al. (36) found that parents with a variety of problems, including incarceration, substance abuse, and stress, had improved empathy, improved understanding of child development, and other improved parenting skills after an 8-week program of interactive classes using a family nurturing program.

The family support needs of parents with an intellectual disability are relatively unresearched. One study reviewed two types of intervention for parents with ID using a literature search of electronic databases: (1) those designed to strengthen social relationships and (2) those teaching parenting skills (37). Only a limited number of evaluative studies were found, and the authors concluded that the evidence for interventions aimed at strengthening social relationships was inconclusive. Although positive changes were observed, there were limitations in study design which restricted the generalizability of the results. The evidence for parental skills teaching suggested that behavioral based interventions are more effective than less intensive forms such as lesson booklets and the provision of normal services, although these studies also had limitations.

THE PRENATAL AND PERINATAL PERIODS

Ray Helfer (38) noted the "window of opportunity" that is present in the perinatal period to enhance parent-child interactions and prevent physical abuse. This period, which he defined as from one year before birth to 18–24 months of life, was determined to be a critical time to teach new parents skills of interaction with their newborns. Several program models have shown promise based upon key periods within this time frame, including pre-pregnancy planning, early conception, late pregnancy, pre-labor and labor, immediately following delivery, and at home with the child. Opportunities for prevention in the early months of life include teaching parents and caregivers to cope with infant crying and how to provide a safe sleep environment for their infant. A recent meta-analysis of several early childhood interventions concluded that the evidence for their preventing child maltreatment in the first year of life is weak, but longer-term studies may show reductions in child maltreatment similar to other programs such as home visiting when longer follow-up can be achieved (39).

Many US state legislatures have enacted legislation to address infant abandonment and infanticide in response to a reported increase in the abandonment of infants (40). Beginning in Texas in 1999, "Baby Moses laws" or infant safe haven laws have been enacted as an incentive for mothers in crisis to safely relinquish their babies to designated locations where the babies are protected and provided with medical care until a permanent home is found. These laws generally allow the parent or an agent of the parent to remain anonymous and to be shielded from prosecution for abandonment or neglect in exchange for surrendering the baby to the safe haven. As of 2013, all 50 states, the District of Columbia, and Puerto Rico have enacted safe haven legislation. While national statistics have not been published, several states have reported hundreds of infants protected in this manner. Michigan, for example, had 170 infants relinquished using safe haven laws during 2001-2015 (41).

HEALTH-BASED SERVICES

Health-based services in early childhood have generally not been shown universally to result in reduced child abuse and neglect. In the hospital in the newborn period, Dias et al. (42) implemented a program in nurseries in western New York designed to teach new parents about violent infant shaking and alternatives to use when infants cry. The incidence of abusive head injuries decreased by 47% during the first 5 years of the program. Another program, The *Period of PURPLE Crying,* uses a brief video and written material to educate new parents about normal crying and how to cope with infant crying. This program has been shown to improve mothers' knowledge about crying and to improve their behavioral response to it (43). Although these programs represent promising models and have been required in more than 15 US states, neither has yet demonstrated strong evidence of effectiveness in the primary prevention of abusive head trauma or child maltreatment. Another in-hospital program, the *No Hit Zone,* has also been used to reduce the use of physical discipline, but it has not been systematically evaluated for CM prevention on a national scale (44).

A randomized trial of screening and anticipatory guidance has shown promise for attaining lower rates of maltreatment, CPS reports, harsh punishment, and improved health services (45). This office-based prevention model, *Safe Environment for Every Child* (SEEK), uses pediatric residents who were trained to recognize risk factors and a team to address them. When tested in a resident continuity clinic over a 3-year period, families had fewer reports of child maltreatment to child protective services, fewer incidents of medical nonadherence and delayed immunizations, and less harsh physical punishment by parents when compared with a control group. Some of the differences between the control group and the intervention group were of modest significance, however, and the program is being systematically evaluated in larger and more varied pediatric practice settings. There are several barriers to widespread implementation (professional time, training, culture, ability to deal with nonmedical issues) that can be addressed by specific strategies, such as the use of handouts and local news stories, to begin a dialogue during routine pediatric visits (46). In addition, there are several high-risk groups that will need focused attention by the health care system, such as adolescent parents, addicted mothers, and depressed or mentally ill parents (47).

The American Academy of Pediatrics (AAP) has developed *Connected Kids: Safe, Strong, Secure* as an office-based intervention (48). Originally known as the *Violence*

Intervention and Prevention Program (VIPP), the program was modeled after the AAP's Injury Prevention Program (TIPP), which uses a resilience-based approach to anticipatory guidance designed to help primary care physicians use their therapeutic relationship to support families as a means of prevention. The Connected Kids program includes a clinical guide, online training materials, and parent education materials to educate both pediatricians and parents about discipline, parenting, and other related issues. The Connected Kids is appealing to pediatricians, feasible to implement, and sustainable over a period of 6 months. A related project, *Practicing Safety*, was conducted by the AAP and funded by the Doris Duke Charitable Foundation to develop expanded anticipatory guidance modules for use in primary care offices. The seven modules provide pediatricians with suggested assessment tools, guidance, and resources to help parents cope with crying, develop parenting skills, ensure their children's safety when they are in the care of others, improve the family environment, provide effective discipline, assist with sleeping and eating, and help with toilet-training. However, neither *Practicing Safety* nor *Connected Kids* led to significant decreases in child maltreatment in national samples.

There are been other promising developments in medical-based parenting programs that are worth mentioning. The *Video Interaction Project* links a parenting intervention with videotaping parents during primary care pediatrics visits; it was associated with less use of physical punishment by parents at 2 years of age (49) which was maintained through age three years (50) with reduced parenting stress. In another analysis, the program improved social emotional development in children and reduced their externalizing behaviors, which may reduce their risk for abuse. Mediation pathways indicate that enhanced positive parenting through reading and play result in improved parent-child relationships, also potentially reducing the risk of abuse (51). When used with a foster care population, a program using similar reflective video feedback during home visits also improved externalizing behaviors among maltreated children (52).

COMMUNITY STRATEGIES

A large body of conceptual theory and empirical research suggests that intervention at the neighborhood level can prevent child maltreatment among children with disabilities. This represents a "fourth wave" in prevention activities, with emphasis on altering communities in ways on par with those aimed at the individual parenting level (53). The two components of intervention that appear to be most promising are social capital development and community coordination of individualized services. Social disorganization theory suggests that child abuse can be reduced by building social capital within communities—by creating an environment of mutual reciprocity in which residents are collectively engaged in supporting each other and in protecting children. This is particularly relevant for disabled children, some of whom are highly dependent on residential or other care provided by specialized institutions. Research regarding the capacity and quality of service delivery systems in these communities underscores the importance of strengthening a community's service infrastructure by expanding capacity, improving coordination, and streamlining service delivery. Community strategies to prevent child abuse and promote child protection have focused on creating supportive residential communities whose residents share a belief in collective responsibility to protect children from harm, and on expanding the range of services and instrumental supports directly available to parents. Both elements—individual responsibility and a strong formal service infrastructure—are important. The challenge, however, has been to develop a community strategy that strikes the appropriate balance between individual responsibility and public investment.

Daro and Dodge (53) have also noted that, in the short run, the case for community prevention is promising on both theoretical and empirical grounds. Community prevention efforts are well grounded in a strong theory of change and, in some cases, have strong outcomes. At least some of the models have reduced reported rates of child abuse and injury to young children, altered parent-child interactions at the community level, and reduced parental stress, and improved parental efficacy. When focusing on community building, the models can mobilize volunteers and engage diverse sectors within the community such as first responders, the faith community, local businesses, and civic groups in preventing child abuse. This mobilization can exert synergistic impact on other desired community outcomes, such as economic development and better health care.

One such program is the *Triple P–Positive Parenting Program*® which was designed as a comprehensive, population-level system of parent and family support with five intervention levels of increasing intensity and narrowing population reach. This system combines various targeted interventions to ensure a safe environment, including promoting learning, using assertive discipline, maintaining reasonable expectations, and taking care of oneself as a parent. These principles then translate into 35 specific strategies and parenting skills. A large-scale randomized trial of Triple P published in 2009 noted lesser increases in substantiated child maltreatment, child out-of-home placements, and child maltreatment injuries in the intervention counties. Recent additional analyses which made use of 5-year baseline data yielded large effect sizes for all three outcomes that converged with those from the original analyses. The authors concluded that the study underscored the potential for community-wide parenting and family support to produce population-level preventive impact on child maltreatment (54).

A public health model follows a common pattern of intervention and evaluation when addressing a variety of conditions. A problem is defined, risk and protective factors are identified, prevention strategies are developed and tested, and if successful, they are widely adopted (12). A key operating assumption in such efforts is that change initiated in one sector will also have measurable spillover effects into other sectors and that the individuals who receive information or direct assistance will change in ways that begin to alter normative behavioral assumptions across the population. This gradual and evolutionary view of change is reflected in many public health initiatives that, over time, have produced dramatic improvement in such areas as smoking cessation, reduction in drunk driving, increased use of seat belts, and increased conservation efforts. The US CDC and the US Maternal Child Health Bureau, for example, have strengthened the public health role and funding for child maltreatment and violence prevention (12). One caution is that the public health model of reducing adverse outcomes through normative change may not be directly applicable to the problem of child maltreatment. In contrast to the "stop smoking," "don't drink and drive," and "use seat-belts" campaigns, child abuse prevention often lacks specific behavioral directions that the general public can embrace and feel empowered to impose on others in their community. Child fatality review has been a promising public health strategy which uses tertiary prevention to identify preventable patterns of CM fatality and near-fatality. Exceptions may exist for specific forms of maltreatment, such as shaken baby syndrome, but much maltreatment is neglect, which is less amenable to identification by this type of state-level public health intervention (55). Also unfortunately, as the US Commission to Eliminate Child Abuse and Neglect Fatalities has found, there are relatively few promising or evidence-based solutions with research evidence showing a reduction in fatalities—one being the Nurse Family Partnership (26). Likewise, they found only a handful of communities that identified reduction of child abuse and neglect fatalities as a goal, implemented efforts to achieve that goal, and demonstrated progress.

All organizations can develop policies and procedures that acknowledge that child abuse occurs in and outside of child-serving agencies. Youth-serving organizations have an implicit responsibility to their clientele. However, even organizations that do not solely or primarily focus on children can and should be involved in the same prevention process. For example, doctors' offices, clinics, hospitals, community mental health centers, and other health care facilities that serve children could also enhance children's safety and decrease their own liability by taking similar actions (56).

Two community risk factors–poverty and substance abuse–have been singled out as particularly important in terms of the strength of their association with physical abuse and neglect (57). Increased recognition and integration of substance abuse treatment into child welfare was found to be an important first step to reduce co-existing substance abuse and CM. A motivationally-based public health approach for potentially at-risk parents could be proactive, brief and repetitive, and would incorporate substance abuse prevention messages into routine public health approaches spread over the parenting years. There is growing evidence that such programs, when implemented in multiple settings without stigmatizing parents, can appreciably reduce substance abuse and its associated CM (57). When children are exposed to violence, some programs of secondary prevention such as group counseling have showed promise (58).

SOCIAL POLICIES

Policies can be powerful tools for prevention given their potential to affect conditions that can improve population-level health. Factors in society that can contribute to child maltreatment include the social, economic, health and education policies that lead to poor living standards, socioeconomic instability, warfare, or hardship as well as social or cultural norms that promote or glorify violence, demand rigid gender roles, or diminish the status of the child with regard to the parent (59). On the global scale, the United Nations Convention on the Rights of the Child offers a framework as a legal instrument for integrating the principles of children's rights with professional ethics and for the policy changes needed to enhance public health responses to prevent maltreatment (60). Each of these rights has specific implications for practice, advocacy, and research that can assist in defining, measuring, legislating, monitoring, and preventing child maltreatment. Achieving appropriate investments in community child abuse prevention programs will require a research and policy agenda that recognizes the importance of linking learning with practice. It is not enough for scholars and program evaluators to learn how maltreatment develops and what interventions are effective, and for practitioners to separately implement innovative interventions in their work. Instead, initiatives must be implemented and assessed in a manner that maximizes both the ability of researchers to determine the effort's efficacy and the ability of program managers and policy makers to draw on these data to shape their practice and policy decisions, which can affect society as well as families and communities (52).

Although evaluating societal CM prevention programs has been discussed for some time, it is only recently that the practice field has begun to develop the necessary capacity to understand and use evidence in decision making. National organizations, such as the US Centers for Disease Control and Prevention, Prevent Child Abuse America, Parents Anonymous, and the National Alliance of Children's Trust and Prevention Funds, have begun to assess and disseminate information about the effectiveness of programs (61). The World Health Organization (18) has also assembled a guide to assist policy makers and program planners in using and developing evidence-based programs. The CDC has promoted evidence in the creation and implementation of family programs, for example, which integrate evidence and evaluation into the program model. Programs should ideally monitor their impact, create and enhance new approaches to prevention based on those results, apply and adapt effective practices, and build community readiness for additional activities (12).

Klevens et al. (62) identified 37 state policies that might have impacts on the social determinants of child maltreatment and used available data to explore effects of 11 policies on child maltreatment rates. These included two policies aimed at reducing poverty, two temporary assistance to needy families policies, two policies aimed at increasing access to child care, three policies aimed at increasing access to high quality pre-K education, and three policies aimed at increasing access to health care. Multi-level regression analyses identified two that were significantly associated with decreased child maltreatment rates: (a) lack of waitlists to access subsidized child care, and (b) policies that facilitate continuity of child health care. These findings were limited by the quality and availability of the data, and future research might focus on a reduced number of US states that have good quality administrative data, population-based surveys on child maltreatment, or reasonable proxies for child maltreatment and where data on the actual implementation of specific policies of interest can be documented. However, the presence of waitlists to access child care had a statistically significant association with child maltreatment investigation rates, with an increase in maltreatment investigations of 3.13 per 1000 children. US states' continuity of eligibility for Medicaid/SCHIP was significantly associated with child maltreatment investigation rates that were 2.55 per 1000 lower than states without continuous eligibility. Klevens et al. theorized that these strategies decrease child maltreatment because child care and medical assistance with enriched early experiences in high-quality care settings can reduce childhood and adolescent behavioral problems that may trigger abusive parenting. Furthermore, continuous health insurance coverage and continuity of the medical home directly affect child health and development by enhancing parents' ability to provide an improved home environment and by removing financial stresses associated with uninsured medical costs.

Pediatricians have long been familiar with therapeutic preschools and with parenting programs. Participation in school-based child-parent centers, which provide extensive family education and support, reduce maltreatment by 50% in high-risk populations (39). Access to affordable health insurance and high-quality early childhood education and child-care programs are additional interventions on a community level that address the problem of toxic stress by creating a healthier environment for children. Policies related to state provision of children's health care insurance such as the State Children's Health Insurance Program (SCHIP) can also potentially reduce maltreatment because children without insurance are less likely to receive health services in a timely manner, which might lead to medical neglect. Continuous insurance eligibility policies have enabled states to ensure continuity of care by providing Medicaid and SCHIP enrollees with continuous coverage for longer periods of time rather than on a month-to-month basis, and they enable states to provide temporary coverage to children and pregnant women until a formal eligibility determination can be made. Other policies with prevention potential include criminalizing fetal exposure to drugs, designating child exposure to partner violence as child neglect, increasing access to abortion, and evaluating the effects of housing policies on stability for children and availability of child care.

Mandated reporting is a societal policy which can result in earlier and better identification of maltreated children. Palusci and Vandervort (63) evaluated the effects of universal mandated reporting laws on child maltreatment reporting rates to determine whether requiring all adults improved CM identification. Using county-level data from the US National Child Abuse and Neglect Data System for the years 2000 and 2010 in linear regression models, they evaluated reporting rates for total reports, confirmed reports, and confirmed maltreatment types in a cross-sectional, ecological analysis while controlling for child and community demographic variables such as child population size, gender, race, ethnicity, school attendance, disability, poverty, housing, high school graduation, parental marriage, religiosity, unemployment and crime. They found that counties in states with laws mandating that all adults must report suspected child maltreatment have significantly higher rates of total and confirmed reports even after controlling for several demographic characteristics previously associated with CM in the literature. When mandates for clergy to report were changed, the results were less clear. They concluded that it is unclear whether changing state law or policy will enhance case identification in states that do not currently require universal reporting.

TARGETING SPECIFIC TYPES OF CHILD MALTREATMENT

Instead of addressing specific methods or populations, some programs have been devised to target specific forms of CM. Several parent education programs, for example, have been evaluated for their association with decreases in physical abuse and neglect. *Family Connections*, a multifaceted, home visiting community-based child neglect prevention program, showed "cost effective" improvements in risk and protective factors and behavioral outcomes (64). To address a specific form of physical abuse, a hospital-based parent education program implemented immediately after birth that has been shown to decrease the incidence of shaken baby syndrome (42). After a similar program delivered to over 15,000 new parents in West Michigan, the number of SBS cases admitted to the hospital dropped from 7 per year to 5.3, a 24% reduction (65). *The Period of Purple Crying* was able to increase maternal knowledge scores, knowledge about the dangers of shaking, and sharing that information with other caretakers, but no significant differences were noted in maternal behavioral responses to crying (43). Counseling and other therapies have been used with families with increased risk for CM, and Parent-Child Interaction Therapy (PCIT) is one evidence-based model which has shown promise in reducing physical abuse and neglect in young children (66).

One area which has historically been targeted with community interventions is the area of sexual abuse prevention. Not all children who have experienced sexual abuse will be clearly identified, or perhaps even identified at all by the community until well into adulthood. Although some cases of sexual abuse are immediately apparent owing to the presence of sexually transmitted infections or acute physical injury, the vast majority of child sexual abuse is discovered through a child's own accidental or purposeful disclosure of abuse. Children often grapple with whether to tell, who to tell, and when to disclose so as to minimize negative outcomes to themselves or their families. These children may be faced with adults who are unprepared to respond appropriately because of lack of information, fears, or adults' own emotional reaction. Even when adults listen, they may respond in ways that upset the child or contribute to a retraction of the report or they may misinterpret the message, either exaggerating or minimizing the situation (67). Parents will react differently than their children and one another, and are critical to healing after abuse. Assessment of and attention to parents may be a critical component of successful intervention. Children with physical disabilities, cognitive impairments, or developmental delays have elevated risk for being sexually abused, and their parents and caregivers need to be especially informed of the need for safety (68). Yet, there is very limited empirical research evaluating methods to teach abuse-protection skills to CWD, and the studies available have focused on female participants with mild to moderate IDDs (69).

The big questions of how best to prevent sexual abuse, how to reduce rates over time, and eventually eliminate sexual abuse remain unanswered. Until recently, few studies actually showed that participation in a prevention program resulted in reduced rates of sexual abuse for participants, with only anecdotal reports on successes and actions taken to stay safe as evidence (70). One study showed that college women who had participated in a child sexual abuse prevention program as children were significantly less likely to experience subsequent sexual abuse than those who had not had such a program (71). Additionally, although some argue that sexual abuse has not decreased as a result of sexual abuse prevention efforts, actual rates of sexual abuse do seem to be decreasing, and one proposed explanation is that sexual abuse prevention efforts may be at least part of the reason. Finkelhor (72) has concluded that these decreased rates and other available evidence do support providing high-quality sexual abuse prevention education programs because children are able to acquire the concepts, the programs promote disclosure, there are lower rates of victimization, and children have less self-blame after attending these programs. Despite this, communities should be wary of relying on children to be solely or primarily responsible for their own safety and protection. All communities must do more than simply educate children about sexuality or abuse.

Despite the prevalence and demonstrated long-term effects of psychological maltreatment, there is little evidence detailing specific programs and practices designed specifically for its primary prevention. Several interventions do promote attachment and enhanced parent-child interactions, which by their very nature should decrease psychological maltreatment. However, given the varying definitions of psychological maltreatment from study to study and difficulty in accurate identification and reporting, it will be inherently problematic to show its reduction after prevention activities. One study did show that providing mental health services after confirmed psychologic maltreatment was associated with a marked reduction in further confirmed psychological maltreatment (73).

IMPORTANCE OF HEALTH PROFESSIONAL INVOLVEMENT

Ray Helfer, a pediatrician who spearheaded the creation of the Children's Trust Funds across the US, suggested decades ago that health professionals should be an important part of a multifaceted approach to prevent violence (74). Historically, approaches used included community commitment, mass media messages, training for new parents, early childhood development programs, interpersonal skills programs, and adult education programs for those caring for children. For children with disabilities, there are several reasons that health professionals should be more involved with prevention efforts. Most health professionals already understand and appreciate the linkages among prevention, intervention, and treatment, and they have an invaluable understanding of the effects of disabilities on children and families. It is critical that health care professionals embrace the importance of their role in prevention beyond merely treating and reporting suspicious injuries.

However, health care professionals are sometimes reluctant to intervene in cases of potential abuse. There are several reasons for this: lack of knowledge, fear of offending the patient (or caregiver), time pressures, discomfort of the patient with questions, fear of loss of control of the provider/patient relationship, and attitudes about accountability. Examining barriers to optimal service provision is important for every health care professional. Because health professionals have unique relationships with families, they have special opportunities to intervene to prevent abuse. Dubowitz (1) has suggested that it is important that physicians be able to ask sensitive questions, gather information, and use astute observation and careful assessment skills if they are to be successful in these endeavors. Keys to effectiveness are professional comfort with hearing sensitive issues, an ability to teach children about sensitive issues their bodies and personal space and privacy, familiarity with normal genital anatomy and routine child and parent concerns, an ability to diagnose and treat suspected maltreatment, and knowledge of the child welfare system (75). Screening for family and community violence should be included in routine health visits, even though some pediatricians need skills to better identify and manage injuries caused by such violence (76).

In addition to good clinical practice, medical providers can use and support a variety of strategies in the office, hospital, and their community to prevent child maltreatment. These include good clinical skills in properly recognizing and reporting suspected maltreatment, as well as educating parents and advocating for community programs and resources that will address the underlying problems that contribute to child maltreatment, such as poverty, substance abuse, mental health issues, and poor parenting skills. Collecting information about possible abuse experiences on intake forms is one way to learn about and create opportunities to address certain problems. Some physicians may be skeptical that patients would reveal information about a history of abuse on health forms, though patients are more forthcoming if asked than if never asked (77). In addition, by mentioning "unmentionable" topics, those providing health care show that they are aware of these issues and probably are knowledgeable about how to be helpful. The American Academy of Pediatrics has developed a violence prevention program called "Connected Kids: Safe, Strong, Secure" (48), which includes a guide for office clinicians, provides 21 parent/patient information brochures and supporting training materials, and encourages implementing a strengths-based approach for clinicians to provide anticipatory guidance to help parents raise resilient children.

Physicians and other medical professionals have now been invited by child welfare and public health officials to become more active in prevention as we think of CM as a long-term, public health problem. Prevention is explicitly not the responsibility of any one agency, profession, or program but is framed as the responsibility of all to create a society less conducive to child maltreatment. In this paradigm, individual skill development, community and provider education, coalition building, organizational change, and policy innovations are all part of the prevention solution for everyone, including health professionals (3).

INTEGRATING PREVENTION INTO PROFESSIONAL PRACTICE

Variability in outcomes after past programming has resulted in efforts to find more effective prevention programs. A current trend is toward "best practices" for ensuring quality, especially for care provided by medical professionals. Several conceptual standards have been suggested to evaluate programs, such as the content and approaches to imparting information to the target group, practice standards, and administrative standards. Recommendations for strategies include being family centered, community-based, culturally competent, and using a strengths-based approach. Other suggestions include being easily accessible, being linked to informal and formal supports, and having a long-range plan and ongoing evaluations. These efforts are promising and may help to build the highest quality into prevention programs that vary greatly in their efficacy and level of comprehensiveness. As we develop our understanding, evidence-based interventions will be useful, but standardizing programs across settings and cultures may not always effectively prevent CM.

Professionals can take several roles in violence prevention, including advocating for resources for effective programs, screening, recognizing and referring at-risk families for services, and promoting nurturing parenting and child-raising styles (78). Beyond this, Plummer and Palusci (11), the American Academy of Pediatrics (3), and the American Professional Society on the Abuse of Children (79) have suggested several opportunities for professionals to integrate CM prevention into their practice (Table 2):

Table 2. Summary of steps to integrate prevention in daily work (72)

Parent Education
Community Awareness about the problem
Bystander Involvement in identification and reporting
Early Behavior Problem Identification
Policy and Organizational Prevention Efforts
Improved Clinical Care and Education
Treatment and Referral to optimal, accessible services
Advocacy for Resources and evidence-based programs
Keeping Up to Date with Practice in the Field

Parent education: Professionals need to give parents effective strategies for discipline and nurturing by providing materials, consultation and referral. Parents should know about Internet safety, supervision, selecting safe babysitters, and choosing quality day care programs. Posters in waiting rooms, take-home brochures, and lists of Internet addresses should be readily available for referrals for parents' use. Additional resources on child abuse prevention programs that exist in and around the community and referrals of parents to area agencies for additional information or assistance are vital prevention interventions.

Community awareness: Professionals need to offer to provide radio or TV public service announcements to build awareness of child abuse as a societal and public health issue and an issue related to physical and mental health. Health care professionals have the credibility to promote awareness of the links between childhood trauma and future health problems.

Bystander involvement: In personal or professional capacities, professionals need to be become involved when they are concerned about a child's safety and to seek supervision or consultation when necessary. Despite great demands on their time, professionals must be willing to make referrals to Child Protective Services based on reasonable suspicion rather than waiting until they are certain to report child maltreatment.

Early behavior problem identification: Caregivers often consult with professionals about behavior problems with their children, who may be exhibiting reactive symptoms of being abused or stress after trauma exposure. Behavioral problems are often nonspecific, but professionals can guide parents to seek additional assistance, while guarding against parental overreaction to self-exploration or developmentally-appropriate behavior.

Policy and organizational prevention efforts: Professionals should be willing to make changes in policy, hiring, supervision, and training in their own office or organization to put proven risk-reduction procedures in place. This can include establishing clinical practice guidelines to address these issues in the hospital, office and clinic.

Improved clinical care and education: Professionals need to recognize risk factors for violence when providing clinic care and be able to identify, treat, and refer violence-related problems at all stages of child development. Professionals need to identify issues with mental illness, substance abuse, stress, inappropriate supervision, family violence and exposure to media violence, access to firearms, gang involvement and signs of poor self-esteem, school failure, and depression. Professionals need to support early bonding and attachment, educate parents on normal age-appropriate behaviors for children of all ages and disabilities, and educate parents about parenting skills, limit setting, and protective factors to be nurtured in children to help prevent a variety of injuries. Consistent discipline practices and body safety techniques should be emphasized.

Treatment and referral: Professionals need to know what they can handle through office counseling and when they need to refer families for help. They must also be cognizant of the resources available in their community to address these risks. This will require knowledge of the child welfare, emergency shelter, and substance abuse treatment systems and how to make referrals to appropriate therapists and mental health professionals.

Advocacy: Professionals should use their given status in the community to advocate for the needs of individual families and for the broader needs of children in society. This includes working on public policy and can best be achieved working in conjunction with organizations that address the needs of children in different arenas. Professionals can endorse and support quality, comprehensive child-focused education and can serve on advisory boards for a local child abuse prevention agency or home visiting program, thereby assisting in networking alliances between prevention programs and the treatment field. Professionals can also be role models and leaders in their communities by offering support for family and neighbors who might need encouragement, help, or referrals and advocating to assure that their communities have resources and services.

Keeping up to date with the field: Professionals can be more effective advocates if they are knowledgeable about the current prevention field and evidence-based strategies for prevention. In CPS, professionals can identify prevention opportunities within the population of families and children who come to their system but who are unsubstantiated or do not require that the children be taken into protective custody. Professionals in other fields of practice can help by recognizing the importance of their prevention work, participating in training, and helping to bridge the gap between research and practice.

PAYING FOR PREVENTION

While there is increasing evidence supporting the effectiveness of many of these universal and selective prevention interventions, a comprehensive assessment should include an analysis of cost and potential financial benefits (80,81). For example, for every $1 spent on childhood vaccinations in the US, $10.20 in disease treatment costs are saved, an estimated $13.5 billion annually in the U.S. (82). Those attempting to justify the cost of CM prevention have often made comparisons to its measurable harms in an effort to show how resources used today can save money later. Every $1 spent on early childhood programs, for example, saves $4-7 for victims and taxpayers (30). All estimations are just that, relying on a series of assumptions about the direct and indirect costs, the costs of programs, the effectiveness of their implementation, and the potential reductions in societal costs as a result of those strategies.

Cost estimation for CM has historically focused on immediate costs in the medical, child welfare and criminal justice systems, but more recent analyses have attempted to estimate costs over the lifespan. In 1988, Deborah Daro (83) estimated a national direct cost of $14.9 million for juvenile delinquency based on its incidence and rate among adolescent victims. She also found that 1% of severely abused children suffer permanent disability. Her analysis projected that the national cost and future productivity loss of severely abused and neglected children was between $658 million and $1.3 billion each year in the US as of 1988, assuming that impairments would reduce future earnings by as little as from 5% to 10%. In 1992, Robert Caldwell (84) looked at a single state (Michigan) and laid out what he thought were total costs in a variety of social systems and the savings that could be had. He estimated that the costs of a home visitor program in Michigan would be 3.5% of the $823 million estimated cost of child abuse, and small reductions in the rate of child maltreatment were thought to make prevention cost-effective. For 2002, he estimated that the yearly loss of tax revenue and productivity due to child maltreatment rose to $1.8 billion (8). Drawing from Maxfield and Widom's work (86), *Fight Crime: Invest in Kids* (30) noted that child abuse and neglect costs Americans at least $80 billion annually and affects taxpayers as well as victims and their families. Potential benefits of prevention included mitigating the direct costs of child maltreatment as well as improving all of our lives through increased productivity and decreased crime and need for social services. Prevent Child Abuse America (87) used "conservative" estimates to calculate direct and indirect costs as $103.8 billion for the US in 2007.

In a more recent analysis of direct and indirect costs in the US, Fang et al. (88) estimated the average lifetime cost per victim of nonfatal child maltreatment to be $210,012 in 2010 dollars, including $32,648 in childhood health care costs; $10,530 in adult medical costs; $144,360 in productivity losses; $7,728 in child welfare costs; $6,747 in criminal justice costs; and $7,999 in special education costs. The estimated average lifetime cost per death was $1,272,900, including $14,100 in medical costs and $1,258,800 in productivity losses. The total lifetime economic burden resulting from new cases of fatal and nonfatal child maltreatment in the US in 2008 was calculated to be approximately $124 billion. In a sensitivity analysis, the total burden was estimated to be as large as $585 billion. They concluded that, compared with other health problems, the burden of child maltreatment is substantial and indicates the importance of prevention to address its high prevalence. Similar conclusions have been reached internationally (89). The potential savings are thought to be substantial if CM is prevented or reduced, yet these savings cross multiple societal systems and funding streams. This acts as a disincentive to investment by segments of the economy such as healthcare unless they can capture potential savings from CM prevention.

One potential source for prevention funding comes from the health care system. On March 23, 2010, President Obama signed into law the Patient Protection and Affordable Care Act of 2010 (Affordable Care Act, ACA, P.L. 111-148), legislation designed to make quality, affordable health care available to all Americans, reduce costs, improve health care quality, enhance disease prevention, and strengthen the health care workforce (90). Through a provision authorizing the creation of the Affordable Care Act Maternal, Infant, and Early Childhood Home Visiting Program, the ACA was designed to use a health insurance model to strengthen and improve the programs and activities carried out under Title V; to improve coordination of services for at risk communities; and to identify and provide comprehensive services to improve outcomes for families who reside in at risk communities. Home visiting is viewed as one of several service strategies embedded in a comprehensive, high-quality early childhood system that promotes maternal, infant, and early childhood health, safety and development and strong parent-child relationships. The longterm effects of the ACA are still being assessed.

Table 3. Cost estimates, risk reductions, and medical savings for select adult conditions and prevention strategies in New Hampshire (NH)

1. Chronic disease costs/savings estimates						
Disease*	Cost(NH)**	RR(4 v 0)	RR(3 v 0)	RR(4 v 3)	PARf(4 v 3)	Savings (4 v 3)**
CA	$220,000,000	1.9	1.0	1.900	0.474	$104,210,526
DM	$90,000,000	1.6	1.2	1.333	0.250	$22,500,000
HD	$180,000,000	2.2	1.4	1.571	0.364	$65,454,545
PD	$170,000,000	3.9	2.2	1.773	0.436	$74,102,564
Total						**$162,057,110**

* CA=Total Cancers; DM=Diabetes Mellitus; HD=Heart Disease; PD=Pulmonary Disorders

** NH annual direct medical cost estimate

*** Calculations: RR(4 v 3) = RR(4 v 0)/RR(3 v 0)

PARf (4 v 3) = (RR (4 v 3) - 1)/RR (4 v 3)

Savings (4 v 3) = Total Cost x PARf (4 v 3)

2. Prevention strategy cost estimates:				$124,130,500	
Strategy	**Unit Cost**	**Target**	**Population**	**Total Cost**	
Newborn Education	$20	Newborns	13,000	$260,000	
Pediatric Screening	$500	Families /children<5y	143,741	$71,870,500	
Home Visiting	$2,000	Children <2y	26,000	$52,000,000	
3. Annual savings:				**$37,926,610**	
PARf calculations use risk ratios from: http://www.cdc.gov/violenceprevention/ acestudy/outcomes.html					

Given recent knowledge about the longterm health effects associated with adverse childhood experiences such as CM, one can look at potential medical savings for the healthcare system associated with reduced adult chronic conditions (see Table 3). One can estimate disease-specific savings over the lifetime related to reductions in adverse childhood experiences (ACEs) to assess whether significant expenditures by healthcare systems for children are justified. Using annual healthcare expenditures in a single US state (NH) for 4 of chronic conditions in adulthood which were analyzed in the original ACEs studies (diabetes mellitus, cancer, heart disease and pulmonary disorders), one can derive direct annual medical costs for each disease from national studies and state data (91). Risk for adult disease based on childhood ACE scores was derived from the original ACEs studies, which found that a score of 4 or more was significantly related to increases in several adult conditions (6,7). Recent research has suggested that these ACE scores are significantly related to adult physical disease in diverse populations, although there is variability (92).

Assuming that a combination of prevention strategies would result in the decrease of at least one adverse childhood experience for each child across the population, we then calculated the resultant decreases in adult disease costs based on changes in the population attributable risk fraction (PARf) using changes in risk associated with ACE score changes from 4 to 3. Using program costs calculated from national data and our prior work, we then estimated the costs for providing three widely-available prevention strategies: homevisiting, office-based parent programs, and hospital-based newborn education. Child population and births were estimated using census data.

The results are impressive. Total medical savings achieved in one year for reductions in healthcare costs associated with four adult chronic conditions amounted to $162 million (see Table 3). The total costs estimated for the three strategies delivered to the eligible populations were estimated to be $124 million, yielding a savings of $38 million annually in direct adult healthcare costs alone. This is likely a large underestimate of savings because it only includes four chronic conditions and does not include mental health or other behavioral issues which result in additional medical costs. This analysis makes several grand assumptions about the accuracy of the ACEs data, the effectiveness of prevention programs in reducing ACEs, the interactions of other risk factors with health and disease, and the economies of scale and program implementation. It is likely that any prevention program would reduce an individual's ACE score by more than 1 point, resulting in a larger decrease in adult disease; however, the efficacy of prevention strategies in reducing ACE scores across populations is still being evaluated.

Despite these reservations, one can conclude that the costs for just these three CM prevention programs were justified if the healthcare system could capture the savings in the future. The return on investment could be substantial, despite the long time frame needed. In addition, given that medical costs are generally estimated to be 10-20% of the total direct and indirect economic burden of CM, an additional $1 billion or more in savings would accrue beyond direct medical costs. Thus, societies which are able to share costs and benefits across systems over time will be able to reap substantial economic benefit by preventing CM.

CONCLUSION

There are a variety of strategies which have been shown to reduce child abuse and neglect, although few studies specifically address their use or outcomes in populations of children with disabilities. Several steps have been taken to improve our identification of maltreatment specifically among disabled children, and children with disabilities who are maltreated are hopefully more readily identified and services are initiated earlier. While research is sparse, it is clinically believed that these interventions reduce the risk of abuse and neglect because of the additional emotional support which benefits child physical and emotional development. Health professionals can confidently support home visiting in their community with appropriate referrals and can work to improve funding and access to affordable child care and prekindergarten interventions as evidence-based strategies which reduce CM. While there are several other strategies available, the evidence supporting these methods is promising but less robust. Regardless of the strategy used, the costs of CM to society are too high, and calculations showing the long-term savings achieved by reducing adverse childhood experiences justify significant expenditures. The medical system can also afford to pay for some prevention strategies for children if medical savings can be captured during adulthood. Our current state of knowledge and the evidence make this plainly obvious.

Yet additional steps can be taken by professionals to reduce CM. Little or no training is currently available specifically addressing the needs of children with disabilities. Clinicians and advocates need to be able to identify and report patterns of maltreatment while excluding mimics and other confounders. Children with disabilities need "medical homes" with professionals who follow them on a consistent basis and are integrated with community services. These reduce the risk of abuse or neglect and permit proactive, preventative services to be put into place. Further analyses are needed to better understand and disrupt the relationships between disabilities and child maltreatment, to answer questions about the causal links between adverse childhood experiences, and whether medically-based prevention programs in hospitals or the community can prevent child maltreatment. With more attention and additional research, we will hopefully demonstrably improve the lives of all children and adults including those with disabilities.

REFERENCES

[1]   Dubowitz H. Preventing child neglect and physical abuse: A role for pediatricians. Pediatr Rev 2002;23(6):191–6.

[2]   Krugman SD. Multidisciplinary teams. In: Krugman RD, Korbin JE, eds. C Henry Kempe: A fifty year legacy to the field of child abuse and neglect New York: Springer, 2013:71–8.

[3]   Flaherty EG, Stirling J, American Academy of Pediatrics Committee on Child Abuse and Neglect. Clinical report: The pediatrician's role in child maltreatment prevention. Pediatrics 2010;126;833–41.

[4]   De Bellis MD. The psychobiology of neglect. Child Maltreat 2005;10(2):150–72.

[5]   Shonkoff JP, Garner AS, the Committee on Psychosocial Aspects of Child and Family Health, Committee on Early Childhood, Adoption, and Dependent Care, and Section on Developmental and Behavioral Pediatrics.The lifelong effects of early childhood adversity and toxic stress. Pediatrics 2012;129(1):e232–46.

[6]   Felitti VJ, Anda RF, Nordenberg D, Williamson DF, Spitz AM, Edwards V, et al. Relationship of childhood abuse and household dysfunction to many of the leading causes of death in adults: the adverse childhood experiences (ACE) study. Am J Prev Med 1998;14:245–58.

[7]   Anda RF, Brown DW, Dube SR, Bremner JD, Felitti VJ, Giles WH. Adverse childhood experiences and chronic obstructive pulmonary disease in adults. Am J Prev Med 2008;34(5):396–403.

[8]   Middlebrooks S, Audage NC. The effects of childhood stress on health across the lifespan. Atlanta, GA: Centers for Disease Control and Prevention, National Center for Injury Prevention and Control, 2008.

[9]   Austin A, Herrick H, Proescholdbell S, Simmons J. Disability and exposure to high levels of adverse childhood experiences: Effect on health and risk behavior. NC Med J 2016;77(1):30–6.

[10]   Palusci VJ. Adverse childhood experiences and lifelong health. JAMA Pediatrics 2013;167(1):95–6.

[11]   Plummer C, Palusci VJ. The path to prevention. In: Kaplan R, Adams JA, Starling SP, Giardino AP, eds. Medical response to child sexual abuse. St Louis, MO: STM Learning Inc, GW Medical Publishing, 2011:365–95

[12]   Centers for Disease Control and Prevention (CDC). Preventing maltreatment: Program activities guide. Atlanta, GA: Author, 2007. URL: http:// www.cdc.gov/ncipc/dvp/pcmguide.htm.

[13]   Bronfenbrenner U. Toward an experimental ecology of human development. Am Psychologist 1977;32:513–30.

[14]   Zielinski D, Bradshaw C. Ecological influences on the sequelae of child maltreatment: A review of the literature. Child Maltreat 2006;11:49–62.

[15]   Daro D. Prevention of child abuse and neglect. In: Myers JB, ed. The APSAC handbook on child maltreatment, 3rd edition. Thousand Oaks, CA: Sage, 2011.

[16] MacMillan HL, Wathen CN, Fergusson DM, Leventhal JM., Taussig HN. Interventions to prevent child maltreatment and associated impairment. Lancet 2009;373:250–66.

[17] Aunos M, Goupil G, Feldman M. Mothers with intellectual disabilities who do or do not have custody of their children. J Dev Dis 2004;10(2):65–79.

[18] World Health Organization. Report of the consultation on child abuse prevention. World Health Organization, Geneva, Switzerland: WHO Press, 1999. URL: http://whqlibdoc.who.int/hq/1999/WHO_HSC_PVI_99.1.pdf.

[19] Patno KM. The prevention of child abuse and neglect. In: Jenny C, ed. Child abuse and neglect: Diagnosis, treatment and evidence. Philadelphia, PA: Elsevier Saunders, 2010:605–9.

[20] Klevens J, Whitaker DJ. Primary prevention of child physical abuse and neglect: Gaps and promising directions. Child Maltreat 2007;12;364–77.

[21] Child Welfare Information Gateway. Child maltreatment prevention: Past, present, and future. Washington, DC: US Department Health Human Services, Children's Bureau, 2011.

[22] Sweet MA, Appelbaum MI. Is home visiting an effective strategy? A meta-analytic review of home visiting programs for families with young children. Child Dev 2004;75(5):1435–56.

[23] Olds DL. The nurse-family partnership: An evidence-based preventative intervention. Inf Ment Health J 2006;27(1):5–25.

[24] Gomby DS. The promise and limitations of home visiting: Implementing effective programs. Child Abuse Negl 2007;31(6):793–99.

[25] Eckenrode J, Ganzel B, Henderson CR, Smith EG, Olds DL, Powers J, et al. Preventing child abuse and neglect with a program of nurse home visitation: The limiting effects of domestic violence. JAMA 2000;284(11):1385–91.

[26] Commission to Eliminate Child Abuse and Neglect Fatalities. Within our reach: A national strategy to eliminate child abuse and neglect fatalities. Washington, DC: Government Printing Office, 2016. URL: http://www.acf.hhs.gov/ programs/cb/resource/cecanf-final-report.

[27] Bugental DB, Schwartz A. A cognitive approach to child maltreatment prevention among medically at-risk infants. Dev Psychol 2009;45(1):284–8.

[28] Dumont K, Mitchell-Herzfeld S, Greene R, Lee E, Lowenfels A, Rodriguez M, et al. Healthy families New York (HFNY) randomized trial: Effects on early child abuse and neglect. Child Abuse Negl 2008;32(2):295–315.

[29] Williams S. Healthy Families Florida evaluation report: January 1, 1999–December 31, 2003. Miami, FL: Author, 2005.

[30] Kass D, Miller C, Rollin M, Evans P, Shah R. New hope for preventing child abuse and neglect: Proven solutions to save lives and prevent future crime. Washington, DC: Fight Crime: Invest in Kids, 2003.

[31] Rigney L, Brown EJ. The use of paraprofessionals in a prevention program for child maltreatment: History, practice, and the need for better research. The APSAC Advisor 2009;21(winter):13–20.

[32] MacLeod J, Nelson G. Programs for the promotion of family wellness and the prevention of child maltreatment: A meta-analytic review. Child Abuse Negl 2000;24(9):1127–49.

[33] Chaffin M, Bonner BL, Hill RF. Family preservation and family support programs: Child maltreatment outcomes across client risk levels and program types. Child Abuse Negl 2001;25(11):1269–89.

[34] Patterson J, Barlow J, Mockford C, Klimes I, Pyper C, Stewart-Brown S. Improving mental health through parenting programmes: Block randomized controlled trial. Arch Dis Child 2002;87:472–7.

[35] Centers for Disease Control and Prevention (CDC). Parent training programs: Insight for practitioners. Atlanta, GA: Author, 2009.

[36] Palusci VJ, Crum P, Bliss R, Bavolek SJ. Changes in parenting attitudes and knowledge among inmates and other at-risk populations after a family nurturing program. Child Youth Serv Rev 2008;30:79–89.

[37] Wilson S, McKenzie K, Quayle E, Murray G. A systematic review of interventions to promote social support and parenting skills in parents with an intellectual disability. Child Care Health Dev 2013;40(1):7–19.

[38] Helfer RE. The perinatal period, a window of opportunity for enhancing parent-infant communication: An approach to prevention. Child Abuse Negl 1987;11(4):565–79.

[39] Reynolds AJ, Mathieson LC, Topitzes JW. Do early childhood interventions prevent child maltreatment? Child Maltreat 2009;14(5):182–206.

[40] Child Welfare Information Gateway. Infant safe haven laws. Washington, DC: US Department Health Human Services, Children's Bureau, 2013. URL: https://www.childwelfare.gov/systemwide/laws_policies/statutes/safehaven.cfm.

[41] State of Michigan Department of Health and Human Services. Safe Delivery Factsheet, January, 2016. URL: http://www.michigan.gov./documents/dhs/SAFE_DELIVERY_STATISTICS __UPDATE__REVISED_as_of_September_7_2011_doc_REV_1_362698_7.pdf.

[42] Dias MS, Smith K, deGuehery K, Mazur P, Li V, Shaffer ML. Preventing abusive head trauma among infant and young children: A hospital-based, parent education program. Pediatrics 2005;115(4):470–7.

[43] Barr RG, Rivara FP, Barr M, Cummings P, Taylor J, Lengua LJ, Meredith-Benitez E. Effectiveness of educational materials designed to change knowledge and behaviors regarding crying and shaken baby syndrome in mothers of newborns: A randomized, controlled trial. Pediatrics 2009;123(6):972–80.

[44] Frazier ER, Liu GC, Dauk KL. Creating a safe place for pediatric care: A no hit zone. Hospital Pediatrics 2014;4:247–50.

[45] Dubowitz H, Feigelman S, Lane W, Kim J. Pediatric primary care to help prevent child maltreatment: The Safe Environment for Every Kid (SEEK) model. Pediatrics 2009;123(3):858–64.

[46] Sege RD, Hatmaker-Flanigan E, De Vos E, Levin-Goodman R, Spivak H. Anticipatory guidance and violence prevention: Results from family and pediatrician focus groups. Pediatrics 2006;117:455–63.

[47] McHugh MT, Kvernland A, Palusci VJ. An adolescent parents programme to reduce child abuse. Child Abuse Rev 2015 Dec 30. doi: 10.1002/car.2426.

[48] American Academy of Pediatrics. Connected kids: Safe strong secure. A new violence prevention program from the American Academy of Pediatrics. Elk Grove Village, IL: Author, 2005.

[49] Canfield CF, Weisleder A, Cates CB, Huberma HS, Dreyer BP, Legano LA, et al. Primary care parenting intervention and its effects on the use of physical punishment among low-income parents of toddlers. J Dev Behav Pediatr 2015;36:586–93.

[50] Cates CB, Weisleder A, Dreyer BP, Johnson SB, Vlahovicova K, Ledsma J, et al. Leveraging health care to promote responsive parenting: Impacts of the Video Interaction Project on parenting stress. J Child Fam Stud 2016;25(3):827–835.

[51] Weisleder A, Cates CB, Dreyer BP, Berkule Johnson S, Huberman HS, Seery AM, et al. Promotion of positive parenting and prevention of socioemotional disparities. Pediatrics 2016;137(2):e20153239.

[52] Pasalich DS, Fleming CB, Oxford ML, Zheng Y, Spieker SJ. Can parenting intervention prevent cascading effects from placement instability to insecure attachment to extenalizing problems in maltreated toddlers? Child Maltreat 2016;21(3):175–8.

[53] Daro D, Dodge DA. Creating community responsibility for child protection: Expanding partnerships, changing context. Future Child 2009;19(2):67–93.

[54] Prinz, RJ, Sanders MR, Shapiro CJ, Whitaker DJ, Lutzker JR. Addendum to population-based prevention of child maltreatment: The US Triple P System Population Trial. PrevSci 2016;17:410–6.

[55] Schnitzer PG, Covington TM, Wirtz SJ, Verhoek-Oftedahl W, Palusci VJ. Public health surveillance of fatal child maltreatment: Analysis of three state programs. Am J Public Health 2008;98(2):296–303.

[56] Saul J, Audage NC. Preventing child sexual abuse within youth-serving organizations: Getting started on policies and procedures. Atlanta, GA: Centers for Disease Control and Prevention, National Center for Injury Prevention and Control, 2007.

[57] Ondersma SJ, Chase SK. Substance abuse and child maltreatment prevention. The APSAC Advisor 2003;15(3):8–11.

[58] Palusci VJ, Bliss R, Crum P. Outcomes after groups for children exposed to violence with behavior problems. Trauma Loss 2007;7(1):27–38.

[59] World Health Organization and the International Society for the Prevention of Child Abuse and Neglect. Preventing child maltreatment: A guide to taking action and generating evidence. Geneva: WHO, 2006.

[60] Reading R, Bissell S, Harvin J, Masson J, Moynihan S, Pais MS, et al. Promotion of children's rights and prevention of child maltreatment. Lancet 2009;373:332–43.

[61] Prevent Child Abuse America. BECAUSE kids count! Building and enhancing community alliances united for safety and empowerment. URL: http://member.preventchildabuse.org /site/PageServer?pagename=research_because_kids_count.

[62] Klevens J, Barnett SB, Florence C, Moore D. Exploring policies for the reduction of child physical abuse and neglect. Child Abuse Negl 2015;40:1–11.

[63] Palusci VJ, Vandervort FE, Lewis JM. Does changing mandated reporting laws improve child maltreatment reporting in large US counties? Child Youth Serv Rev 2016;55:170–9.

[64] DePanfilis D, Dubowitz H, Kunz J. Assessing the cost effectiveness of Family Connections. Child Abuse Negl 2008;32(3):335–51.

[65] Palusci VJ, Zeemering W, Bliss RC, Combs A, Stoiko MA. Preventing abusive head trauma using a directed parent education program. Presented at the Pediatric Academic Societies Meeting. Atlanta, GA, May, 2006.

[66] Funderburk BW, Eyberg S. Parent-child interaction therapy. In: Norcross JC, Vandenbos GR, Freedheim DK, eds. History of Psychotherapy: Continuity and Change Second edition. Washington, DC: American Psychological Association, 2011:415–20.

[67]   Jensen TK, Gulbrandsen W, Mossige S, Reichelt S, Tjersland OA. Reporting possible sexual abuse: A qualitative study on children's perspectives and the context for disclosure. Child Abuse Negl 2005;29:1395–413.

[68]   Andrews AB, Veronen LJ. Sexual assault and people with disabilities. Special issue: sexuality and disabilities: A guide for human service practitioners. J Soc Work Hum Sex 1993;8:137–59.

[69]   Doughty AH, Kane LM. Teaching abuse-protection skills to people with intellectual disabilities: A review. Res Dev Dis 2010;31:331–7.

[70]   Plummer CA. Prevention of child sexual abuse: A survey of 87 programs. Violence Victim 2001;16(5):575–88.

[71]   Gibson L, Leitenberg H. Child sexual abuse prevention programs: Do they decrease the occurrence of child sexual abuse? Child Abuse Negl 2000;24(9):1115–25.

[72]   Finkelhor D. Prevention of sexual abuse through educational programs directed toward children. Pediatrics 2007;120:640–5.

[73]   Palusci VJ, Ondersma SJ. Services and recurrence after psychological maltreatment confirmed by child protective services. Child Maltreat 2012;17(2):153–63.

[74]   Helfer RE. A review of the literature on the prevention of child abuse and neglect. Child Abuse Negl 1982;6:251–61.

[75]   Finkel MA. Child Sexual abuse prevention: Addressing personal space and privacy in pediatric practice. AAP SCAN Newsletter 2014;25(1):2,10–2.

[76]   Trowbridge MJ, Sege RD, Olson L, O'Connor K, Flaherty E, Spivak H. Intentional injury management and prevention in pediatric practice: Results from 1998 and 2003 American Academy of Pediatrics Periodic Surveys. Pediatrics 2005;116:996–1000.

[77]   Diaz A, Manigat M. The healthcare provider's role in the disclosure of sexual abuse: The medical interview as a gateway to disclosure. Child Health Care 2000;28:141–9.

[78]   American Academy of Pediatrics, Task Force on Violence (AAP). The role of the pediatrician in youth violence prevention in clinical practice and at the community level. Pediatrics 1999;103(1):173–81.

[79]   APSAC Prevention Taskforce. Practice guideline: Integrating child maltreatment prevention into professional practice. Elmhurst, IL: American Professional Society on the Abuse of Children, 2010.

[80]   Mikton C, Butchart A. Child maltreatment prevention: A systematic review of reviews. Bull World Health Org 2009;87:353–61.

[81]   Plotnick RD, Deppman L. Using benefit-cost analysis to assess child abuse prevention and intervention programs. Child Welfare 1999;78(3):381–407.

[82]   Shurney D. Immunizations, prevention and lifestyle. J Managed Care Med 2016;19(Suppl 1):5–10.

[83]   Daro D. Confronting child abuse: Research for effective program design. Washington, DC: National Academy Press, 1988.

[84]   Caldwell RA. The costs of child abuse vs. child abuse prevention: Michigan's experience, 1992. URL: https://www.msu.edu/~bob/cost1992.pdf.

[85]   Noor I, Caldwell RA. The costs of child abuse vs. child abuse prevention: A multi-year follow-up in Michigan, 2005. URL: https:// www.msu.edu/ ~bob/cost2005.pdf.

[86]   Maxfield MG, Widom CS. The cycle of violence: Revisited six years later. Arch PediatrAdol Med 1996;150(4):390–5.

[87] Wang CT, Holton J. Total estimated cost of child abuse and neglect in the United States. Chicago, IL: Prevent Child Abuse America, 2008.

[88] Fang X, Brown DS, Florence CS, Mercy JA. The economic burden of child maltreatment in the United States and implications for prevention. Child Abuse Negl 2012;36:156–65.

[89] Ferrara P, Corsello G, Basile MC, Nigri L, Campanozzi A, Ehrich J, et al. The economic burden of child maltreatment in high income countries. J Pediatrics 2015;167(6):1457–9.

[90] Affordable Care Act Maternal, Infant and Early Childhood Home Visiting Program. URL: http://www.hrsa.gov/grants/apply/assistance/homevisiting/homevisitingsupplemental.pdf.

[91] DeVol R, Bedroussian A. An unhealthy America: The economic burden of chronic disease charting a new course to save lives and increase productivity and economic growth.Santa Monica, CA: Milken Institute, 2007.

[92] Wade R, Cronholm PF, Fein JA, Forke CM, Davis MB, Harkins-Schwarz M, et al. Household and community-level adverse childhood experiences and adult health outcomes in a diverse urban population. Child Abuse Negl 2016;52:135–45.

SECTION THREE: ACKNOWLEDGMENTS

In: Child Abuse: Children with Disabilities
Editors: V. J Palusci, D. Nazer et al.

ISBN: 978-1-53612-035-6
© 2017 Nova Science Publishers, Inc.

Chapter 14

ABOUT THE EDITORS

Vincent J Palusci, MD, MS, FAAP is professor of pediatrics at New York University School of Medicine and a pediatrician at the Bellevue Hospital Frances L Loeb Child Protection and Development Center and NYU Langone Medical Center in New York City. He serves on the executive committee of the American Academy of Pediatrics Section on Child Abuse and Neglect and the American Board of Pediatrics Child Abuse Pediatrics Subboard. He is also program chair for the AAP provisional Section on Child Death Review and Prevention and president of the Society of Alumni of Bellevue Hospital. He has served on of the board of directors of the American Professional Society on the Abuse of Children and was the Editor-in-Chief of the APSAC Advisor. Dr Palusci was named a founding member of the Ray E Helfer Honorary Society and received the 2004 Ray Helfer Award from the National Alliance of Children's Trust and Prevention Funds and the American Academy of Pediatrics. He serves on the editorial boards for Child Abuse and Neglect, Child Maltreatment, and Pediatric Radiology and has edited several books. A graduate of New Jersey Medical School and Bellevue Hospital in New York, Dr Palusci is a board-certified clinician in general pediatrics and child abuse pediatrics who teaches medical students, residents and fellows, and consults with New York City's Children's Services as a senior medical consultant in the ACS Medical Clinical Consultation Program. He is a member of the International Society for the Prevention of Child Abuse and Neglect and the British Association for the Study and Prevention of Child Abuse and Neglect, and has provided training for universities, medical, law enforcement and child welfare professionals nationally and internationally. His research interests include studying medical issues in child maltreatment and reporting, health services for maltreated children, child fatalities, and the impact of services and prevention in hospital and child welfare populations. E-mail: vincent.palusci@nyumc.org

Dena Nazer, MD, FAAP is an assistant professor of pediatrics at Wayne State University, Chief of the Child Protection Team at Children's Hospital of Michigan and performs medical evaluations for children suspected of being maltreated at the Kids-TALK Children's Advocacy Center (CAC) in Detroit. Dr Nazer graduated from the University of Jordan Medical School. She completed her pediatric residency, chief residency, and fellowship in child abuse pediatrics at the Children's Hospital of Michigan. She is certified by the American Board of Pediatrics in both general pediatrics and child abuse pediatrics. Dr Nazer is a member of the American Professional Society on the Abuse of Children (APSAC) and both a board member and the membership chair of the Michigan Professional Society on the Abuse of Children (MiPSAC). She is a board member of the Wayne County Child Death Review Team, the Kids-TALK Children's Advocacy Center Advisory Board, and an executive board member of the Windsor-Essex Children's Aid Society. Dr Nazer was appointed by Governor Rick Snyder as a member of the Human Trafficking Health Advisory Board. She is also a member of the Michigan Department of Health and Human Services (MDHHS) Medical Advisory Committee (MAC), which serves as the advisory committee on medical matters specific to the abuse and neglect of children. She has been named as one of the Hour Detroit Magazine's Top Docs as voted by peers for the past seven consecutive years and was featured as one of the Ambassador Magazine "Top Docs, Metro Detroit's Finest Physicians" in 2015. She teaches nationally and internationally for medical, legal, law enforcement and child welfare professionals. In 2014, she was awarded the first BRANCH (Building Regional Alliances to Nurture Child Health) Partner Grant to expand her ongoing work in training health professionals on the diagnosis and treatment of child maltreatment in Amman, Jordan. In 2016-2017, she will act as the American Academy of Pediatrics Leonard P Rome CATCH Visiting Professor to implement an educational program on child advocacy and child maltreatment at Hurley Children's Hospital in Flint, Michigan. E-mail: dnazer@med.wayne.edu

Donald E. Greydanus, MD, Dr. HC (Athens), FAAP, FSAM (Emeritus), FIAP (HON) is Professor and Founding Chair of the Department of Pediatric and Adolescent Medicine, as well as Pediatrics Program Director at the Western Michigan University Homer Stryker MD School of Medicine (WMED), Kalamazoo, Michigan, USA. He is also Professor of Pediatrics and Human Development at Michigan

State University College of Human Medicine (East Lansing, Michigan, USA) as well as Clinical Professor of Pediatrics at MSU College of Osteopathic Medicine in East Lansing, Michigan, USA. Received the 1995 American Academy of Pediatrics' Adele D. Hofmann Award for "Distinguished Contributions in Adolescent Health", the 2000 Mayo Clinic Pediatrics Honored Alumnus Award for "National Contributions to the field of Pediatrics," and the 2003 William B Weil, Jr., MD Endowed Distinguished Pediatric Faculty Award from Michigan State University College of Medicine for "National and international recognition as well as exemplary scholarship in pediatrics." Received the 2004 Charles R Drew School of Medicine (Los Angeles, CA) Stellar Award for contributions to pediatric resident education and awarded an honorary membership in the Indian Academy of Pediatrics—an honor granted to only a few pediatricians outside of India. Was the 2007-2010 Visiting Professor of Pediatrics at Athens University, Athens, Greece and received the Michigan State University College of Human Medicine Outstanding Community Faculty Award in 2008. In 2010 he received the title of Doctor Honoris Causa from the University of Athens (Greece) as a "distinguished scientist who through outstanding work has bestowed praise and credit on the field of adolescent medicine (Ephebiatrics)." In 2010 he received the Outstanding Achievement in Adolescent Medicine Award from the Society for Adolescent Medicine "as a leading force in the field of adolescent medicine and health." In 2014 he was selected by the American Medical Association as AMA nominee for the ACGME Pediatrics Residency Review Committee (RRC) in Chicago, Illinois, USA. Past Chair of the National Conference and Exhibition Planning Group (Committee on Scientific Meetings) of the American Academy of Pediatrics and member of the Pediatric Academic Societies' (SPR/PAS) Planning Committee (1998 to Present). In 2011 elected to The Alpha Omega Alpha Honor Society (Faculty member) at Michigan State University College of Human Medicine, East Lansing, Michigan. Former member of the Appeals Committee for the Pediatrics' Residency Review Committee (RRC) of the Accreditation Council for Graduate Medical Education (Chicago, IL) in both adolescent medicine and general pediatrics. Numerous publications in adolescent health and lectureships in many countries on adolescent health. E-mail: donald.greydanus@med.wmich.edu

Joav Merrick, MD, MMedSci, DMSc, born and educated in Denmark is professor of pediatrics, child health and human development, Division of Pediatrics, Hadassah Hebrew University Medical Center, Mt Scopus Campus, Jerusalem, Israel and Kentucky Children's Hospital, University of Kentucky, Lexington, Kentucky United States and professor of public health at the Center for Healthy Development, School of Public Health, Georgia State University, Atlanta, United States, the medical director of the Health Services, Division for Intellectual and Developmental Disabilities, Ministry of Social Affairs and Social Services, Jerusalem, the founder and director of the National Institute of Child Health and Human Development in Israel. Numerous publications in the field of pediatrics, child health and human development, rehabilitation, intellectual disability, disability, health, welfare, abuse, advocacy, quality of life and prevention. Received the Peter Sabroe Child Award for outstanding work on behalf of Danish Children in 1985 and the International LEGO-Prize ("The Children's Nobel Prize") for an extraordinary contribution towards improvement in child welfare and well-being in 1987. During 1984-1996 on the international council of the International Society for the Prevention of Child Abuse and Neglect (ISPCAN) and chairperson of the Journal Committee. E-mail: jmerrick@zahav.net.il

In: Child Abuse: Children with Disabilities
Editors: V. J Palusci, D. Nazer et al.

ISBN: 978-1-53612-035-6
© 2017 Nova Science Publishers, Inc.

Chapter 15

ABOUT THE FRANCES L LOEB CHILD PROTECTION AND DEVELOPMENT CENTER, DEPARTMENT OF PEDIATRICS, NEW YORK UNIVERSITY SCHOOL OF MEDICINE, NEW YORK, UNITED STATES

INTRODUCTION

The Frances L Loeb Child Protection and Development Center (CPDC) opened on November 15, 2000 as a component of the Bellevue Hospital Pediatric Resource Center, a national model for preventive health care for high-risk families. The director, Margaret T McHugh, MD, MPH, is a leader in the field of child abuse and adolescent health, as well as the author of the New York State protocols for the identification and treatment of child abuse and neglect. The Center is an integral component of city-wide child protection services.

Within the Loeb Center, the child abuse team evaluates children from the Greater Metropolitan area. The interdisciplinary nature of this service, the techniques, and the comprehensive nature of the evaluations make the Center unique among hospital-based child abuse evaluation programs. Its goal is to minimize trauma to children and provide treatment interventions that are developmentally appropriate.

The CPDC opened as the result of several gifts from the Loeb family. Frances Lehman Loeb (1907-1996) had spent a dozen years as New York City's liaison to its vast corps of foreign diplomats and a lifetime maintaining a family tradition of philanthropy. In addition to money, Mrs Loeb gave time. For 12 years in the 1960s and 70s during the administrations of Mayors John V Lindsay and Abraham D Beame, Mrs Loeb was New York City's unsalaried commissioner for the United Nations and for the Consular Corps.

Directing a staff of nine full-time and six part-time employees, Mrs Loeb eased cultural shock and fostered amity in a foreign diplomatic community that numbered 35,000 people from 197 missions and 91 consulates. She helped found the Children of Bellevue Inc, a nonprofit organization, founded in 1949 to initiate, develop, and fund special programs and to advocate for children and their families within Bellevue Hospital Center. She died in May, 1996.

Child protection

At the CPDC, we address the unique needs of approximately 300 physically and sexually abused children in the greater Metropolitan area every year. Our multidisciplinary child protection team, consisting of specially trained pediatricians, nurses, social workers, child development specialists, and psychologists, seeks to minimize psychological trauma by providing evaluation and treatment that is age-appropriate, child-focused, and comprehensive. Dr McHugh first developed and initiated the practices at Bellevue in the 1970s that became statewide protocols for the identification and treatment of child abuse and neglect in hospital settings. Associated with NYU Langone Medical Center, the Center offers specialized clinical services for NYU and its broad network of hospitals, centers and practices throughout the metropolitalm area.

A safe haven

The interdisciplinary nature of this service, their techniques, patients served, and the comprehensive nature of the evaluations make the CPDC unique among hospital-based child abuse evaluation programs in NYC. Clinical and didactic training opportunities are provided to medical personnel and other interested professionals, and the CPDC provides the physical setting for the hands-on application of material presented in training sessions. While other programs take place in the chaotic environment of the emergency room, the CPDC is a safe haven for doctors, nurses, social workers, patients and their families. It is complete with quiet exam rooms as well as special interview rooms with one-way glass. Social work and forensic medical services are also provided for adolescents who have been victims of a crime such as assault, stab wounds, gun shot wounds, date violence, rape/sexual assault are also available. Services include crisis intervention, short-term counseling, referrals, and advocacy with law enforcement and the district attorney's office.

A unique approach

The CPDC is unique among hospital models in that the psycho/social component of care begins during the initial evaluation and continues throughout the child's follow-up treatment. It also is the only facility of its kind that provides specialized services for developmentally and intellectually disabled children and teenagers for abuse and neglect, rather than sending these patients to the unprepared emergency rooms and clinics. The Loeb Center marked its 15th anniversary in November, but Dr McHugh and the Child Protection Program at Bellevue have been providing comprehensive medical, psychological and social intervention to abused and neglected children and their families for more than 35 years.

Dr McHugh is the director, founder and driving force behind the center. "She recognized that abuse was a problem and that doctors were in a unique position to identify and treat abused children," said Barbara Paxton, Chief Development Officer for Children of Bellevue, a non-profit organization that partially funds the center. "She also recognized that abuse was not just one incident in a child's life, but something that would impact their whole life." "The challenge is to devise an intervention so these youngsters don't get stuck developmentally," Dr McHugh said. "You help them cope with the child abuse and move on. You help them heal themselves."

The team includes Dr McHugh and board-certified child abuse pediatricians doctors, two social workers, two child life development specialists, and a clinical psychologist. They also work with NYC Children's Services, law enforcement agents and prosecutors to provide training on how to interview and work with young victims.

Bellevue Hospital Center has been providing quality healthcare in an urban setting since its founding in 1736. It is the oldest and one of the largest public hospitals in the United States and provides services without regard to a patient's ability to pay.

The Center

The Frances L Loeb Child Protection and Development Center provides the following services:

- Comprehensive evaluations in a child-focused environment to reduce unnecessary trauma caused by repeated medical examinations and interviews
- Advocacy and coordination with child protection and law enforcement agencies including joint interviews
- Forensic child sexual abuse assessment

- Collection and documentation of evidence
- Crisis intervention
- Short-term and group treatment for children and non-offending parents; referrals
- Expert consultation and testimony
- Non-abuse related medical care for pediatric and adolescent gynecological complaints
- Utilization of other medical resources available within Bellevue Hospital Center
- Assistance with filing New York State Crime Victims Board claims

Contact

Margaret T McHugh, MD, MPH
Director, Frances L Loeb Child Protection and Deveopment Center,
Bellevue Hospital, Room GC-65
462 First Avenue
New York, NY 10016, United States of America
E-mail: Margaret.McHugh@nyumc.org

In: Child Abuse: Children with Disabilities
Editors: V. J Palusci, D. Nazer et al.

ISBN: 978-1-53612-035-6
© 2017 Nova Science Publishers, Inc.

Chapter 16

ABOUT THE CHILDREN'S HOSPITAL OF MICHIGAN AND THE WAYNE STATE UNIVERSITY SCHOOL OF MEDICINE, DETROIT, MICHIGAN, UNITED STATES

The Wayne State University School of Medicine (WSUSOM) currently hosts an enrollment of more than 1,000 medical students in undergraduate medical education, master's degree, PhD, and MD-PhD programs and courses encompass 14 areas of basic science. WSUSOM traces its roots through four predecessor institutions since its founding in 1868. According to United States News ranking, the school ranks 179th in its Research activities, and 85th in primary care. The School of Medicine's mission is to provide first-rate medical education while leading the field through research and patient care. The faculty consists of over 2,000 physicians, many who are members of the Wayne State University Physician Group, and provide care at eleven affiliated hospitals, clinics and training sites throughout the area. The school's ties to the community are very strong. WSU has a stated mission to improve the overall health of the community. As part of this mission, the School has established with the help of a $6 million NIH grant the Center for Urban and African-American Health to seek new ways to redress health disparities by identifying preventive strategies and therapeutic approaches to chronic diseases that plague this population, namely obesity, cardiovascular disease and cancer. Perhaps the most significant contribution the School provides to the community is care to area residents who are under- or uninsured. Along with the Detroit Medical Center, WSU faculty physicians provide an average of $150 million in uncompensated care annually.

Although the school's faculty offer expertise in virtually all medical fields, the institution's areas of research emphasis include cancer, women's and children's health, neuroscience and population studies. Many are academic leaders at national and international levels in editorial roles. WSUSOM sponsors a number of community-service and health-awareness programs in southeastern Michigan, including mental-health screenings, Diabetes Day, the Community Health Child Immunization Project, the Detroit Cardiovascular Coalition and Brain Awareness Week. In addition to faculty-sponsored programs, WSU medical students are among the most active in the country for community outreach. The medical students, with supervision, regularly provide free medical care for homeless and unemployed patients at Detroit's Cass Clinic. Student-sponsored outreach programs also include Senior Citizen Outreach Project, Adolescent Substance Abuse Prevention Program and Teen Pregnancy Education Program.

With more than 40 specialties, the Children's Hospital of Michigan sees more kids and trains more pediatric medical and surgical experts than any other hospital in the state. Since 1886, the Children's Hospital of Michigan is the hospital where all we know and everything we do is just for them. Children's Hospital of Michigan is recognized by US News and World Report as one of the Best Children's Hospitals and as one of Americas Best 25 Children's Hospitals by Parents Magazine. The pediatric medical and surgical specialties share common values--to provide the highest quality of care for children, to inform that care through research innovations, and to ensure that children have access to the care they need. Through an academic affiliation with Wayne State University and Michigan State University, Children's Hospital of Michigan is an innovator in education and research. From appendectomies to transplants, the Children's Hospital of Michigan is proud to offer the state's widest range of pediatric surgery options with a multidisciplinary team of surgeons on staff and other health care providers delivering an unparalleled level of pediatric surgical care.

The Kids-TALK Children's Advocacy Center (CAC) is a community-based program that serves children through 17 years of age, providing comprehensive treatment to suspected child victims of sexual abuse, physical abuse, neglect, or other forms of psychological trauma. The Kids-TALK CAC utilizes a multidisciplinary and collaborative approach to coordinate the investigation, assessment, treatment and prevention of child abuse in Wayne County. Services provided to children and their non-offending family members include forensic interviewing, advocacy, onsite medical evaluations, mental health services and outreach and prevention services. The Kids-TALK CAC partners with The Guidance Center, the Office of the Wayne County Prosecuting Attorney, the Wayne County Association of Chiefs of Police, the Wayne County Department of Health & Human Services, Child and Family Services, the Wayne County Office of the Attorney General, Detroit Wayne Mental Health Authority, Children's Hospital of Michigan, Wayne State University and the medical and mental health community to reduce the trauma experienced by the child victims of suspected abuse. Together these partners make the Kids-TALK CAC a safe and child-friendly environment where abused and traumatized children receive the protection, support and treatment they need to heal.

In: Child Abuse: Children with Disabilities
Editors: V. J Palusci, D. Nazer et al.

ISBN: 978-1-53612-035-6
© 2017 Nova Science Publishers, Inc.

Chapter 17

ABOUT THE DEPARTMENT OF PEDIATRIC AND ADOLESCENT MEDICINE, WESTERN MICHIGAN UNIVERSITY HOMER STRYKER MD SCHOOL OF MEDICINE (WMED), KALAMAZOO, MICHIGAN USA

Mission and service

The Western Michigan University Homer Stryker MD School of Medicine was started in 2012 and its first class of medical students began in 2014. The Department of Pediatric and Adolescent Medicine has a pediatric residency program which is accredited by the Accreditation Council for Graduate Medical Education (ACGME) in Chicago, Illinois, USA and the current residency program in Pediatrics started in 1990.

The WMED Department of Pediatric and Adolescent Medicine has a commitment to a comprehensive approach to the health and development of the child, adolescent, and the family. The Department has a blend of academic general pediatricians and pediatric specialists. Our Pediatric Clinic team provides a broad spectrum of general well and sick child care (birth through 18 years) including immunizations, monitoring general physical and emotional growth, motor skill development, sports medicine (including participation evaluations and evaluation of common sports injuries), child abuse evaluations, and psychosocial or behavioral assessment. WMED Pediatrics believes in immunizations as a protection against preventative disease processes. Our Pediatrics Clinic is undergoing a transformation to a patient-centered medical home (PCMH). A patient-centered medical home is a way to deliver coordinated and comprehensive primary care to our infants, children, adolescents and young adults. It is a partnership between individuals and families within a health care setting, which allows for a more efficient use of resources and time to improve the quality of outcomes for all involved through care provided by a continuity care team.

Research activities

The Department has a variety of research projects in adolescent medicine, neurobehavioral pediatrics, adolescent gynecology, pediatric diabetes mellitus, asthma, and cystic fibrosis. The WMED Department of Pediatric and Adolescent Medicine has published a number of medical textbooks: Essential adolescent medicine (McGraw-Hill Medical Publishers), The pediatric diagnostic examination (McGraw-Hill), Pediatric and adolescent psychopharmacology (Cambridge University Press), Behavioral pediatrics, 2nd edition (iUniverse Publishers in New York and Lincoln, Nebraska), Behavioral pediatrics 3rd edition (New York: Nova Biomedical Books); 4th Edition: In press. Pediatric practice: Sports medicine (McGraw-Hill), Handbook of clinical pediatrics (Singapore: World Scientific), Neurodevelopmental disabilities: Clinical care for children and young adults (Dordrecht: Springer), Adolescent medicine: Pharmacotherapeutics in medical disorders (Berlin/Boston: De Gruyter), Adolescent medicine: Pharmacotherapeutics in general, mental, and sexual health (Berlin/Boston: De Gruyter), Pediatric psychodermatology (Berlin/Boston: De Gruyter), Substance abuse in adolescents and young adults: A manual for pediatric and primary care clinicians (Berlin/Boston: De Gruyter), and tropical pediatrics (New York: Nova); Second edition in press.

The Department has edited a number of journal issues published by Elsevier Publishers covering pulmonology (State of the Art Reviews: Adolescent Medicine—AM:STARS), genetic disorders in adolescents (AM:STARS), neurologic /neurodevelopmental disorders (AM:STARS), behavioral pediatrics (Pediatric Clinics of North America), pediatric psychopharmacology in the 21st century (Pediatric Clinic of North America), nephrologic disorders in adolescents (AM:STARS), college health (Pediatric Clinics of North America), adolescent medicine (Primary Care: Clinics in Office Practice), behavioral pediatrics in children and adolescents (Primary Care: Clinics in Office Practice), adolescents and sports (Pediatric Clinics of North America), and developmental disabilities (Pediatric Clinics of North America). The Department has also edited a journal issue on musculoskeletal disorders in children and adolescents for the American Academy of Pediatrics' AM:STARs; in April of 2013 a Subspecialty Update issue was published in AM:STARs.

The department has developed academic ties with a variety of international medical centers and organizations, including the Queen Elizabeth Hospital in Hong Kong, Indian Academy of Pediatrics (New Delhi, India), the University of Athens Children's Hospital

(First and Second Departments of Paediatrics) in Athens, Greece and the National Institute of Child Health and Human Development in Jerusalem, Israel.

Contact

Professor Dilip R. Patel, MD, current chair and Professor Donald E Greydanus, MD, founding chair, Department of Pediatric and Adolescent Medicine
Western Michigan University Homer Stryker MD School of Medicine
1000 Oakland Drive, D48G, Kalamazoo, MI 49008-1284, United States
E-mail: dilip.Patel@med.wmich.edu and Donald.greydanus@med.wmich.edu
Website: http://www.med.wmich.edu

In: Child Abuse: Children with Disabilities
Editors: V. J Palusci, D. Nazer et al.

ISBN: 978-1-53612-035-6
© 2017 Nova Science Publishers, Inc.

Chapter 18

ABOUT THE NATIONAL INSTITUTE OF CHILD HEALTH AND HUMAN DEVELOPMENT IN ISRAEL

The National Institute of Child Health and Human Development (NICHD) in Israel was established in 1998 as a virtual institute under the auspices of the Medical Director, Ministry of Social Affairs and Social Services in order to function as the research arm for the Office of the Medical Director. In 1998 the National Council for Child Health and Pediatrics, Ministry of Health and in 1999 the Director General and Deputy Director General of the Ministry of Health endorsed the establishment of the NICHD.

Mission

The mission of a National Institute for Child Health and Human Development in Israel is to provide an academic focal point for the scholarly interdisciplinary study of child life, health, public health, welfare, disability, rehabilitation, intellectual disability and related aspects of human development. This mission includes research, teaching, clinical work, information and public service activities in the field of child health and human development.

Service and academic activities

Over the years many activities became focused in the south of Israel due to collaboration with various professionals at the Faculty of Health Sciences (FOHS) at the Ben Gurion

University of the Negev (BGU). Since 2000 an affiliation with the Zusman Child Development Center at the Pediatric Division of Soroka University Medical Center has resulted in collaboration around the establishment of the Down Syndrome Clinic at that center. In 2002 a full course on "Disability" was established at the Recanati School for Allied Professions in the Community, FOHS, BGU and in 2005 collaboration was started with the Primary Care Unit of the faculty and disability became part of the master of public health course on "Children and society". In the academic year 2005-2006 a one semester course on "Aging with disability" was started as part of the master of science program in gerontology in our collaboration with the Center for Multidisciplinary Research in Aging. In 2010 collaborations with the Division of Pediatrics, Hadassah Hebrew University Medical Center, Jerusalem, Israel around the National Down Syndrome Center and teaching students and residents about intellectual and developmental disabilities as part of their training at this campus.

Research activities

The affiliated staff have over the years published work from projects and research activities in this national and international collaboration. In the year 2000 the International Journal of Adolescent Medicine and Health and in 2005 the International Journal on Disability and Human Development of De Gruyter Publishing House (Berlin and New York) were affiliated with the National Institute of Child Health and Human Development. From 2008 also the International Journal of Child Health and Human Development (Nova Science, New York), the International Journal of Child and Adolescent Health (Nova Science) and the Journal of Pain Management (Nova Science) affiliated and from 2009 the International Public Health Journal (Nova Science) and Journal of Alternative Medicine Research (Nova Science). All peer-reviewed international journals.

National collaborations

Nationally the NICHD works in collaboration with the Faculty of Health Sciences, Ben Gurion University of the Negev; Department of Physical Therapy, Sackler School of Medicine, Tel Aviv University; Autism Center, Assaf HaRofeh Medical Center; National Rett and PKU Centers at Chaim Sheba Medical Center, Tel HaShomer; Department of Physiotherapy, Haifa University; Department of Education, Bar Ilan University, Ramat Gan, Faculty of Social Sciences and Health Sciences; College of Judea and Samaria in

Ariel and in 2011 affiliation with Center for Pediatric Chronic Diseases and National Center for Down Syndrome, Department of Pediatrics, Hadassah Hebrew University Medical Center, Mount Scopus Campus, Jerusalem.

International collaborations

Internationally with the Department of Disability and Human Development, College of Applied Health Sciences, University of Illinois at Chicago; Strong Center for Developmental Disabilities, Golisano Children's Hospital at Strong, University of Rochester School of Medicine and Dentistry, New York; Centre on Intellectual Disabilities, University of Albany, New York; Centre for Chronic Disease Prevention and Control, Health Canada, Ottawa; Chandler Medical Center and Children's Hospital, Kentucky Children's Hospital, Section of Adolescent Medicine, University of Kentucky, Lexington; Chronic Disease Prevention and Control Research Center, Baylor College of Medicine, Houston, Texas; Division of Neuroscience, Department of Psychiatry, Columbia University, New York; Institute for the Study of Disadvantage and Disability, Atlanta; Center for Autism and Related Disorders, Department Psychiatry, Children's Hospital Boston, Boston; Department of Pediatric and Adolescent Medicine, Western Michigan University Homer Stryker MD School of Medicine, Kalamazoo, Michigan, United States; Department of Paediatrics, Child Health and Adolescent Medicine, Children's Hospital at Westmead, Westmead, Australia; International Centre for the Study of Occupational and Mental Health, Düsseldorf, Germany; Centre for Advanced Studies in Nursing, Department of General Practice and Primary Care, University of Aberdeen, Aberdeen, United Kingdom; Quality of Life Research Center, Copenhagen, Denmark; Nordic School of Public Health, Gottenburg, Sweden, Scandinavian Institute of Quality of Working Life, Oslo, Norway; The Department of Applied Social Sciences (APSS) of The Hong Kong Polytechnic University Hong Kong.

Targets

Our focus is on research, international collaborations, clinical work, teaching and policy in health, disability and human development and to establish the NICHD as a permanent institute in Israel in order to conduct model research and together with the four university schools of public health/medicine in Israel establish a national master and doctoral program in disability and human development at the institute to secure the next generation of professionals working in this often non-prestigious/low-status field of work.

Contact

Joav Merrick, MD, MMedSci, DMSc
Professor of Pediatrics
Medical Director, Health Services, Division for Intellectual and Developmental
Disabilities, Ministry of Social Affairs and Social Services, POB 1260, IL-91012
Jerusalem, Israel.
E-mail: jmerrick@zahav.net.il

In: Child Abuse: Children with Disabilities
Editors: V. J Palusci, D. Nazer et al.

ISBN: 978-1-53612-035-6
© 2017 Nova Science Publishers, Inc.

Chapter 19

ABOUT THE BOOK SERIES
"DISABILITY STUDIES"

Disability studies is a book series with publications from a multidisciplinary group of researchers, practitioners and clinicians for an international professional forum interested in the broad spectrum of disability, intellectual disability, health and human development.

- Reiter S. Disability from a humanistic perspective: Towards a better quality of life. New York: Nova Science, 2008
- Knotkova H, Cruciani R, Merrick J, eds. Pain. Brain stimulation in the treatment of pain. New York: Nova Science, 2010.
- Prasher VP, ed. Contemporary issues in intellectual disabilities. New York: Nova Science, 2010.
- Lotan M, Merrick J, eds. Rett syndrome: Therapeutic interventions. New York: Nova Science, 2011.
- Satgé D, Merrick J, eds. Cancer in children and adults with intellectual disabilities: Current research aspects. New York: Nova Science, 2011.
- Knotkova H, Cruciani RA, Merrick J, eds. Neural plasticity in chronic pain. New York: Nova Science, 2011.
- Prasher VP. Down syndrome and dementia. A comprehensive and historical review. New York: Nova Science, 2012.
- Merrick J, Aspler S, Morad M, eds. Disability and chronic disease. New York: Nova Science, 2013.
- Tse MMY, Merrick J. Pain and the elderly. New York: Nova Science, 2013.
- Brown RI, Faragher RM, eds. Quality of life and intellectual disability: Knowledge application to other social and educational challenges. New York: Nova Science, 2014.
- Grenon I. From one century to the next: A history of Wrentham State School and the Institutional Model in Massachusetts. New York: Nova Science, 2014.

- Sharkey PM, Merrick J, eds. Virtual reality: People with special needs. New York: Nova Science, 2014.
- Sharkey PM, Merrick J, eds. Virtual reality: Rehabilitation in motor, cognitive and sensorial disorders. New York: Nova Science, 2014.
- Merrick J, Greydanus DE, Patel DR, eds. Intellectual disability: Some current issues New York: Nova Science, 2014.
- Pareto L, Sharkey PM, Merrick J, eds. Technology, rehabilitation and empowerment of people with special needs. New York: Nova Science, 2015.
- Sharkey PM, Merrick J, eds. Recent advances on using virtual reality technologies for rehabilitation. New York: Nova Science, 2016.
- Omar HA, Patel DR, Greydanus DE, Merrick J, eds. Pediatric pain: Current aspects. New York: Nova Science, 2016.

Contact

Professor Joav Merrick, MD, MMedSci, DMSc
Medical Director, Health Services, Division for Intellectual and Developmental Disabilities
Ministry of Social Affairs and Social Services, POBox 1260
IL-91012 Jerusalem, Israel
E-mail: jmerrick@internet-zahav.net

SECTION FOUR: INDEX

INDEX